# fortysomething

# fortysomething

## CLAIMING THE POWER AND THE PASSION
## OF YOUR MIDLIFE YEARS

ROSS E. GOLDSTEIN, PH.D.
with Diana Landau

JEREMY P. TARCHER, INC.
Los Angeles

Library of Congress Cataloging-in-Publication Data
Goldstein, Ross E.
     Fortysomething: claiming the power and the passion of your midlife years/
Ross E. Goldstein with Diana Landau.—1st ed.
     p.   cm.
     ISBN 0-87477-590-6
     1. Middle aged persons—United States—Life skills guides.
2. Baby boom generation—United States. 3. Midlife crisis—United States.
I. Landau, Diana, 1950–     . II. Title.
HQ1059.5.U5G65 1990                                                  90-19846
305.24 ' 4—dc20                                                           CIP
Copyright © 1990 by Ross Goldstein

Jeremy P. Tarcher, Inc.
5858 Wilshire Blvd., Suite 200
Los Angeles, CA 90036

Distributed by St. Martin's Press

Manufactured in the United States of America
10   9   8   7   6   5   4   3   2   1
First Edition

*For Nancy and Chase*

# Contents

# Acknowledgments

This book is built on the wisdom and support of many people. I would like to take this opportunity to thank some of them.

David C. McClelland, Ph.D., Robert W. White, Ph.D., and Stanley King, Ph.D., taught me an appreciation for the art as well as the science of psychology. Their emphasis on the study of life histories has shaped my professional development long past the time I spent with them at Harvard.

My wife and son, Nancy and Chase, carried so much of the weight during the completion of this manuscript. Writer's block has never known such diversion and encouragement. All those early mornings they were there with me . . . like it or not.

Margaret Williams, Ph.D., was instrumental in developing the concept of this book and provided much of the research and information for the chapters on the family and the physiology of aging. She was there from the beginning of this project, and I am extremely grateful for her efforts. Also, thanks to Frederic Hudson, Ph.D., whose seminal work at MDI was both enlightening and encouraging.

Jeremy P. Tarcher was willing to listen to my ideas and gave me the chance to bring them to life.

My editor, Diana Landau, was so often my voice through this project. Like a partner singing perfect harmony, she blended her writing with mine seamlessly. I watched her grow into and through the material until even I could not tell where my ideas ended and hers began. My thanks, also, to Tom Farber, for his suggestions and encouragement, and for directing me to Diana.

If completing a project like this is said to be one percent inspiration and ninety-nine percent perspiration, then I want to acknowledge the sweat and vision of Rick Benzel, who lived this book as I wrote it. His organization and clarity were a help from beginning to end. Also, my thanks to Victoria Pasternack, whose comments influenced us at a critical time.

My deepest appreciation also to the Galens, Helene and Lou, who watched, supported, and believed in the project. Helene's feedback on the first chapters were important in helping me to bring my *self* to my work.

To Mayme, Joel, Sandra, Jessica, and Hilary Goldstein I offer a special thanks that transcends any piece of work. This book is only a reflection of your support along the way.

To Pierre Mornell, my deepest gratitude for helping me separate the forest from the trees. His grasp of the simple truths was profoundly enlightening.

Finally, my bicycling training buddies, Ron, Tom C., Peter, Jim, Pamela, Jerry, Tom B., Tom W., and Andre, kept me spinning, quite literally, during the time I wrote this book. You guys were an inspiration, my ongoing research group, and a resource for me. Thanks for showing me the folly of acting your age.

# Preface

The comic strips are always a good barometer of what is on our minds. In an episode of the daily strip *Cathy*, published as this book was being prepared for press, the heroine's fortysomething boyfriend, Irving, raises his nose from the grindstone one day, notices life passing him by, and flips out. Succeeding panels lampoon his stereotypical midlife crisis—he gets a permanent, signs up for a trek to the Himalayas, outfits himself to the max in day-glo neoprene clothing and personal electronics to pursue his quest for lost youth.

On the same page within the same month, Michael J. Doonesbury is being kept awake by voices telling him it's time to get out, after his boss in the advertising agency has offered him yet another account that totally offends his values.

The subject of midlife is like sex: we joke about it endlessly for the very reason that we take it so seriously. Jokes about the midlife crisis have been around for a long time, but in just the last half-decade or so, they seem to be everywhere. And not just jokes, but newspaper and magazine articles, advertising pitches aimed at the aging baby boomer market, and of course, books.

It happened that society's intensifying focus on this phenomenon converged with my own midlife experience. In short, my life was changed profoundly, on the level where my persona and professional identities were inextricably joined. When it was more or less over, midlife became the unifying theme of my psychotherapy practice, writing, and consulting work. I am now probably more at ease with myself than at any time in my life, and I look forward to tomorrow with a sense of excitement I couldn't have begun to imagine when I was struggling in the early stages of the transition.

Thus, out of my own experiences, those of my clients and countless other people I talked to during that time, and the reading I did to make sense of what was happening to me, came this book. Yes, there already exists a wealth of published material about the midlife passage, yet I felt none of it was written from the exact perspective I was seeking. That's because when we speak of midlife today, we are speaking of midlife for the baby boom generation specifically. We baby boomers, the largest, most closely watched group of Americans ever—76 million born between 1946 and 1964—have been pioneering social trends since adolescence. As we now enter or stand poised on the brink of our forties, it is clear that we are rewriting the script for midlife transition, confounding society's (and our own) expectations about what should happen at this time of life.

This book takes the point of view that baby boomers are experiencing midlife in a significantly different way than any earlier generation. That premise defines its readership; I am writing for anyone in the plus-or-minus-forty age group who wants to understand what is happening to them, or about to happen to them, and turn those potentially troubled times into the golden opportunities they actually are. This book will also be useful to anyone close to a midlife voyager who wants to understand that person better. I wish I could have given it to my wife a few years ago.

Another primary assumption based on my own experience and observations is that the midlife passage has enormous potential for life-enhancing transformation, if it is actively managed. Much of my aim is to help you realize that promise, by providing skills and strategies for dealing with the issues you'll undoubtedly encounter.

The first chapter describes my own midlife passage and presents some of the reasons why midlife is different for our generation, and is such an important time for us. Chapter 2 offers a more detailed portrait of the baby boom generation as it heads into midlife. We'll look at traditional theories of adult development and why they don't fit our unique profile in many ways. And we'll see how boomers today are remaking middle age to their liking.

Chapter 3 focuses on the nature and dynamics of life transitions. We'll take apart a "typical" midlife transition and describe what you can expect at each stage. People vary greatly in how they deal with change, and these patterns affect how each individual experiences midlife. The behavior of several common types, such as the Stimulation Junkie and the Change Resister, are profiled, to help you recognize your own patterns.

Chapter 4 delves into the inner workings of midlife—the conscious and unconscious psychological changes we go through. Midlife is a time of seeking to redefine our identity, of giving up the illusions of our youth, so understanding this process is vital if we are to forge a new self-image to carry us through the second half of life.

Chapter 5 presents a series of *master skills* for midlife transition, targeted to the various change types. Some are *global skills*, necessary for personal growth at any stage of life. Others are more directed to the practical, day-to-day effort of coping with midlife. The emphasis of the skills is on how you can take an active role in establishing new goals and life plans.

Chapter 6, "Staying Alive," surveys the current information about the many physical changes associated with midlife and how people come to terms with them (or don't). There's good news about a few scientific advances that will help us age more gracefully. There is also valuable information about handling midlife stress, an inescapable part of this transition.

Chapters 7 and 8 look at the impact of the fortysomething transition in the two major arenas of life: relationships and work. Midlife tests these elements severely; it's a time when many marriages fail and career paths are abandoned. We'll see how midlife's energy can be used to facilitate changes you may need to make, but also how to decide whether they *are* needed and so minimize the likelihood of a serious mistake.

In the last chapters, we'll examine the final stage of midlife: the task of developing a specific, long-term mission to guide you as you enter the second half of life. In this, finding your *passion* is the key to making a commitment to your vision. Finally, we'll glance into the future of life after midlife—what a successful resolution to this transition feels like, and how it serves as the foundation for satisfaction and harmony in later life.

My clients today are mainly people in midlife, and the information and insights gained through working with them are the essence of this book. I have also drawn heavily on the input of friends and acquaintances in midlife, people not necessarily in therapy.

I have not attempted to conduct empirical scientific studies with control groups, percentages, and questionnaires (though I do use questionnaires in my work with clients). The case studies you encounter here are people who have come to talk about their midlives, or they are composites of several clients, as well as friends and acquaintances polled informally.

I have made generous use of existing studies, especially on adult development and social demographics, of popular articles on midlife and the baby boom, examples from pop culture, and literary works that have something eloquent or enlightening to say on the subject of midlife. My hope is to synthesize these sources into an investigation of midlife that is lively, accessible, and useful to all readers.

More than anything else, I want to share with readers my personal sense of discovery about what the fortysomething years can be, and their potential for changing lives in unexpected but deeply satisfying ways. With all my reading, all the talking and interviews I've done in the course of preparing this book, the most important things I've learned about midlife have come out of my own experience.

One major realization is that we can't rush change. I'm aware that I'm actually still in the midst of this transition, though there have been times when I longed for it to be over, all the doubts gone and the decisions made; when I wanted to push for a resolution—any resolution. I've also felt the typical impulse to escape back into the tried and true, the predictability and financial security of my previous life. Part of me said I was crazy to switch off a winner, so I kept flogging that horse until I had to accept that it simply had nothing more to give.

I know now that I really had no options about going through this transition. There were choices aplenty to be made during the course of it, but whether to take the journey or not—that was beyond choice. In fact, I've come to see midlife as an offer we can't refuse, but rather, should embrace.

# 1

## Am I Grown Up Yet?

## The Midlife
## of the 90s

*When they tell you to grow up, they
mean stop growing.*

TOM ROBBINS

In 1979, when I was thirty-three, I decided to leave Aspen,
Colorado, where I had been practicing as a psychologist for
five years and relocate to San Francisco. There were many reasons behind the move. Some were fairly easy to understand
and talk about: for example, the woman I was involved with
no longer wanted to live in the mountains, and I still wanted to
be with her. I had also grown weary of the good-time resort
mentality that characterized Aspen society. Those years had
been a wonderful decompression from the intensity of graduate school, but now I felt ready for a larger, and deeper, pond.

But other issues were harder to fathom. I was beginning to
have serious questions about my career. I don't know that I
had ever really considered what being a psychologist meant,
but after five years I knew that it was less rewarding than I'd
anticipated. I had begun with an illusion, encouraged by
movie portrayals of psychologists, that once I came up with
the right interpretation, a change in the client's behavior

would naturally and immediately follow. Of course, this wasn't the case in real practice, and I was feeling frustrated.

I thought maybe what I needed was to integrate my work with my other interests, and since sports had always been a big part of my life, I took steps to establish a practice in sports psychology in San Francisco. Unfortunately, few psychologists were making a living at sports psychology in 1979. By the time I learned this, my savings had run out, my relationship had ended, and I had hit a low point in my life.

This was a dark time for me, perhaps a precursor of what was to come. Fortunately, I was soon offered a job working for a psychiatrist who consulted with a group of orthopedic surgeons specializing in back problems. Within a couple of years I'd moved out on my own again, with a thriving practice in behavioral medicine, pain management, and psychotherapy. I consulted with one of the leading spine centers in the country, and even got to counsel some of my sports heroes who came there for treatment. I told myself I was content—and certainly I *was* content with the authority and power and the trappings of success.

But as time went on, I felt less and less engaged by the work and brought less and less energy to it. One question began to nag at me, at first quietly, then more and more insistently: Is this all there is? I resolutely pushed my doubts aside. Like so many people whose lives are in transition, I expended a lot of energy in denial. In my case, I bought more: a bigger house, cars, clothes, the latest and best sports gear and electronic toys. I joined a fancy health club and traveled, the more exotic the destination the better. I was well and truly caught up in what writer Lawrence Shames calls "the hunger for more" that typified the 1980s.

But reshuffling the pieces and accumulating more of them didn't get at the heart of what was wrong inside me. It's taken a lot of hindsight to figure out what was happening then. There I was, nearing forty and feeling that what I was doing wasn't particularly special, or important, or passion-inspiring. I was the quintessential baby boomer in my need to feel that I made a difference. My expectations, like those of many boomers, were probably unrealistically high.

It took two more years to summon enough courage to change things. I had become very attached to the money and averse to risk, but I was getting messages from inside me that couldn't be ignored. My moods swung wildly from anger to bleak depression to resentment. The people close to me noticed too, in spite of all my efforts to act like things were okay.

In July of 1988 I decided to leave my hospital-based consulting practice. The decision crystallized around several factors. I had finally turned forty and it was as if an urgent internal alarm went off; if I didn't take a chance now, I might be stuck forever. I had remarried and was lucky to be in a secure and supportive relationship; my wife actually thought I *deserved* to feel satisifed in my work. We'd had a baby, and my little boy was part of the picture too. Being with him was the only time I could submerge my negative feelings, but the pleasure I found there made my work seem even less satisfactory by contrast. Somehow, I felt I owed it to all three of us to find meaning in what I was doing with my life.

Beyond that, my family was making me more aware of my need for connection with others. The separateness that I had cherished all my life was beginning to seem unnecessary, even a handicap. Before I had a family, I thought mine would be unique, that I would avoid the cliches and patterns all parents fall into. For the first year or so after my son's birth, I was even self-conscious about carrying pictures of him. But the resistance gradually melted away, and I began to take comfort from the idea of being a parent like millions of other parents, with its predictable trials and rewards.

But these insights came much later. When I first confronted my dissatisfaction, all I had was negativity about my life. In an effort to get unstuck, to make some sense of what I was feeling, I began to read the existing literature about the age forty, or midlife, transition—the seminal writings of Jung, the academic theories of Erik Erikson and Daniel Levinson, and Gail Sheehy's popular bestseller, *Passages,* among others.

I was already aware, both as a psychologist and simply as someone living in our culture, of the generally accepted view about midlife: that it's usually a time of change, of restless seeking, of wanting to break away, of discovering new values. Like everyone else, I had laughed at the jokes about victims of midlife anxiety and their portrayals in movies, like Bruce Dern in *Middle Age Crazy,* who runs off with a cheerleader.

In fact, as I became more aware of midlife, it seemed I couldn't get away from the subject. Whenever I opened a newspaper I'd be confronted with stories like "Midlife Crisis Hits Mr. Control"—about baseball player Steve Garvey and his philandering—or about the drug-related arrest of violin prodigy Eugene Fodor, which his manager blamed on midlife stress, or the continuing romantic adventures of forty-plus superstar Cher.

I read the existing midlife studies hungrily and felt grateful that at least some of the characteristics of this powerful transition had been catalogued. I took some comfort from knowing that my restless feelings were natural and predictable, though part of me still resisted the idea that *my* midlife transition could be like anyone else's!

But I was also disappointed with much that I read, because it didn't seem to speak to me and the circumstances my generation—the baby boomers—faced as we approached midlife at this time in history. It didn't allow for many of the social changes we had caused and come through in our own lives. The fundamental message I kept reading was: just muddle through the crisis and things will turn out okay. But in this I found little specific guidance, and not much hope.

I wanted to compare my experience with that of other people around my age, so I started asking my friends and clients to tell me what it was like for them to be crossing the forty-something threshold, and what the concept of midlife meant to them.

Many people I talked with spoke of feeling stuck, out of gas, depleted of the youthful energy, excitement, and dedication they had once brought to their work and lives. A client named Jenny said: "In my thirties, I felt like a firecracker. Now I feel like a firecracker that's fizzled—a dud."

Some feel betrayed by midlife's unexpected urges, and by the motives that had kept them moving in one direction up until then. "It seems like I got too focused on making it in my thirties. I lost perspective on what I was doing and why. It annoys me to have to rethink it all—it's like some sort of cruel trick."

Another client, Cass, expressed the common wish to escape deadening fatigue. "I've got this train of responsibilities to pull, and just getting by takes all my energy. I have lots of fantasies about escaping—just taking off to that proverbial island. Of course, I'd never do that; I'm too conscientious. But I can't help thinking about it and wishing there were some way to bring that feeling of relief into my life."

Ian was a classic case. He came to see me after learning that his rise in corporate marketing had been derailed due to a takeover. The news hit him hard, yet he'd been denying that anything was really wrong—feeling as if he should quit but afraid to make the move.

He recounted to me that one night at dinner with his wife and several other couples the talk turned to aging, with the usual jokes about wrinkles, pot bellies, baldness, and the miracles of modern cosmetic surgery. Ian listened with rising emotion and finally it spilled over. "Yeah, it's easy to change the outside, but what about what's inside? What if that feels old and tired? How do you get a 'spirit lift'? I'm almost forty and I feel like I'm stuck . . . just when I need the energy to make something happen, there's none left."

What really struck me about the comments I was hearing, and about my own situation, wasn't that baby boomers entering midlife felt tired, or trapped in an unsatisfying life structure. In past generations it was taken for granted that once you reach a certain age, you settle in, accept what life has given you, and after a slight struggle at midlife, simply plod onward into the sunset. But the stories I heard were more marked by an unwillingness to settle down, a rebellion against staying in the groove, a fierce drive to recover some of the passion people had felt at earlier stages in their lives.

One client expressed this feeling succinctly.

> I just turned forty-three. My husband gave me a party when I turned forty, as if that was a big number. I didn't feel too much about it then. But forty-three . . . for some reason the mid-forties seem so much older.
>
> I'm really feeling concern about aging. The physical part bothers me a little, though I'm in pretty good shape, and I try to stay on top of my weight. But it's more a matter of how I feel about my age.
>
> What I'm trying to say is that there's still much much more I want out of life, so much I always thought I'd have by now that I don't have. I don't feel the game is over by any means. When I look at my parents, by the time they were forty-three, they were so set in their lives. They had their house, they already had me and my brother. They just seemed very settled in. I think that's the way they wanted it, or maybe they just fell into the trap.
>
> But my life is different from theirs. I know there are many more changes to come for me. I'm definitely not ready to call the game at this point. I look around, and I see that most of my friends are at the same place in their lives. So I feel pretty optimistic about what the future holds for me. I'm not being naive about it; I know I won't get it all, but I sure won't settle for what I have now.

Several of those I talked to recognized that their values were changing in midlife, and they were struggling to bring their lives into sync with this shift. This too seemed different from our parents' generation, whose values seemed to become only more ensconced with time. A marketing vice president in his early forties had been recently bumped off the fast track, fired from his software firm. He'd once told me that his goal was to make $17 million by age fifty. "I know I've got to give up the path I'm on. The things I want now are different from the things I wanted before. But I have no experience in how to get them."

Then there's the whole physiological issue, the changes in what was once a youthful body. My friend Bruce told me about being at a party in a house he wasn't familiar with. "I was wandering around and caught a glimpse of someone else in the room, and wondered idly who that old guy was. Then I realized I had just walked by a mirror!" The shock was obviously still reverberating as he recalled it.

For some, the awareness of physical aging made midlife seem like "the last chance to make certain choices," as one woman put it. A corporate executive who chose to become a single mother, she had postponed the childbearing issue like so many fortysomething career women, and then made a radical choice. She also expressed the anxiety and bewilderment many people feel on discovering a sharp change in their values and what they want from life: "Everything before seems to have been leading to this point, and I feel like I'm about to take a test I haven't studied for."

Men as well as women were hearing the urgent ticking of the body's clock and reacting to it in various ways—some pushing their workouts harder, others opting to try a high-risk sport or a Himalayan trek or a Harley-Davidson *before it's too late.* In general, people seemed to be aware of their bodies changing and needing more upkeep, but were resistant to the idea that turning forty meant resigning themselves to serious physical decline.

As I continued to collect the midlife stories of my contemporaries and read further into the literature, it also happened that more and more clients were coming to see me about issues of aging and change. More and more articles were appearing in the popular press with titles like "Over Forty and Sensational" or, "Baby Boomers Seek Meaning."

It gradually became clear to me, with the kind of upwelling excitement I hadn't felt about my work in years, that I wanted to investigate this phenomenon as thoroughly as I could, to discern the new shape of the midlife transition for myself and my generation, and what its effects would be on us and our world. Two things were obvious already: that the first wave of baby boomers was feeling the impact of midlife profoundly, and that they were reacting to it in different ways than any previous generation.

## This is Not Your Father's Midlife Crisis

In the 1989 hit movie *Field of Dreams,* the main character struggles to explain to his wife why he's building a baseball diamond in their cornfield. It has something to do with being thirty-six, he says, and afraid of turning into his father. Why was that so bad, his wife wonders? and he replies: "I never forgave him for growing old."

He wasn't talking about simple physical aging, but about growing old in spirit. Many people in the post–World War II generation perceive that their parents gave up on the possibility of growth when they hit forty, settled into a life structure that was as safe and secure as possible, resisting all change and shunning all risk.

There were good reasons for our parents to approach the middle of their lives conservatively. Their formative experiences were those of worldwide economic depression and war. Little wonder that they reacted with gratitude to the prosperous calm of the 1950s and tried to freeze time, clinging tenaciously to the material assets and the mindset associated with that era.

Although Carl Jung had identified the midlife passage as far back as the 1920s, for most people in our parents' time it was perceived as little more than a blip on the big screen of an adult life, a short-lived dislocation in the predictable course of growing older and more settled. Occasionally, vague feelings of middle-aged restlessness would erupt into full-blown trauma, but flagrant acting-out was discouraged in those days.

Consider also that in nearly all the classic portrayals of midlife crisis, the people going through it were men. In the typical scenario, young man goes out into the world, makes a place for himself, acquires a family, and loses sight of his youthful dreams and energy in the process—a realization that abruptly smacks him in the face at forty. Women did not have such a crisis, since their fate as wives and mothers was preordained, and they had no dreams worth mentioning to mourn. Or, if they did feel a sense of loss around forty, it was about losing their beauty and their fertility. So went the prevailing assumption. Popular perception was reinforced by science: until quite recently, studies of adult development after age thirty focused exclusively on men.

And in most portrayals, even the man's experience was trivialized. Walter Mitty in James Thurber's wonderful stories was an ordinary middle-aged guy with a hyperactive fantasy life, but his dreams could never be realized. Movie characters like Jack Lemmon's in *Good Neighbor Sam* or Tom Ewell's in *The Seven Year Itch* were permitted a brief, harmless fling before settling back into their humdrum, domestic routines. The midlife itch just wasn't taken seriously as part of the overall process of maturation.

This image of what happens at fortysomething is alien to our generation, and our rejection of it is the essence of why midlife will be different for us. Just consider the history of the baby boom generation, raised in prosperity and then assaulted by the social and political upheavals of the sixties and seventies—civil rights, assassinations, Vietnam, Watergate. We contributed to the decline of once sacred institutions: the church, the state, the family. We embraced the women's movement, which has repatterned the fabric of society. We saw the end of America's domination of the world economy and felt its effects in our own lives. We witnessed a dark period in our country's history, leading us to question the values we'd grown up with and to create a counterculture that groped toward a new vision of what society should be. And in the 1980s we saw the idealism of that vision give way to the realities of achieving what we wanted from life.

Clearly, we grew up in a different mind space than our parents did. But did we grow up? Certainly many of us don't seem to qualify as adults by our parents' standards. Our roots are not planted as deeply as theirs. The benchmarks of the American Dream have been harder to attain in recent years. We couldn't afford to buy a house, so we rented, creating an enduring sense of impermanence.

We delayed marriage, or if we did marry, the soaring divorce rate robbed the institution of its stability. We postponed having children, depriving many marriages of the glue that holds them together. We joined a company, but two or three years later left to join another one, or left work altogether to move to the verdant hills of Vermont or Oregon.

And even those of us who did the things we thought adults were supposed to do—find a good career, get married, get a house, have kids—still found that a sense of adulthood eluded us. It's a case of perception defying reality, for which *Boston Phoenix* writer Caroline Knapp has coined the term the "Gilligan Syndrome" (after that forever-young hero of the TV generation, played by Bob Denver). "The patented domain of baby boomers," writes Knapp, its victims "feel youthful, aware of but oddly estranged from [their] chronological age. Equipped with a sense that there's loads of time ahead: time to change, time to [screw up], time to play, and—at some distant, ill-defined point—time to settle down."

There are lots of reasons why baby boomers feel unwilling

to live out their parents' script for adulthood. Chief among these is that we were raised and educated to believe we had limitless choices. It is a fact that we do have many more options in life than our parents had (this is especially true for women), but our sense of being without limits goes way beyond this. A thirty-eight-year-old financial analyst quoted in Knapp's article wondered, "How can you know what you really want when you can only touch three out of the three thousand possibilities out there? I still feel like I'm waiting to find out what I'll be when I grow up." The sense that we can do anything is a strong force in our generation.

When I started writing about midlife, my mother, who is seventy-six, read my first magazine article. She was proud of me but also troubled by what I wrote. "In my day," she told me, "we slept in the beds we made." She meant that her generation made their choices and stuck with them, even if they didn't work out. This wasn't really news to me, but I was struck by the pride with which she said it. This seemed to be at the heart of the generation gap: that hers took pride in suffering the consequences of their choices, wearing them like a badge of courage, whereas ours sees absolutely no need for such suffering, preferring to celebrate the virtues of continual innovation and change.

Our generation questions a host of other inherited assumptions about the fortysomething passage and the negative connotations it holds. Start with the basic vocabulary: the word *middle-aged* is anathema to baby boomers. The term *midlife* didn't really come into common use until after Gail Sheehy's *Passages* appeared in 1976. Until then, middle-aged was how we described anyone between about forty and sixty, and that term was associated with loss, resignation, lack of movement, the desire for comfort, and risk avoidance. No wonder baby boomers dropped it like a hot potato when we began to cross the frontier of forty.

A recent study found that most Americans now think that

middle age is anything past forty-six and less than sixty-seven—certainly a higher starting point than such a survey would have found a few decades ago. Again and again I hear from people around forty comments like, "I just don't feel as if I'm at the middle of my life"—when statistics say that they are. Our self-perception leads us to push the deadline for middle age up, perhaps indefinitely. One of my fortysomething clients remarked that he thought of middle age as "ten years older than me."

Sheehy tried carefully to distinguish between *midlife* and *middle age,* restricting the former to the turbulent period of transition and describing the latter as a calmer, better adjusted, more evolved stage that follows. Indeed, that is what should follow from the passage, but boomers' aversion to the term middle age probably means that it is doomed to fall out of popular use. We just haven't found a satisfactory replacement yet.

Or take the coupling of midlife with crisis, a word that's come to have very scary associations. For the older generation, who felt committed to their choices and roles in life at all costs, the pressure for change that midlife brings was likely to build up like a head of steam with no escape valve. Surprisingly, this did sometimes lead to an explosive crisis—a wrecked marriage, a sabotaged career, an escape into alcohol abuse.

However, crisis doesn't necessarily imply trauma. According to one definition, it can simply be a turning point, a crucial stage at which future events are determined. That's not a bad description of midlife, yet because we are conditioned to shun crises, I prefer linking midlife to the more encouraging idea of transition. Getting past the fear of change is the first step in taking the crisis out of midlife.

Much of the traditional vocabulary for middle age refers to physical aging—a reality that baby boomers are strongly resisting and with considerably more success than our parents.

Phrases like "over the hill," "seen better days," "no spring chicken," "out to pasture," and "on the shady side" all basically convey the message that the best is over; get ready for that big downhill slide. It's a message fiercely rejected by our generation, which is more likely to look toward models of midlife health and vigor, like Jane Fonda or basketball great Kareem Abdul-Jabbar, who said on retiring from the game at forty-two, "My life is just beginning."

## The New Midlife

As I've come to understand it, the unique shape of the midlife transition for the baby boom generation will be determined largely by two forces: our previous life experiences and how they conflict with the values and assumptions we've inherited from our parents. Of course, there are other factors, such as individual personality and personal history. These have always been important, but it is how they intersect with our generation's experiences and values that make midlife today vastly different.

Based on my own experience and information gathered in my research and interviews, here are some observations about what I'm calling the *new midlife*.

On the positive side, the new midlife reflects the world we live in today; it acknowledges who we are, where we have been, and where we're headed. It is less closely tied to chronological age than midlife used to be, because baby boomers have been breaking all the rules about when we're supposed to get out of school, get married, have children, and establish a career. Social changes brought about by the women's movement are a major force shaping the new midlife; both men and women today are less trapped in traditional roles. It is also less irrevocably tied to physical decline, because of advances in health care and longevity. And it shares the distinguishing characteristic of this generation: a refusal to set limits to growth, an urge to constantly refine and redefine the quality and shape of life, to push the envelope of meaning a little farther.

At the same time, there's a flip side to this picture that may cause baby boomers trouble in midlife. Aging imposes some limits that are futile to struggle against, so our continuing youthful identification is bound to run into some roadblocks sooner or later. Also, we were the "me generation"; but our self-preoccupation will conflict with certain psychological needs of this time of life, like being realistic about our expectations in life and offering something back to the world. Baby boomer narcissism will run counter to the natural psychological urges of midlife . . . to be more connected to others and to express that need in nurturing actions.

But for the most part, the new midlife is an optimistic vision that holds out an irresistible promise: that the second half of life can be longer, richer, and more satisfying than ever before. The synergy of the baby boom hitting midlife will be powerful, because boomers are generally equipped to take advantage of the potential for growth. We already have the skills to cope with a rapidly changing world, and these align nicely with the natural midlife impulses toward change and experimentation. The baby boom's passage through midlife will establish new parameters and expectations in the arenas of health, family, work, and education.

In the year 2000, the last of the baby boomers will be closing in on age forty. The 1990s, when many millions of boomers will cross that threshold, might justly be called the *midlife decade*. Our first task, as we embark on it, will be to take the crisis out of midlife. Viewing the passage as an opportunity and not an ordeal will be the key to fulfilling its potential. As we'll see in the next chapter, we are trained and primed to do so.

# 2

## Our Midlife Profile

### Pros and Cons
### for Baby Boomers

*Just remember, we're all in this alone.*
LILY TOMLIN

W hat is midlife, anyway? There is no universally accepted definition; people think of it as anything from an isolated point on life's timeline to an emotional syndrome with a cornucopia of symptoms: anxiety, depression, self-doubt, and so on. It's a time when perfectly normal people seem to go crazy.

In trying to determine what makes the midlife experience unique for the baby boom generation, we need to look at how people have defined it in the past. Age is a convenient way to demarcate life's big events, so the first question many have asked in searching for a definition of midlife is: When does it happen?

### The Numbers Game

Forty is the number that most resonates with people's idea of the middle of life. One's fortieth birthday, the big 4–0, symbolizes for many baby boomers a last-ditch deadline for growing up in their parents' terms—to be established in one's career, married, parents, homeowners. And forty, or thereabouts, is when many start to become aware of physical aging: we can't stay up as late, bounce back as quickly, run as many miles in a week.

Daniel Levinson, a Yale University psychologist whose book *The Seasons of a Man's Life* is one of the best-known works on adult development, pegs the age range for midlife at forty to forty-five. But Levinson's studies were mostly of men. For women, the passage generally seems to begin earlier, around age thirty-five. Women are likely to notice the signs of aging sooner, and those who haven't yet had children hear the biological clock ticking ever louder. Besides, women are generally more attuned to their emotional state than men are, and more inclined to pay attention to midlife's earliest whispers.

There's a strong focus on forty right now, with the leading edge of the baby boom already passing this marker. Between 1980 and 1990, the age thirty-five to forty-four segment of Americans increased by a whopping 42 percent.

But in truth, the numbers game has been the first criterion to go. Because boomers have taken such varied paths through life, paying scant attention to the timing of traditional key events like marriage and childbearing, the parameters of midlife have expanded. Some people don't experience midlife symptoms until they are nearing fifty. Under other circumstances—say, the person who raced down a burnout career path in their twenties, or for someone such as the athlete whose living depends on physical prowess—the midlife transition may arrive closer in the mid-thirties.

The fact that we don't resemble our parents at forty also weakens the strict connection between that number and midlife. One friend told me, "For our parents, midlife meant that life was over. I'm forty-four, and I know I'm not a mirror image of them, so now I think that midlife must happen at fifty or so."

And so, any attempt to get a firm chronological fix on midlife today is doomed to confusion, for the new midlife is more accurately seen as a response to our personal history and situation. What we're doing with our lives, the degree of satisfaction we derive from them, the stresses we're subjected to—these rather than chronological triggers are the main determinants of midlife today.

## Ages and Stages: Doctor Spock for Grown-Ups

Whenever it comes, midlife in our time has grown into much more than a small bump in the road to late adulthood. Both in popular culture and in psychological science, it is now viewed as an extended period of adult development for men and women, with a psychology and set of feelings all its own, a discrete stage that largely determines how the second half of life will unfold.

The term *stage* has in fact taken on a specific meaning in developmental psychology, the science that seeks to understand human life by diagramming it in timelines, from birth to death. It's simply a quantitative approach to the age-old human urge to comprehend by categorizing. Shakespeare expressed it in his famous speech about the "seven ages of man"—the one that begins "All the world's a stage," and goes on to describe the different roles we play at each stage of life.

The various systems that psychologists have come up with to subdivide our lifespan are grouped under the general heading of *stage theory*. In the parlance of developmental psychology, midlife is a *transition,* a period of change between relatively stable stages of life, or *life structures.*

Obviously midlife has become a major life transition only since old age became a significant stage. The overall pattern and rhythm of the human lifespan has shifted radically in less than a century. Life expectancy for Americans in 1920 was only 54.1 years; a child born in 1980 can expect to live 73.2 years, on the average. And the figure goes up for those who live to midlife. If a man reaches forty today, he'll probably live past seventy-five; for women it jumps to eighty. Twenty to thirty more years to live—no wonder we require more of a midcourse adjustment than our ancestors did!

The evolution of various theories about adult development has coincided with this stretching of the human calendar. Sigmund Freud, the great progenitor of psychological science early in the century, had remarkably little to say about adult development, and many consider it his chief shortcoming. He believed that the primal experiences of infancy and childhood crystallized the outline of adulthood—that personality was essentially determined by late adolescence. Freud's influential ideas probably delayed the emergence of other theories that explored continuing personality development in adulthood. But emerge they did, and the psychological consensus today is that, while childhood remains crucial, we *are* capable of personality change as adults—both unconsciously and consciously directed.

Carl Jung, Freud's chief disciple who later dissented from his master, is probably the seminal writer on adult development and midlife in particular. In an essay called "The Stages of Life," written around 1930, he observes that "in this phase of life—between thirty-five and forty—an important change in the human psyche is in preparation." He went on to describe some of the characteristics of this change—a rising sense of discomfort felt by people once content with their lives, nostalgia for youth and fear of physical decline, and the way men and women seem to grow more like each other around midlife.

Jung offered an insightful metaphor for the journey of life: the sun tracing its course through the heavens, reaching its zenith at midlife and gradually waning in the afternoon. This image may not fit the vigorous post-midlife years we're likely to enjoy today, but Jung's central point still rings true: that "we cannot live the afternoon of life according to the programme of life's morning."

Jung also noted that midlife's changes come as a surprise to most people.

> . . . are there perhaps colleges for forty-year-olds which prepare them for their coming life and its demands . . . ? No, there are not. Thoroughly unprepared we take this step into the afternoon of life.

## THE PROGRAMMED LIFE

Later psychologists expanded on the ideas of Freud and Jung, and proposed entire systems of life stages linked to specific age ranges, thus giving the numbers game scientific validation. The leading figure was Erik Erikson, who in his *Childhood and Society* (published in 1950) identified eight stages he believed we all pass through. Only three of those belonged to adulthood; however, Erikson's emphasis, like Freud's, was largely on child development.

Central to Erikson's theory—and to most others that followed—was the idea that the stages must build on one another. Each stage brought with it some task, some set of psychic hurdles that must be overcome in order to proceed to the next stage. For example, in adolescence the task was to establish one's identity by acquiring distinct values, roles, and behaviors. In early adulthood, it was to develop the capacity for intimacy by choosing a mate and bonding. Middle adulthood posed the challenge of *generativity,* a time where we give back to the world by nurturing our offspring or by playing a mentoring role to younger people. And late in life, we must struggle to maintain *ego integrity* as we become less engaged with the outside world, and contemplate the significance of our lives as its end nears.

It was Erikson who popularized the term *crisis* to refer to the passage from one stage to the next. "Psychosocial development proceeds by critical stages," he wrote, ". . . moments of decision between progression and regression, integration and retardation." In a sense, Erikson's view of growing through life amounted to a pass/fail course. If you failed to accomplish the appropriate coursework at each stage, you'd get left back, stuck in an earlier stage, emotionally unequipped for the next. Though more recent psychologists have modified Erikson's scheme, the strongly recurring theme of stage theory remains that we're expected to do certain things at certain times of our lives, and if we fail to do so, it is at our great psychic peril.

### BLOWING THE SCHEDULE

However, this core principle of stage theory is crumbling under the weight of numerous social trends initiated by the baby boom generation. Life schedules today resemble anything but a straight-line march. For our generation, the identity crisis that Erikson thought should be resolved in adolescence now often persists well into the twenties; the bonding stage that is thought to typically occur in the mid-twenties may be delayed until the thirties, or experienced more than once. People who have pursued careers with a vengeance may find the generativity crisis coming earlier than it's supposed to; and people of advanced age may be too busy with a second marriage or a third career to evaluate ego integrity.

The changes in women's life patterns, in particular, demonstrate the increasing irrelevance of stage theory centered on age. Women entering the workplace en masse, delaying marriage and childbirth, and the many women beginning careers in midlife have thrown these predictable tasks and crises way off schedule. "Give me a roomful of 40-year-old women," declares adult development observer Nancy Schlossberg, "and you have told me nothing."

Many low-income and minority individuals don't fit the

stage theory mold well either. A childhood characterized by parental neglect and the myriad problems of the disadvantaged is obviously an undependable foundation on which to build later stages of life. If you haven't been able to move into the world successfully in young adulthood, there's not much room for the introspective urges of midlife. Even white, middle-class men aren't moving neatly through the stages anymore: baby boomer males who have experienced Vietnam, a constricting economy, lack of job security, and the psychic fallout of the women's movement are likely to diverge from the model.

The urge to organize, subdivide, and discern patterns in human development is an intellectual response to a biological reality. We are all mortal creatures with finite lifespans, and certain powerful biological and social drives in common. So the stage theories of developmental psychology contain a core of truth and usefulness. But we must use them as an outline rather than a catechism, a point of departure rather than a roadmap. The pace of social change in the last several decades has been too fast for any system to keep up with.

As Janet Wolff notes in her book *Lifetrends,* "There is a strong likelihood that adult developmental psychology will undergo a major overhaul in the next decades because of the influence and ascendency of baby boomer women . . ." Acknowledging the catalyst role of women, we can extend this statement to baby boomers generally. What is it about this generation that makes us so resistant to following a pre-set, well-mapped path, and how will it affect us as we pass through the portals of middle age?

## *Talkin' 'Bout My Generation: Boomers in Profile*

"The combination of education and affluence has made them a Superclass with an economic power that outstrips the GNP of most countries. The baby boom is consumer society's R and D division—testing new products, new fads, new drugs, new morality, even new ideas about marriage and children."

Landon Jones
*Great Expectations: America
and the Baby Boom Generation*

The Depression and World War II were the formative experiences for our parents, and both these historical events kept the birth rate down for many years. Then, after the war, came the pregnancy explosion between 1946 and 1964, hitting a peak of more than four million new births each year from 1954 to 1959.

Among the factors causing the baby boom was that people got married younger after the war. Fertility was also on the rise, due to better health and nutrition. From 1940 to 1957 the fertility rate among American women aged twenty to twenty-four doubled. During the same period the median age of women having their first child dropped from twenty-three to twenty-one. All this added up to a 46 percent increase in families with two or more children over the decade 1948–1958. And it wasn't just that people were having more babies; it was that everyone was taking part in the trend.

The baby boom generation is really made up of two waves: the first wave born from 1946–1955, and the second wave between 1956–1964. There are some key differences between these two groups that will influence how each will experience midlife, even though they are really of the same generation.

The leading-edge boomers have had an advantage over the second wave, coming on the scene while the postwar economy was still vigorous. They got the jobs before competition drove salaries down, and bought their homes before demand drove prices up. The average monthly mortgage payment for a boomer who bought a home in 1979 is $450; for the second wave buying today, the average payment is $900. The values of the first group were also shaped by the dramatic events of the sixties: the civil rights struggle, Vietnam, and the climate of freedom and experiment in lifestyles.

The younger segment of baby boomers (42.3 million of the 76 million total) will be reaching midlife as we enter the next century. They tend to be more serious about money and more conservative than their older counterparts. They've had to work harder to make economic progress; the workplace has had fewer opportunities to accommodate their numbers, and the real-estate market has become harder to break into. These handicaps are only partly offset by the larger proportion of double-income households in this group, another legacy of the women's movement.

Socially, the younger half of our generation has ignored many of the issues that concerned those who came of age in the sixties. In 1967 only 44 percent of college students rated being "very well off financially" as an important goal. By 1982, 69 percent of the second wave endorsed financial security as a primary goal. In 1967, 83 percent of students said that "developing a philosophy of life" was important; in 1982 that number had declined to 47 percent.

But despite these and other significant differences, the two waves of baby boomers are more like each other than they are like any other generation, and midlife for both groups will be different from our parents' generation because of the following characteristics of our collective psyche.

## GREAT EXPECTATIONS

Baby boomers were raised during an economic boom. While we were children, our families experienced a tremendous rise in the quality of life, and we came to expect the same.

This assumption of success has had a profound effect on our psychology. We grew up being told that we could achieve anything we worked hard enough for—whether it was good grades, financial rewards, a sense of fulfillment, a perfect body, or a perfect world. We are people who don't take well to settling for less.

Never having experienced economic hardship encourages a willingness to take risks. A friend of mine was recently laid off at age forty-one from his longterm position in the front office of a big-league sports franchise. Nick was taking his time finding new employment, shopping around for a situation that met his wish list, which included personal fulfillment, respect for the work and his colleagues, and equity opportunity in the company. He told me that his standards for what he did around the middle of life were powerfully influenced by memories of his father at the same age.

> I remember going with my mother to meet him at the subway station when he came home from work in those sweltering New York summer days. I'd see him come up out of the ground, looking like a goddamned mummy, something not really alive. He just looked like a beaten guy, coming out of that hole. He'd been a leftist lawyer in the thirties, worked with the pro-republican brigades in the Spanish Civil War and all that, but now he was doing work he hated. He had sacrificed what he believed in for security, and all he was living for was his family. I knew even then that I never wanted to be like that.

Job satisfaction—feeling that one's work is meaningful and enjoyable, not just monetarily rewarding—is a powerful motivation for boomers. And we don't mind risking security to get it, as was apparent in Nick's attitude toward job hunting. "Maybe because I never went through the Depression," he said, "I have confidence that I won't fail, that I can survive setbacks."

The baby boom is also the best-educated group of Americans ever, a big factor in its *I can do anything* mentality. By 1981, when the tail end of the boom hit college age, 35 percent went on to college, compared with only 9 percent in the forties and fifties. Higher education has given us more real choices, and also encouraged our sense of unlimited opportunity. It also made us less settled, due to postponement of decisions about career and family while we finished our schooling.

Great expectations do sometimes fall short, and the flip side for boomers is a similarly high level of disappointment, frustration, and cynicism. A *New York Times* study in 1989 found that 29 percent of baby boomers felt that they had accomplished less in life than they had originally anticipated when they were in high school. This exceeds the usual level of disillusionment characteristic of aging: only 13 percent of the group ahead of the boomers reported such a sense of failure. A *Los Angeles Times* study reported similar results: only half the people polled between the ages of eighteen and forty-nine described themselves as satisfied with their lives, compared with two-thirds of those over sixty-five.

Nonetheless, a sense of optimism generally persists among boomers. While we have had to revise specific expectations to fit changing social and economic realities, we don't feel we must compromise our high standards of satisfaction. We take the pursuit of happiness seriously, and we take it to mean seeking a balance of work, family, and recreation. The belief that we can achieve such a diverse, well-balanced life is a positive stance from which to approach aging.

## A LONG AND HEALTHY LIFE

Baby boomers are the beneficiaries not just of extended longevity, due to this century's great strides in disease control, but of the more recent emphasis on personal health management through nutrition, fitness, and lifestyle changes. High-risk behaviors such as smoking are declining: the average forty-year-old man smokes less now than when he was thirty. Alcohol consumption too is down in nearly all age groups and both genders.

Raised on a high-protein, high-calcium diet that made us

the biggest and strongest Americans ever, we have learned early on from the lessons of our parents' generation, who suffered health declines in middle age due to lack of knowledge about self–care, especially about heart disease. Recent studies indicate that many health problems thought to be inevitably connected with old age can be avoided by improving health habits at midlife. This only confirms what boomers have discovered on a personal level: that they feel better and look better when they pay attention to staying healthy and fit. And we've made our physical needs a priority by adjusting the balance of work and leisure time to accommodate them.

So a long and healthy life, like affluence, is assumed as a birthright by baby boomers. But our success at combatting physical aging has its flip side too: aging is a fact of life and resisting it is futile. A study found that 55 percent of female baby boomers felt unhappy with their weight in 1986, compared with 48 percent in 1972; for men the numbers were 41 percent and 35 percent, respectively. Cosmetic surgery—including male hair replacement—has risen tremendously in the last decade. There's no doubt that this generation continues to think of itself as youthful and is having difficulty parting with that image in midlife.

### CHILDREN OF CHANGE

Baby boomers also have the advantage of being weaned on rapid change. We are accustomed to society reinventing itself every few years; "stay loose" is our motto. We are less threatened than our parents were by the prospect of major changes in the world as we grow older.

Our life patterns have also undergone a profound shift. Instead of proceeding through life's major landmarks in an orderly, successive fashion—education, marriage, career, retirement—and leaving each one inexorably behind, we may experience one or more stages several times, in different ways.

This shift from a linear to a cyclic lifestyle is evident all around us. Education, rather than being limited to the adolescent period, now continues throughout life, with periods of learning becoming briefer but more frequent. We've seen the growth of university extension courses and specialized training schools. A concurrent shift toward multiple careers in a single lifetime is also in progress. Some predict that male boomers will change careers up to six times, and women four times.

This pattern occurs in our relationships, too. Serial marriages resulting in mixed families have already become common. Lastly, a cyclic lifestyle is making the concept of retirement, or finally having some time to enjoy life, nearly obsolete. Just as work increasingly continues after retirement age, so boomers have made leisure a priority throughout their lives. It's even likely that the midlife transition—or something that resembles it—will be a repeat experience in later life.

Growing up in this whirlwind of social change has contributed to our tolerance for diversity. We went to integrated and ethnically mixed schools; participated in student exchange programs; made friends with kids of divorced parents and kids from across the country; traveled with our families; and went to colleges far from our hometowns, sometimes with a year or two abroad. We are a generation raised in an open world, and we don't think in provincial terms. This background makes us more open to midlife as yet another opportunity for learning and innovation.

### THE TRASHING OF TRADITION

Every generation has primary events that define its character, lending commonality to its psychology and motives. For the Depression generation it was an extended time of deprivation, producing a high concern for security and an attitude of gratefulness for whatever came one's way.

For the baby boom generation, marker events have come thick and fast, but have tended to deconstruct rather than construct traditions. Our events have included assassinations, Vietnam, the civil rights movement, Watergate, and perhaps most important, the women's movement.

A common thread working its way through these marker events is the demise of institutions. At no other time in history has a generation seen so many major institutions dwindle into near irrelevance: marriage and the traditional family, the church, the all-powerful state, the paternalistic corporation, even the Boy Scouts. Baby boomers have had an active hand in this process, but we're also reacting to forces outside our personal control.

The corporation, for example, used to be a fraternity that the working man joined for life (as it still largely is in Japan). If you were basically contented and competent in your job, you could look forward to continued advancement up to retirement age. That pattern is changing, especially in the management ranks. Intense competition and less job security, due to a contracting economy and the merger-and-takeover mania of recent years, have seriously eroded corporate loyalty. People tend to view a job in corporate management today as a treacherous platform from which, with luck, one might vault higher, not as a benign and protective fortress. This trend has also stimulated the rise of entrepreneurism. Even if we don't go out on our own, we may seek more control of our workplace, what my friend Nick calls "equity opportunity."

The demise of these institutions has given boomers some freedom, but we may have to pay the piper as we go through midlife. This is traditionally a time when the individual, feeling considerable self-doubt, turns to the support of cultural institutions. But since we have left families behind as we became mobile, since we have rejected organized religion, big government, and the big-brother corporation, we are left vulnerable. The cult of the self is a rather flimsy shelter against midlife's storms.

## THE GROUP: A LOVE/HATE RELATIONSHIP

The baby boom went to elementary school in classes of thirty or split shifts, to camp in floods, and to college in the largest freshman classes ever. (One client told me, "I waited in line at the pediatrician's office; then I waited in line for the classes I wanted to get into. Now I'm waiting again—to get a house.") We were bonded as a generation by rebellion, rock music, and getting high. Growing up in the age of mass media also has intensified the sense of an entire generation doing the same thing at the same time. We and television came of age simultaneously, and modern media has shaped us all profoundly. Since we were all exposed to trends and ideas almost simultaneously, we are prone to the *cohort effect*—doing what everyone else is doing.

Going through life in lockstep has made us very group-dependent, yet at the same time we fear being swallowed up by the group. Individualism and insecurity are at odds in this approach-avoidance situation. In midlife, the need for group support is strong, and since we've abandoned so many institutions, we may need cohorts. But the need to bond is counteracted by the drive to be unique.

## AREN'T WE SPECIAL?

The attention lavished on the baby boom as a phenomenon, the kind of child-rearing we experienced, and the power in numbers we became aware of as young adults—all these have given our generation a sense of uniqueness. Advertisers have sold to us throughout our lives. We have been studied, analyzed, and written about more than any group in history.

But this specialness has also fostered a narcissism that can be dangerous in midlife, making it harder to accept the inevitable shortfall from our youthful expectations. Even the high-achieving baby boomer may feel frustrated by some elusive *more*.

Modest doses of narcissism can help one stand out from the crowd and motivate the drive to care for oneself, to keep growing, to live a full life. But the process of aging is stronger than any individual, and an increasing need for connection with others comes with it. There's a fine line between feeling unique and feeling alienated. And in the relationship issues that arise during midlife, narcissism makes it harder to focus on another person's needs and problems.

## Fit for Midlife: How Do We Score?

While this profile of the baby boomer is far from exhaustive, it's clear that our generation is coming into midlife equipped with a distinct set of advantages and disadvantages.

On the plus side, the flexibility bred into our outlook on life, which we have extended to our family structures and working environments, can serve us well in a time that requires a capacity for change. Boomers as a rule are psychologically better equipped to handle change than earlier generations; we are skilled adapters. We have been educated and encouraged to seek personal satisfaction and fulfillment as a basic human right. So while an unknown future still makes us apprehensive, we also see it as potentially better; we tend to be optimistic. When midlife restlessness strikes—the feeling that familiar roles don't fit anymore—our need to cultivate satisfaction in many arenas will give us the courage to try new paths.

Our generation is the first to be fluent in psychological concepts and vocabulary; introspection and communication about psychological issues are valued and validated. Getting our fears about midlife out of the closet and into the open will help ease the strain. Our preoccupation with physical health and fitness, if not taken to extremes, will endow us with the energy to cope with a major life transition. And our group identification can provide support at a time when it is sorely needed.

For better or worse, baby boomers also have the benefit of highly visible models—*age scouts,* they've been called—to turn to for examples of vigorous and vital aging. The most visible are show biz folk who have held onto their appeal well into their forties or beyond: Cher, Jane Fonda, Warren Beatty, Robert Redford, Joan Collins, Sean Connery, Susan Sarandon. (Fonda is a special case because she's also an example of a woman achieving business success in midlife.) Aging pop music stars like the Rolling Stones, the Grateful Dead, Paul McCartney, Paul Simon, and Bonnie Raitt are admired for their powers of survival and revival against formidable odds.

In other fields we might include the writer Nora Ephron, who made the risky transition from journalism to screenwriting in her forties, and politician Tom Hayden, who bared his midlife angst in a long *Esquire* article—a new man if there ever was one. Broadcast journalist Bill Moyers is admired for his intellectually stimulating and personally revealing reports, and the "Today" show's Jane Pauley for striking out in new directions when NBC replaced her with a younger anchorwoman. But our age scouts needn't be celebrities of any stripe. We all know family members and friends who have somehow retained a youthful vitality that transcends their biological age.

On the downside, the handicaps of baby boomers in midlife will include narcissism, our often unrealistic expectations, and the lack of a sense of limits. Midlife entails acknowledging that certain youthful goals probably won't be attained, that careers and personal capacities are not infinitely expandable.

A classic case was a client of mine, a partner in a big-name engineering firm with a six-figure income. He wasn't getting enough from his work and was anguishing over a move to another firm, thinking that more money might be the answer.

But as with many people in midcareer transition, the real problems are not financial: in his case, a growing awareness that he had gone as far as he could in his organization. His learning curve had flattened out; he simply wasn't being challenged. My client was unable to act on the real issue, however. So he began to stir things up everywhere else in his life: becoming hypercritical of his wife, flirting with alcohol abuse, alienating his fifteen-year-old daughter—who responded by getting even in typical teenage fashion. Although he was sufficiently self-aware to know that he was being a jerk, he felt helpless to change his behavior.

Similarly, baby boomers' preoccupation with physical youthfulness is a two-edged sword: we have a better chance of staying vigorous long past midlife, but we cannot forever postpone coming to terms with an aging body. We will have a keen struggle letting go of our youthful selves and illusions, and acknowledging our mortality, both essential to the evolution of a strong postmidlife identity. Not recognizing the inevitability of this process is a sure prescription for midlife depression.

In the long run, most of our generational traits are neither intrinsically useful nor harmful in midlife; what really matters is what we make of them. The failure of youthful expectations, for example, need not be a demotivating force. Depending on the individual personality, it can motivate by increasing our receptivity to change, because we've been trained to believe that change equals progress.

Our early experience of affluence, or at least comfort, can also work both ways. It has encouraged boomers to take risks, but also to postpone going after financial security—a choice that starts to bring more anxiety around midlife. Similarly, our history of burning bridges, of shunning the institutions that once supported people through transitions, has deprived us of some support, yet it has stimulated our search for other options such as networks of friends, extended families, and interest-based associations.

## REMAKING MIDLIFE IN OUR IMAGE

Though the downside will present challenges, boomers are basically facing midlife from a position of strength. Part of the reason is the overall *aging of America,* a well-documented trend produced by the combined effect of three demographic facts: the baby boom, the birth dearth that followed it, and the increased longevity of the older generation.

This is causing an important shift in the center of power in American society. There are more older people in relation to the entire population than ever before; the median age crossed thirty in 1979 and is expected to be thirty-six by 2000. In short, baby boomers will have the unprecedented experience of aging in a society where older people are the majority, which is making a profound impact on our perception of growing older. As one friend put it, "It's not so scary to turn forty when even the sixty-year-olds don't look old."

The huge population bulge of the baby boom—the sheer weight of our numbers—has made this generation influential since adolescence. We are accustomed to holding center stage, and now we are moving into what is traditionally the most powerful age group, economically and politically. The age thirty-five to forty-four segment of the population spends the highest per capita amount on consumer goods and services, rivaled only by the next oldest group, those forty-five to fifty-four. This double whammy of numbers and timing guarantees that boomers will remain society's prima donnas, our tastes catered to by business, our concerns exhaustively scrutinized by academia and the media.

"Don't trust anyone over thirty," used to be our motto. Now it might be something more like, "Don't trust anyone under thirty or over sixty." In other words, baby boomers have always related to each other much more than to other generations, made our own choices for good or ill, set our own course. It won't be any different in the fortysomething years:

we'll bend the rules of the midlife passage to fit our widely varying situations and needs, with the confidence that the rest of our generation is doing likewise.

## CHANGING THE WORLD . . . AGAIN?

We can trace the baby boom's uniquely self-defined path through the familiar history of our social involvement. Middle age used to be the time when people came to prominence in the tribe, the community, the church, the government, but these institutions have lost much of their meaning for baby boomers. Or had, until recently.

In the 1960s, our youthful belief in our own special destiny and the power of our numbers took us into the streets to change the world. Then came a period of disillusionment and retreat from social activism, which probably climaxed around the time of Watergate and the oil crisis. After that, boomers more and more withdrew from public life to focus on gaining control of our personal destinies. We became the "Me Generation," seeking our full human potential during the seventies, and nirvana through consumerism in the money-mad eighties.

But boomers seem to be reengaging with society as they enter midlife—not so much as citizens of the global village, but by taking better care of our own backyards. Having children, however belatedly, has been an impetus: things like library closings or the prospect of a polluted water supply tend to get parents involved. Volunteerism is up, and environmental activism is a growing force.

One of midlife's strongest urges is making connections with others, part of what Erik Erikson called the *generativity urge*—and boomers are evidently feeling it. In a 1990 *New York Times* article, Daniel Goleman reports that studies indicating the fortysomething reassessment "often leads to a more compassionate attitude . . . [and] a sharp rise in people's altruism," part of an overall reordering of priorities. Psychologist Martin Seligmann, in a *Psychology Today* article called "Boomer Blues," suggests that the antidote for an epidemic of midlife depression is "an attachment to something larger than the lonely self. . . . A balance between individualism, with its perilous freedoms, and commitment to the common good should lower depression and make life more meaningful."

Journalist Laurence Shames, writing about the baby boom at midlife in the magazine *7 Days,* calls for "a new idea about what success means."

> By sheer numbers, we have been shaping the country as we've gone along—from a hotbed of adolescent unrest to a scramble of young adults' ambitions. It's time to change it again. Here at midlife . . . it's time to work toward an idea of the well-lived life that has less to do with more and more to do with better.

He suggests that the money chase of the 1980s was a red herring in our quest for "a vision of the well-lived life," and that boomers have a responsibility to redefine that vision for an age of scaled-back expectations. If anyone can do it, we can.

As social circumstances have shaped our experience of midlife, so baby boomer midlife has the potential to reshape society. Boomers are subject to many of the same biological, psychological, and social pressures that drove midlife for earlier generations, yet our unique position in history is driving us to break new ground. We don't go through life stages on time because we believe we have all the time in the world. We have more of just about everything it takes to handle transition successfully—mobility, education, options, resources, familiarity with change—than any previous Americans.

Midlife will be a very conscious event because of our penchant for tracking our progress as a generation and for doing things en masse. We also face some tough challenges in growing past our egocentrism and our attachment to being young. Boomers will resist fiercely the idea that midlife is the beginning of life's decline. We will not "go gentle into that good night," resigning ourselves to a slow slide into golden invisibility.

This is both our great advantage and potential liability: how do we maintain our positive stance toward aging while learning to live with our limitations? For better or worse, our experience of midlife transition will be powerfully influential, both for our own lives and those that follow us. It seems to be part of our destiny as a generation.

# 3

# Blueprints For Change

## Transitions and How We Respond to Them

*For all that moveth doth in Change delight.*
EDMUND SPENSER

C hange is an eternal fact of life, never more so than in our fast-forward century. Most of us accept the fact, but we don't always delight in it, by any means. Even when we feel discontented with the shape of our lives, the safety of familiar ground, however barren, may be easier to live with than the risks of uncharted territory. One of my midlife clients, a corporate human resources executive who thought about leaving to start her own personnel agency, put it this way:

> I feel like I keep bouncing back and forth between being bored and being frightened. When the boredom gets out of hand, I resolve to change. Then I think it over and say, "Whoa, wait a second! What if it doesn't work out? You only get so many chances; at least you're surviving now." That lasts a while, and then I get down about being stuck again.

## Life Structures and Transitions

The dynamic tension between the known and the unknown is more or less constant during adult life, though the balance is usually weighted on one side or the other. The times in which we are most grounded, with the major pieces of life in place and satisfying our emotional needs, are known in developmental psychology as periods of stable life structure. Times when the urge to change becomes dominant are called transitions. These two are the basic components of the life cycle, the DNA and RNA of human experience.

While a stable life structure is in place, a person's inner work focuses on sustaining and enriching the structure, and pursuing goals within it. Within an established structure such as a career in medicine, for example, there will be further decisions regarding advanced training in one's specialty, about setting up a practice or joining a larger one, furthering one's career through conferences, published work, and partnerships. In a thriving family structure, constant small shifts and adjustments are made in response to the growth and development of individual members.

In a strong life structure, all the key elements—work, family, behavior, values, beliefs—fit together in a self-sustaining ecosystem of identity. A litmus test for the stable life structure is the question: Does what you do—at work, home, or play—fit reasonably well with your sense of who you are? If so, then the structure is solid enough to maintain its equilibrium even if one or another part of the system suffers damage—a family quarrel, a missed promotion. The weak spot can be tolerated or repaired. But if your actions are out of sync with your feelings and values, it's a signal that change is due.

During transitions, our tasks are to reappraise the existing structure, explore new possibilities, and make choices that promote the establishment of a new structure. Transitions are

inherently unsettling, tumultuous, experimental, and exciting. They are about destructuring and reassembling the building blocks of identity—and the longer you've spent putting
those together in a certain way, the scarier that prospect is. But
the work of taking apart can be just as important as the work
of putting together.

## MOVING OUT OF THE COMFORT ZONE

In a major transition such as midlife, we feel conflict between
the desire to stay in our *comfort zone* and the need to keep
growing. In the comfort zone, the challenges we face every day
are familiar; our capabilities exceed the demands on us. If we
try to remain in this state when transition knocks, however,
we grow bored and stagnant; our general outlook and performance ultimately suffer. A good example is the person who
has "topped out" in a job and no longer gets the stimulation of
learning from it—and doesn't look for stimulation elsewhere
in life.

On the other hand, when we're pushed too far out of the
comfort zone by cumulative change and stress, when demands
far outstrip our capacities, we experience overload and frustration. In extreme cases, such as the loss of someone close
through death or divorce, combined with other stresses like
a job change, an illness, a legal battle, or a financial crisis,
we may completely shut down, resisting change in order to
protect ourselves. During times of heightened stress, staying within the comfort zone can be a temporary coping
mechanism.

The optimum condition for growth is when we're operating
at the limits of our capacities, or slightly beyond. In this state,
we are expanding and thriving, exercising our skills. We feel
stimulated, enthusiastic and fully alive, in control, and capable of commitment. Most of us have experienced these

feelings at some time during our twenties and thirties, that period of mastering challenges, of building and consolidating careers and families. The drive to go on experiencing them is strong.

But here's the big catch of midlife: we can't seem to get that charge anymore from the things that used to provide it. Maybe the kids are out of the house and you no longer need to leap to the challenge of organizing several lives every day; or maybe they're just old enough that the primary task of setting them on the right path is accomplished. The prospect of another business trip makes you tired just thinking about it. Going for the big real estate score used to be your biggest high, but wouldn't it be nice to have Sunday off instead of holding another open house?

Depending on how you react to change and use its energy, the midlife transition can be an experience of renewal. If your fear of change is stronger than your need to break out of old patterns, the result more likely will be stagnation.

### IS IT TIME FOR TRANSITION?

In childhood and adolescence, transitions come so frequently that there is almost no quiet space in between. Psychological development is closely tied to biological growth; hence infancy, during which there are nearly daily gains in motor and cognitive skills, is a period of constant transition.

As we move through childhood and adolescence into early adulthood, the frequency of transition slows, because it is driven less by physiological change and more by social and psychological forces. It becomes a more conscious process: by the time we make the transition from adolescence to the first life structure we set up outside our birth family, we are keenly aware of the multitude of turbulent feelings accompanying this change—from the soaring euphoria of liberation to the deflating despair of loneliness.

As transitions occur with less frequency, they gain in potential energy. Like the forces that build up around an earthquake fault, the longer the wait between transitions, the more power is released when one finally hits. By the time we approach the midlife transition, we've usually been engaged in building our life's most complex structure: the matrix of career and relationships that gives form to our adult identity. The force that shakes this edifice is a powerful one indeed.

Until the last few decades, adult development experts gave little attention to transitions as a distinct stage in the overall picture. Erik Erikson's system basically sent people from one stage into the next without a break, assuming they successfully resolved a crisis of no specified time duration. Daniel Levinson, who followed Erikson, put more emphasis on adult stages and especially on the transition periods separating them. Rather than leaping directly from one stage into the next, people would go through a sort of molting phase that might last several years.

In general, stable life structures are becoming more short-lived and will continue to shrink as the pace of social change revs higher, making transition ever more the norm. Life structures, Levinson thought, could last no more than seven or eight years, and transitions might take nearly as long.

### PUSH VERSUS PULL

Looking closely at what impels us into transition can help predict how successfully we will resolve it. All transitions can be described in terms of a push/pull dynamic: there are negative factors that *push* us to escape from our comfort zone, and positive factors that *pull* us toward a vision of satisfaction and fulfillment.

In midlife transition, the big push is provided by our fear of aging, boredom with the restrictiveness of old roles, awareness of limited time, regret for lost opportunities, and a sense of loss of our vital, youthful self. On the pull side, we are attracted by the prospect of continued health, vitality, and growth; the excitement of trying out new identities; the urge to use our time most effectively; and the hope that we can achieve inner harmony by integrating what we do with what we most value.

Both kinds of motivation are useful, though it is better to respond to the positive charge. The pull is fueled by healthy ego needs for growth and stimulation, curiosity, self-actualization; the push is driven by fear and neurotic compulsions. We often respond to the push reflexively, taking the quick way out of an uncomfortable situation—quitting a job or abandoning a relationship—whereas in answering the pull—moving toward an attractive goal—we tend to make healthier, more sustainable decisions.

An encouraging fact of the new midlife is that the positive pull is strong and accessible to most people. Visions of a healthy, productive, and well-integrated life beyond midlife are becoming easier to imagine and more widely validated by society.

## Have It Your Way: Transitions For All Seasons

There is no single blueprint for midlife transitions—they vary greatly in form, degree of intensity, and causes. The shape of a transition depends on one's age, background, and personality type. Some are precipitated more by external circumstances, others by internal rhythms. Before we take apart a typical transition to examine its inner stages, let's look at a few of these variations in the larger pattern.

The most subtle transitions are hard to notice because they don't cause any great tumult or crisis in one's life. Sometimes, through a series of small adjustments, you can fine-tune an existing life structure so that it remains stable and functional while allowing room for growth. This might happen around midlife, for example, if you reorganize your responsibilities at work to assume a mentoring role by managing a team of younger people, while doing less of the day-to-day selling, designing, dealing with clients, or seeing patients. Or, you might cut down on work time to pursue volunteer activities or an interest long simmering on the back burner.

A similar, though less subtle, kind of transition, is when sustained progress produces a positive change in one's life structure. These might be a career success that leads to relocation, an offer from a new employer, or a new business venture. In relationships, it might be when a sound marriage leads to the decision to have children. These changes are smooth steps onto a new ladder rather than continuing up the same one.

In the reverse pattern, changes within a life structure can produce a negative transition. One classic example happens in relationships where people are basically incompatible or haven't really worked at compromise and communication, and the relationship declines. It may be internal, a kind of character deterioration that results from consistently making unworkable choices or pursuing self-destructive behavior—as when substance abuse leads eventually to a career collapse. Transition may be triggered abruptly by a serious setback such as the death of a spouse or getting fired.

The most dramatic form of transition—what people usually think of when they talk about a midlife crisis—is *breaking out*—deliberately and thoroughly rejecting an old life structure and searching for a new one. This top-to-bottom transition is often accompanied by a definitive ending (quitting a job, selling a home, getting a divorce) and sometimes an identifiable beginning (returning to school, moving to another place), and it usually happens in one's mid to late thirties or early forties; radical change after that time is rare, though probably becoming less so.

Radical transitions may be appropriate if an old life structure was deeply entrenched, profoundly unrewarding, or resistant to change short of such a major break. But such transitions are full of difficulties and sacrifices, and people who undertake them must spend an extraordinary amount of effort setting up a new life structure. A model, or at least a metaphor, is the political refugee who cuts lifelong personal and cultural ties in the quest for freedom—even for life itself. Few of us will ever face such an all-or-nothing choice, but any person who feels trapped in his life structure understands the comparison. He too may feel the need for desperate measures and be willing to make sacrifices of friendships, family, status, or possessions in exchange for freedom.

Levi became a midlife refugee at forty-five. He had an extremely successful cardiology practice, was on the teaching faculty of an Ivy League school, and was a mover and shaker in his field with an international reputation. He related his experiences:

> When my dissatisfaction started to peak I thought I was just overworked so I did what I'd always done—scheduled a vacation. This time, though, I went without my wife and kids; she couldn't get away from her job anyway. And I did something different. I went on a backpacking trip with a medical school buddy who lived in Denver.
>
> We took off for a week into the backcountry. We did a lot of talking about our lives, our work, what we wanted, things like that. I can't really explain how it happened, but as we were heading back to the car, getting closer to civilization, all the feelings I'd gotten away from came back at me like a ton of bricks. It was as though I hadn't really allowed myself to feel them before; I was so deadened. But at that moment I knew for sure it wasn't just overwork. It was much bigger and deeper. I was so tired, of me and of my life.

Levi tried to work things out when he got home. His wife was very threatened by the feelings he expressed; she was heavily invested in their current lifestyle and it was meeting her needs. They went to counseling, and Levi also started therapy by himself. He had endless meetings with his partners, trying to make the system bend to his needs, but he might as well have been speaking a foreign language. His wife continued to resist any change in their roles. The demands of his work were overwhelming, and soon he was back to 12-hour days, six days a week of teaching, office hours, writing.

> It never seemed to let up. My life was running me. To make a long story short, I picked up and left—went to the [San Francisco] Bay Area and started over with a residency in psychiatry. It was incredibly hard at times, and sometimes I wondered if I'd lost my mind. My family certainly thought so! Sheila and I separated—she decided she couldn't leave Boston and all her ties there—but our college-age son moved out with me.
>
> It was terrific being with residents fifteen years younger; I suppose my age gave me some authority, and I felt special. Whatever—it was great to be learning again.
>
> I still miss some things, but the bottom line is I've never regretted it. Now [more than a dozen years later] I hardly recognize the person I used to be. I was driven by what others thought of me, fixed on the outer wrapping of success, and my beliefs, my expectations were set in concrete. It took a total break to see that.

Levi was fortunate, but there's a fine line between a successful break-out transition such as his and escapist behavior. Escape fantasies can resemble bold and creative choices from the outside, but are usually attempts to shortcut the transition process. The root of escapism is the mistaken conviction that changing the wrapping will change the contents. We've all seen the results of this belief, from the trivial to the tragic: buy a new car, get a facelift, change your wardrobe, find a new mate. The Porsche will restore youth—so goes the delusion— the younger lover will restore vitality. Regrettably, the new lover often loses his or her luster before the new car does.

Escapes only delay resolution, diverting energy needed for the real creative work of midlife.

A hallmark of escapist behavior, and a way to distinguish it from a difficult but necessary break-out transition, is its re-etitiveness—one false move leads to another. People also tend to rush into escapes before giving the old life structure a fair chance to change, and without living with their feelings long enough to understand their source. It may be difficult to tolerate discomfort, but it is essential if we're to learn from it—in fact, this is one of the master skills of managing transitions.

There are also what might be called *pseudo-transitions.* We all know someone who gets involved in one business venture after another but somehow can't see any of them through the tough times. These are people who have never really created a stable life structure. They may be the right age for midlife, and they're certainly going through changes, but for them it's the norm—just part of a continuing effort to grow out of adolescence and establish some kind of viable life structure.

## Situational Transitions

University of Maryland psychologist Norma Schlossberg takes a *situational* approach to categorizing transitions, keying them to changes in our roles and situations. It is an approach that reflects today's social reality, where people are ignoring the rules about the timing of life events.

The following transitions are not time-linked, except insofar as specific circumstances (like retirement) will occur at certain times of life. They may or may not overlap with midlife transition. In fact, what Schlossberg describes are *events* that precipitate change, rather than the process of the change itself. They are easy to recognize from your own experience; you might use them as another palette of colors to shade in your own picture of midlife transition.

*Anticipated transitions* are events that we plan for: going to college, getting married, starting a career, raising a family, retiring at sixty-five. As the traditional *marker events* of adult life, they call for some adjustment but they usually aren't traumatic—unless they either fail to happen, or all happen simultaneously, which can cause stress.

*Unanticipated transitions* are the changes that take you by surprise: learning your spouse has a terminal illness, having a baby after you thought you couldn't, being fired or forced to retire early, getting a job offer you can't refuse that involves moving to a new place. Whether positive or negative, such curveballs can throw you off balance.

*Nonevent transitions* are the things you counted on happening that don't come to pass. You never marry; your spouse doesn't want children; you reach a plateau on your path to the top; you'd like to take early retirement but can't do without the income. Unfulfilled expectations can be transitions in themselves, because they require our conscious adjustment and adaptation.

*Chronic hassle transitions* are ongoing stressful situations that can be tolerated, but which may eventually call for decisive action. Marital strife is among the most common, though it might be a parent with Alzheimer's, a boss or a coworker who strains your good will at work, or a troubled teenager in your family.

As you can see, transitions can be as varied as individuals. In reviewing the above definitions and categories, you'll likely recognize a style of transition you've gone through in the past. This will provide useful guideposts along your path through midlife.

## *Plotting the Curve: The Anatomy of a Transition*

There is an overall pattern to the way people go through transitions, which is composed of a series of stages. I sometimes describe it as a circle where we begin by descending one arc and continue around and back up to the top. Each transition stage is a segment of the curve, and the unbroken circle implies that we will take this journey cyclically.

Not everyone proceeds through the stages of transition in an orderly sequence, but for clarity, let's begin by looking at it that way. The following is a good outline for midlife or any adult transition.

### THE DESCENDING CURVE OF DISCONTENT

In this phase we start to notice cracks in the foundation of our life structure. Most events and feelings we experience seem to erode our happiness rather than support it. Boredom sets in; we crave novelty. We feel out of step with our identity; perhaps our work or family role seems no longer congruent with our sense of who we are. We become more urgently aware of the passage of time.

Some of the things people say to themselves during the early part of transition are:

> I used to be excited about going to work, but lately it's all I can do to drag myself there. My lifestyle depends on the money, but the thrill is gone. I don't think I can face doing the same damn thing for the rest of my life.
>
> My wife is holding me back. She doesn't understand what I'm feeling. We don't seem to have anything to talk about anymore, or even want the same things.
>
> My back bothers me a little every morning when I get up now. How can my body be getting old when I'm still playing rock-and-roll on my car radio?
>
> If I'm ever going to try hang-gliding, I'd better do it soon.

I get really depressed when I see a happy couple with kids. It's probably not going to happen for me at this point, and I don't think my work is enough anymore.

This period of growing discontent is often triggered by a key event, either external or internal. Some critical change—a death, illness, accident, divorce, or sudden departure from a job—may serve as the flashpoint that lets us see our world, or ourselves, differently, showing how deep those cracks in the foundation really are.

Jerry, a photographer, has a story that paints a classic picture of early midlife and shows the impact of such catalytic events. He had started shooting pictures for fun and ended up with a career. Most of his friends in their late twenties were settling into occupations, and he thought he should do likewise, but didn't; even after earning some recognition in his early thirties, he remained ambivalent about his craft—it was still half business, half hobby.

At thirty-five he married, and his wife soon became pregnant, which galvanized Jerry into a more professional attitude and forced him to pay more attention to the business side of his work. He was in his early forties when some subtle but persistent feelings began to surface.

I never really made the choice to be a professional photographer. It seems like circumstances made the decision for me . . . getting married, having a baby, needing a bigger house. Sometimes I feel angry toward my family, as if they made me do it, even though I know this isn't true . . .

It's not that I don't like photography, especially compared to other ways of making a living. But it's been a real struggle to take it seriously, to run a business. I guess I resist it because I haven't really accepted that this is what I will always do or who I am. These feelings are affecting how I do my work; I seem to lack the energy to go out and get the jobs, promote myself. It's almost like I don't want the work, and yet I need it. I should hang a sign around my neck that says, "Hire me at your own risk."

A couple of things happened in the last year. My father had a stroke and we had to put him in a nursing home. It's been real hard for a lot of reasons, including the extra responsibility on me—I'm the oldest son—to help my mother. But something else . . . seeing him compromised, needing so much help, reminds me how important your health is. I look at him and wonder: will I end up that way? And if so, shouldn't I make sure that every second now counts?

Also, a couple that my wife and I were very close to, our best friends, just split up after ten years. Watching them go through their divorce really shook me. If there's no permanence to things, what's the point? I'm not looking for a guarantee—but you make compromises, in work, family, everywhere, because you expect that it will all work out in the long run. Then you look around and see that it doesn't.

I know I've been unhappy with different parts of my life for a long time, but I never really expressed it or took it seriously—just hoped things would work out for the best. I'm really questioning that now. I feel like I have an obligation to make some decisions before time runs out.

Denying that anything is wrong or different is also typical of the first stage of transition. If we're good at denial, we can remain stuck at this stage for a long time. Denial is usually expressed through behavior that will distract us from our feelings: workaholism is a common example, or, as in my own case, spending money on expensive toys, trips, and other transient pleasures. Even an activity as physically beneficial as exercise can be used in the service of denial.

### DEEP IN THE HEART OF TRANSITION

Sooner or later, all the energy that was gathering in the first stage is liberated as if in a breaking wave. Now we move into the heart of transition, its most tumultuous stage. The first important step of this stage is to let go of the old life structure, and is often accomplished through some symbolic act like quitting a job, leaving a relationship, or changing locations. The mood of this stage, especially early on, is often negative. Feelings of anger, despair, fear, anxiety, loss, confusion, and alienation are common, but working through these feelings—by which I mean letting yourself live with them, explore them, get to know them—is essential. The intensity of these feelings can be frightening, but if they are run away from and not resolved, they can poison the next life structure.

Around the time I was getting ready to leave my hospital-based practice and go out on my own, I was experiencing scary mood swings. One day in the morning, I'd be furiously angry because I wasn't recognized or satisfied with my work, and would spread the blame around on my wife, my colleagues, whomever was handy. The same day in the afternoon, I might become euphoric over a promising phone call. The next day I'd simply be in despair, feeling alienated, convinced I was a fraud with nothing to offer the world or my family (except the income I knew I was capable of earning at a job that was making me miserable) and wondering, on the most basic level, who the hell I was anyway, and what I was doing here.

At this stage we really get down to the guts of transition: the question of identity. As the process unfolds, more and more aspects of our life come up for reconsideration. While midlife turmoil may be initiated by job dissatisfaction, for example, eventually its embrace can widen to include family, friendships, and other pieces of a life structure we thought was unshakeable. Gradually we understand that no single factor is responsible for our confusion and unhappiness.

Later in this stage we come to realize that the answers we seek aren't outside of ourselves somewhere, but inside. This awareness is the fulcrum on which the successful resolution of transition turns. Eventually our negativity and turbulent emotions subside and become easier to live with as we recognize their role in reshaping our identity.

Tolerance for ambiguity and indecision is a key skill at this stage; rather than racing ahead toward any resolution, we need to spend some time living with a range of possibilities. Solitude and introspection are important tools now—we need to dust them off and give them space to operate. For the most part this movement inward happens on its own, and we should let it happen, not sabotage it with more denial.

The work of *individuation*—Jung's term for the lifelong evolution of the individual, distinct self—requires that we make some quiet space in the hurly-burly of our lives to listen to our hearts. In this calmer environment, the work of individuation gets rolling: the critical issues of identity and values are examined.

Jerry, for example, considered how his various roles—those of the first-born son, the creative artist, the businessman, the head of a family, his parents' caretaker—fit together, and how they related to the person he wanted to be. One unexpected detail that emerged was his rediscovery of a childhood love of fishing. He began making a point of going on short trips— sometimes with others but more often alone. He realized he'd been feeling resentful about spending so much of his time doing what others wanted of him; this activity was purely *himself.* While his solution, fishing trips, may seem trivial, it is truly a part of the picture that forms once the fine-tuning begins.

## RESURRECTION AND RENEWAL

After the storm of negativity has passed and the ship of identity been given a thorough going-over in its aftermath, a new stage of growth begins. We have more energy and a more positive outlook. New possibilities and priorities surface, reflecting a clearer sense of values, and we begin to make decisions more confidently, based on this newly emerging sense of what matters most to us. Our life structure and behavior may not change much, but how we feel about them does; we have come out of the forge with a tempered, more refined sense of self.

Emboldened by redefining *who* we are, we can get to work on *what* we want. At this point people tend to go through a certain amount of experimentation to either build a new life structure, or simply remodel the present one. A woman who has concentrated on caring for her family may try her wings in the business world; a man may take on an expanded family role. Both may practice a new stance with regard to their parents or boss, or behavior that leads to better fitness and health. Such actions give us critical feedback: what works, what doesn't.

As we come full circle in transition, a new *mission*, a vision of what we want our lives to be, may be conceived and launched. It starts with a vague, unformed desire or inspiration; if this is firmly rooted in our values, plans will inevitably coalesce around it. The fully formed mission includes a goal or set of goals linked to a timetable, and contingency plans to deal with the inevitable surprises and derailments. The launch, as with the end of stage one, is often marked by a symbolic act.

Jerry's journey through transition led him to change course somewhat, though not in a radical way. He recognized that he needed to take better care of himself. His father's stroke—plus a family history of high blood pressure—led him to change his diet and lifestyle. Like a lot of baby boomers, he'd been very ambivalent about becoming a parent himself, and this changed in a more subtle process of acceptance. Much later, he acknowledged: "This is what I've done, and it's not so strange; in fact, I'm enjoying it; I like feeling protective and reliable toward my kid."

Perhaps the hardest realization for Jerry was that he did not like the business side of photography. He had assumed, from most of the examples he'd seen, that after you worked for a while as an assistant, you went out and opened your own studio. Finally, he faced his persistent reluctance to compete in the marketplace. At first, he tried going into partnership with another photographer who was a more aggressive promoter. It was a good try, but his partner soon grew convinced that he didn't need Jerry and promoted him right out the door. Then Jerry heard about a job as a corporate photographer, and landed it. He was concerned that he'd find the work—shooting for newsletters, brochures, training materials, annual reports—unchallenging, but it didn't prove so. He got to travel, which he enjoyed (and which took him to some new fishing locales), and managed to exercise his creative chops in his free time.

At the end of our transition, we've climbed back up the opposite arc of the circle to a period of stability, with a new or revised life structure in place. If the essential work of the previous stages has been done adequately this structure will have credibility, vitality, and durability. True to our wheel of life metaphor, another transition will come along sooner or later, but won't be needed right away.

### PATHWAYS AND PITFALLS

A typical adult transition can take from two to three years to complete. This time frame is probably growing shorter as transitions become more *situational*—that is, as they become less linked to age and more related to the major life moves that people now undertake with dizzying frequency: new jobs, new primary relationships, relocations.

However, a major transition still requires an extended period of time to unfold. Long-standing patterns and behaviors don't change quickly. In fact, new research on the nervous system indicates that in order to change long-established habits, our synaptic pathways must be reshaped—new connections formed and old ones allowed to weaken. New pathways may even need to be created. Our brains retain enough plasticity in adulthood to do this, although not as quickly as when we were young. It takes conscious practice of a new behavior—eating more healthily or interacting emotionally with someone in a different way—to rewire the neurological circuits.

Not everyone goes through the transition stages in exactly the same order, but if you skip large chunks entirely, you're likely to miss out on the self-exploration that's vital to a successful resolution. Some people, out of fear or impatience, leap directly from the first to the last stage, bypassing much of the scary *deep transition* work. An unmarried woman feeling the chill of age may rush into family life ill-prepared; the person whose work has grown stale may jump ship without even trying to patch what may be a basically sound vessel. They try to fire up a new life structure before the ashes of the old one are cold, without taking the time to live through the emotional catharsis, the interior search, the test phase for new values. Opting for the short cut usually leads to energy-wasting escapist behavior.

On the other side of the coin from those who want to move too quickly toward resolution are people who get stuck in a certain stage of transition, due to fear of change or inability to confront their feelings or question their values. They may attempt, against all evidence, to deny that a life structure is ending or needs changing—clinging to a failed marriage or relationship is a typical case. That person ends up trapped in a lifeless structure and loses the potential that transition holds.

## Patterns of Change: What's Your Type?

Different personalities react differently to transition. Some resist change, are uncomfortable with the unknown, and spend a lot of energy trying to control or ignore an inevitable process. It's my experience that such people often unconsciously sabotage their situation so that circumstances finally dictate a change.

Others do well with change; they have a high tolerance for ambiguity and thrive on the stimulation of roller-coaster emotions. The change-lover may seem better adapted to deal with transition, but we've all known *change junkies* who can't seem to make the commitments needed to establish and maintain a viable life structure.

Your individual *change profile* is the template of your personal blueprint for midlife transition. It's the product of everything in your background: genetics, upbringing, education, your present circumstances, and your history of past transitions. While each profile is unique, we can nevertheless identify several typical patterns of change. No one is a pure type, though you probably know people who closely resemble one or another of the examples described below.

These profiles describe the ways in which people defend themselves against change or use it to their advantage. We sketch the strengths and weaknesses of each type, and the critical work each needs to do in midlife. Becoming familiar with these types can help you chart your own course as well as understand those close to you who are facing transition.

### THE STIMULATION JUNKIE

The Stimulation Junkie thrives on change. No two days are the same—not necessarily because the situation changes, but because she makes it change. She grows very uncomfortable when forced to live in anything resembling a predictable way. Change doesn't frighten her, stability does.

Such people seem to be in their element in midlife. They see transition as a legitimate cover for getting rid of whatever they don't like about their life structure. In truth, however, they are often guilty of throwing the baby out with the bathwater.

The Stimulation Junkie's favorite defense is a combination

of denial and impulsive acting-out. Move to a new city? No problem! End a fifteen-year marriage? "I was bored anyway." More accurately, they're in touch with only the positive side of their feelings, denying any that smack of negativity. This one-sidedness keeps them off balance, unable to look at reality, but midlife requires an unflinching assessment of pros and cons. Sometimes pain is useful to help make real choices; hurt and loss are part of the real process of reassessing identity.

Margaret was a forty-one-year-old vice president of human resources at a major bank. She had worked there for three years when she decided to leave, and her resume indicated that this was the longest she'd stayed in any position. She liked challenges. So far she had been lucky, overcoming any doubts about her ability and stability through exuberance and keeping her sights on what she felt was the big picture. Her personal life likewise reflected her addiction to change. She had never married because she felt it would be too confining. "What if I want to take off on a trip and my husband doesn't? What if his work demands a move and I'm not ready?" she asked.

In midlife and facing another job transition, Margaret wanted some help on what the next step should be. But our work was difficult because she consistently blocked my attempts to find out what she didn't like about her prior positions, insisting that the past was "old business, irrelevant."

Margaret's forward-looking perspective is a useful but incomplete approach to midlife. We need to use our past; denying its validity is denying a big chunk of our identity. Trying to construct a future without reference to the past is an exhausting and fruitless endeavor. In Margaret's case, as with other Stimulation Junkies, the challenge was getting her to slow the frenetic hubbub of her life and focus on what was going on inside her. When we finally did that, what emerged was a feeling that she was flawed and would never find happiness. It went deeper than her immediate situation—she had little sense of her core identity and feared that she wouldn't like any of herself if she had to live with it for too long.

Such doubts are typical of the Stimulation Junkie. In midlife their critical work starts with believing their feelings are worth listening to, and then slowing down enough to hear them. Learning that they can survive unhappy feelings is important too.

Margaret stopped seeing me soon after we got to the heart of the matter. Leaving therapy precipitously wasn't really surprising, given her compulsive need for novelty, but by understanding her change pattern better, she was better equipped to make choices about her next move. And she left with my words, "Look before you leap," in her ears.

## THE CHANGE RESISTER

On the other side of the fence is the Change Resister. "If it ain't broke, don't fix it," might be the motto of this type. The problem is that, for them, things are hardly ever "broke" enough to warrant fixing. Change Resisters will try anything to make an old life structure seem solid and enduring. They fear the future and have only warm feelings for the past; when pressed, they'll settle for the present. They would much rather accept an evil that is known than a potentially better unknown.

Though his conservative behavior is the opposite of the Stimulation Junkie's, the Change Resister uses similar defenses: denial and rationalization. Out of touch with his feelings, denying discomfort and dissatisfaction, he is a *minimizer*—someone who downplays the strength of his reaction to any emotional stimulus. The minimizer's motto is "It's all right."

The strength of Change Resisters is in their ability to continue investing an existing life structure with value. This makes them less prone to escapist ploys. Their chief liability is their negativity. When forced to move forward, they often react with anger, like a sleeper awakened too early, not realizing that their negativity subverts the changes they're trying to make. This pessimistic, prove-it-to-me mindset becomes a self-fulfilling prophecy, making positive change more difficult to accomplish.

In my counseling work with corporations, I often come across Change Resisters, whose skepticism can sap energy from the group's adaptive efforts. One such was Stan, a line supervisor at a fruit canning plant. When new equipment came in, Stan's response was cynical. "These new machines," he complained, "break down one after the next. I spend more time fixing them than I do running them." It sounded like a reasonable gripe—until I found out that the new equipment hadn't even been installed yet. Stan's attitude naturally affected the people he supervised: some were looking forward to the changes but were intimidated about expressing it.

Change Resisters in midlife can be identified by withdrawal and alienation. The passage of time is inevitable; since they can't stop it, they stop participating instead. This leaves them feeling outside the circle, abandoned and alone. They get stuck in the second stage of transition, in a mood of loss and sadness. Claire, at forty-three, felt like this now that her children were gone and her husband more than ever consumed by his work after a promotion to company president. "They've all moved on to greener pastures. It seems like all the work I put in to create a home, a place for everybody, is just wiped away. I don't know what to do next."

What Claire did at first was take to the living room sofa, a subtle message of reproach. Since no one was around to get the message, Claire, basically a healthy person, gradually shifted into introspection and began fantasizing about a career. When a chance came along to work as a landscape architect's assistant, and eventually do a project on her own, she was scared but went for it. She observed later that she was "really saying 'yes' to a whole new way of seeing myself."

The critical work for the Change Resister in midlife is to find something that *pulls* them toward a vision of the future. The Change Resister is very much a hands-on learner. He needs to be shown that change can work for him before he trusts it. But beware of the Change Resister's resolve. He can be very convincing that life as it is—however boring and dissatisfying—is better than life as it might be.

## THE NOSTALGIA BUFF

The Nostalgia Buff is a close cousin to the Change Resister. Rather than being openly hostile to change, he is more subtle. Passive resistance, a kind that's hard to pin down, is his forte. This person's point of view is that, while change may be inevitable, the past sure was wonderful. He moves into the future with his eyes on the past, like a person crossing the street backward. He may get where he's going, but not with any sense of purpose or determination.

The major handicap of this personality type is *lack of motivation*. People are usually motivated by the discomfort of old situations that need changing and from the positive attraction of future possibilities. The Nostalgia Buff may feel discomfort but his vision is drawn toward the past. Seeing his history through rose-colored glasses, he may lose all sense of why he decided to make a change in the first place.

Jeff was a good example. At forty-nine, his marriage was hitting the rocks. He and his wife found they had little left to connect them after their kids left for college; parenting had obscured the problem for some time. By the time Jeff came to see me, his wife had decided to move out; she was ready to make changes and wanted action.

Jeff didn't disagree with her assessment of the marriage, but his solutions were inappropriate, rooted in nostalgia for their joint past. At one point he even suggested they adopt a child.

While she was planning to return to school for her masters and go on to teach, he was romanticizing the image of her pregnant, and still attached to his home and children.

Even after she moved out for an agreed-on trial separation, he continued to passively resist any real change. It took him a long time to realize that his wife was truly growing and moving on, but finally he began to let go of the past and see how a new life structure could work for him. A breakthrough came when he realized that his wife's return to work might enable him to cut down on his own working hours. When he saw what was in it for him, he began to share some of her enthusiasm, and this served as the basis for a renegotiated relationship.

The Nostalgia Buff cannot be confronted out of his position. His passivity acts like the oil on a duck's feathers: one's best efforts at motivation simply roll off his back. Because his main defense is a romantic view of his history, critical scrutiny of the past is lost on him. He usually needs time to work through it on his own. Sometimes it takes a crisis, but a better approach would be to consciously work at envisioning some future scenario that would be an improvement over both past and present.

### THE ESCAPE ARTIST

Anyone who says you cannot change the contents of the package by changing the wrapping hasn't met the Escape Artist. Mercurial and energetic, flying off in a hundred directions at once, she has undeniable charisma.

Unlike the Change Resister, who digs in his heels when transition beckons, or the Stimulation Junkie, who leaps in headfirst, the Escape Artist misses the point altogether by moving too fast to see what's happening. Her escape routes may be seductive and thrilling, but usually run sideways and rarely toward the resolution of transition. At best, they are harmless entertainment, at worst counterproductive, siphoning off the energy needed to adapt or restructure one's situation.

The Escape Artist is particularly vulnerable to being sidetracked by material possessions and new experiences. Marissa is typical. She decided to celebrate her fortieth birthday by buying a sportscar. She had always owned a practical sedan, but when she started feeling old, the antidote was a new set of wheels. This is a common impulse in our car-oriented culture and not inherently a harmful one. She enjoyed the car, and it was a reasonable investment; it just didn't solve the problem. There was no magic in the machine: she still felt forty and tired.

The next escape was quitting her job and taking a trip around the world. Again, there is nothing wrong with that unless you expect too much from it. The trip was fun, but Marissa landed literally back in the same place where she'd started. And it had more serious consequences than the car: not only were her savings depleted, but she had given up the means to replenish them. Now she was broke, out of work— and forty-one.

At this point she finally started confronting her feelings about her situation. She returned to her career, and began working in a volunteer program with runaway kids. And where the latter may sound like an odd way to deal with feelings of being old, it suited Marissa well. She could identify with the desire to run away—after all, she was a master of it. Being a resource for younger people made her feel connected and valuable, satisfying her mentoring urge, and contact with the kids exposed her to new styles and ideas, which her personality thrived on.

The main defense of the Escape Artist is displacement, that is, misidentifying the true source of one's feelings or directing them toward inappropriate targets. Marissa displaced her feelings about growing older onto her possessions, and when that failed, onto her physical surroundings. Again, these solutions are not in themselves wrong or pernicious. They simply miss the point. Real change happens from the inside out, and Escape Artists need to focus their energies on self-exploration and acceptance of themselves and their situations.

## THE ANTICIPATOR

The Anticipator deals with transition by getting ready. Unfortunately, that's often all he does. The perpetual student, he takes classes, attends workshops and seminars, investigates, experiments, and becomes an expert in the potential benefits of change. All this is fine, but it's all just preparation. What he doesn't do is make a commitment and follow through with it.

The Anticipator's strength is his intellectual understanding of the need for change. He may even display the right emotional reactions, expressing and working through all the appropriate feelings. His liabilities are procrastination and a fear of risk. He feels that you can never be too well-prepared for change, and wishes that success could be guaranteed and risks avoided. He has a strong obsessive-compulsive streak, which can be maddening to those waiting for him to take the leap.

Carl was an Anticipator. At thirty-seven, he was getting ready for midlife. He wasn't quite there yet, he said at our first meeting, but thought he soon would be. I believed him: he was showing signs of boredom with his work as comptroller in a large corporation, and was considering going out on his own as a financial planner. Two years earlier, his fiancee had ended their engagement without warning, and Carl was just beginning to feel ready to start dating again.

Carl prepared in similar ways for both these major changes in his life. He thoroughly researched the fields—finance on the one hand, women on the other. So far, though, he had gone no further with either, staying at a distance and making no commitments.

Underlying his reluctance was fear of failure. "What if I make a choice and it doesn't turn out right? I'm thirty-seven: I only have so many choices left. If I pursue a 'wrong' avenue and it takes me two or three years to find out, then I'm forty and have even more pressure and less time. No, I've got to make sure this time."

Carl's sense of urgency about time and choices is not unusual in midlife, but his need for certainty is unrealistic. Sometimes the best you can do is minimize the chance for error and then take the leap, assuming that you can correct in mid-jump if necessary. Anticipators like Carl underestimate their ability to adapt. There's no such thing as a sure thing, especially in midlife, but a dream has its own self-correcting power. It sweeps us along and alerts us when we stray off course. A useful practice is to pick a small challenge and see it through—even if you fail, the consequences won't be dire or irreversible.

## THE RECONSTRUCTIONIST

A subset of the Anticipator, the Reconstructionist is active to excess, all too willing to move on to new and better things, always busy learning, always getting ready. What distinguishes the Reconstructionist is that her compulsion for newness and change is directed almost entirely inward. The Anticipator may be preparing for external changes; the Escape Artist also looks outside the self for answers. But the Reconstructionist believes that the act of continually recreating and perfecting the self will protect her from the emotional buffeting of midlife transition.

The human-potential movement of the seventies encouraged this mindset toward self-improvement. Judith Viorst gives an astute profile of the type in her poem "I've Finished Six Pillows," which reads in part:

I've finished six pillows in Needlepoint,
And I'm reading Jane Austen and Kant,
And I'm up to the pork and black beans in
     Advanced Chinese Cooking.

I don't have to struggle to find myself
For I already know what I want.
I want to be healthy and wise and extremely good-looking.

I'm learning new glazes in Pottery Class
And I'm playing new chords in Guitar
And in Yoga I'm starting to master the lotus position.

I don't have to ponder priorities
For I already know what they are:
To be good-looking, healthy, and wise,
And adored in addition.

I'm improving my serve with a tennis pro,
And I'm practicing my verb forms in Greek,
And in Primal Scream Therapy all my frustrations
     are vented.
I don't have to ask what I'm searching for
Since I already know that I seek
To be good-looking, healthy, and wise,
And adored.
And contented.

Reconstructionists tend to blame themselves rather than external factors for midlife's troubles. In their case, a little outward projection wouldn't hurt: maybe it *is* time to look for another job; maybe your needs and your spouse's *are* irreconcilable. Instead of chasing an impossible standard of inner self-perfection, they can make progress by focusing on what's improvable about their external situation.

### THE CHANGE SUFFERER

The Change Sufferer goes even farther than the Anticipator in doing the right things during transition. She anticipates change, does the research, and follows through with appropriate action. She takes risks—about the right amount. She gets her support system together. The Change Sufferer's problem isn't failing to come to grips with transition. It's that she believes the only way to do so is to suffer a lot. She feels something is missing if she isn't miserable during midlife.

This is actually one of the less maladaptive approaches to midlife, since the Change Sufferer is essentially well-grounded in what she does and how. While it's rare that transition doesn't bring some unhappiness, a high degree of visible suffering needs to be scrutinized. On one level, it can be simply a holdover from the time when midlife was more widely seen as the beginning of the end, the gateway to old age, inevitably accompanied by menopausal misery, for both genders.

A Change Sufferer named Paula moved from New York City to the San Francisco area to be with a man with whom she'd fallen in love, giving up her precious-as-gold rent-controlled apartment and a well-established social life. The love affair soon ended, but, meanwhile, Paula had found a good job in her field and decided to stay. She complained inordinately, though, about how different her new environment was from what she was used to—how much less rewarding culturally and personally. It became clear that this was her mode of reacting to most new experiences. Never married, she was eager to be in a relationship but quick to find fault with new prospects, and usually relieved to move on. Whether it was finding a new doctor or buying a new car, any change was traumatic and caused pain.

Suffering publicly can be a way of assuaging guilt about going after what you really want. It serves as a shield against criticism from people who resent the changes you're making. Usually this kind of suffering has little basis in reality—but it nevertheless has an effect on those around the sufferer. Paula's job, for instance, called for a fair amount of travel abroad—usually a welcome perk. But in talking about it, she tended to emphasize the woes of jet lag, worry about hijackings, and fret about falling behind in her work.

Change Sufferers need to remember the following points. We teach others how to assess what we're going through by expressing how we feel about it. We have a lot of control over what we hear from people and the kind of support they offer. If we complain about transition, we communicate that it's a painful experience, and those who care about us will often mirror our feelings back to us. We in turn evaluate our experiences partly through their reactions, and thus our negative feelings are validated. So suffering creates a feedback loop: we send it out, we get it back.

## THE SOMATICIZER

The Somaticizer lets his body do the suffering for him. He develops a series of ailments, often exaggerated, as a way of expressing psychological symptoms he can't acknowledge; for example, his anger and fear about aging. This is not to say that the suffering isn't real. Psychosomatic illnesses are not imaginary but often true organic dysfunctions whose origins are mainly in the psyche—as with the worrier who develops an ulcer.

Strangely, the Somaticizer's symptoms often serve to get him what he wants but is too inhibited to ask for. After all, illness is a great way to satisfy dependency needs: you get nurturance, sympathy, and genuine concern. You also get off the hook for unrealized (and unrealistic) expectations and goals. Who can criticize the somatic sufferer for wanting to leave his job if it has produced so much stress? The Somaticizer usually is not consciously malingering, but subconsciously expressing something his conscious self won't accept.

Gene was a highly competitive, fifty-one-year-old auto mechanic referred to me by his doctor, a respected orthopedic surgeon. In telling me his story, Gene emphasized that he'd always been able to do twice the work of anyone else in the shop. He would be still, he assured me, if his back hadn't gone bad. The problem, his doctor told me, was that there were no organic indicators for pain as disabling as he described.

Like other midlifers referred to me by medical doctors, Gene was at first resistant to the idea of seeing a psychologist. He felt that his doctor didn't believe him, and that I was supposed to find out if the pain was all in his head. Articulate and insightful, he was challenging to work with because he wouldn't even admit the possibility of a psychological connection.

My first tactic was to reassure him that I didn't think he was a malingerer or a faker or a wimp; I merely wanted to understand how he was experiencing the pain and what impact it was having on his life. Once Gene accepted this—which took several hours of hurdling obstacles—he began to look inward at the function of the pain.

Gene's father, also a hardworking mechanic, had wanted him to go to college, but Gene left school after a semester and started working at a garage. The owner saw him as a cut above the other employees and gave him responsibility and promotions. Soon Gene was running the shop. He had managed to live with his back injury, a legacy of high school football, until the past six months. The pain became intolerable right around the time that the owner—whom Gene had come to see as a father figure—had a stroke, and his family approached Gene with an offer to sell him the garage. He assumed his back flare-up was coincidental.

Reviewing how he felt about the offer, Gene expressed tremendous ambivalence. It was flattering to have been asked, yet to assume ownership would mean giving up some barely formed ideas about doing something else for a living before it was too late. He'd talked it over with his father, who had told Gene how foolish it would be to look this gift horse in the mouth. The conflicting feedback was tearing Gene apart:

there seemed no way to please himself, his family, and his mentor.

As he described his internal conflict, Gene began to see that the back pain had been his way out of it. He could reject the offer without offending either his father or father-figure. Who could blame him for starting off in a new direction if his back would no longer support his work in the garage? Indeed, his desire to change course in late midlife would be seen as brave and industrious. The insight didn't make his decision to leave easier, but it did allow him to make it with a sense of conviction and commitment. A year later, his back pain was still with him but was no longer disabling.

Somaticizers are lucky in that they receive a very loud signal that something needs changing in their life. They must, however, be able to make the connection between their physical malaise and their mental tasks. They could save themselves unnecessary pain by not suppressing their feelings so ruthlessly, but permitting them other outlets. They need to give themselves permission to feel depressed, anxious, bored, or alienated in midlife. Otherwise, resolving their transition will be stymied by a lot of wasted energy and pain, not to mention the toll their illness takes on others.

## What Makes the Midlife Transition Different?

Given these various types of transitions and personality profiles of changers, what really sets midlife apart from other passages? It resembles other adult transitions, yet is distinct. The quintessential adult transition, its importance is reflected in the metaphors we use: the watershed of adult life, the crest of the hill, or in Jung's image, the zenith of the sun in its course. The danger (as well as a certain truth) of these comparisons lies in the implication that life after midlife is all downhill. But as a guide to postmidlife behavior, especially today, the old metaphors are lacking, and we need to find new ones.

Perhaps what most sets midlife apart from other transitions is that it's such a supremely conscious one. We may sleepwalk through other passages, but the temblor of midlife's onset rarely fails to jolt us awake. Something in us needs and welcomes the irresistible urge to examine ourselves and our lives under a magnifying glass, to take stock of where we've been and where we're going.

Passion—intensity of feeling—is a hallmark of midlife. As we mentioned earlier, the pace of transitions slows as we progress through our thirties, and the stresses of building and maintaining a life structure pile up heavily. When we hit midlife, they are unleashed with more power than other transitions. We acknowledge this power and try to defuse it with jokes about turning forty, with escape fantasies, and with endless talking to relieve the tension. These tactics are natural and helpful, yet they aren't enough to harness the power. Most of that work goes on inside.

Whereas the young adult transitions were about moving out into the world, learning to adapt to the larger social context, the psychic movement of midlife is inward. This transition is about introspection, slowing down, turning inward to engage in intense self-scrutiny.

If the transitions of the twenties and thirties are driven mainly by psychological and social factors, midlife also has a stronger physiological theme—more like an adolescent transition. Not that it's a purely physiological event, but much of the psychology of midlife follows from the physical fact of aging. The awareness that our time is limited is the single most potent motivation behind the impulse to change.

Sometimes this can be counterproductive; we tell ourselves that we have only so much steam left and can't afford to waste it on side trips like learning a new skill or pursuing an interest outside work. In retrospect, such explorations often prove to be the catalyst of the midlife journey and failing to undertake them is like putting on a set of golden handcuffs: you remain trapped in a secure but dead life structure.

If we've made earlier transitions successfully, we can come to midlife with enough self-knowledge to ground us during the upheaval. Often at the lowest point on the wheel, the most difficult stage of the passage, the typical midlifer is reassured to discover a strong core of identity that buffers the loss of illusions and the shift in values, and enables him to strike an attractive deal with the constant of aging. This gives us renewed energy to continue on our journey.

# 4

## The Well-Tempered Self

### Our Continuing
### Search for Identity

*In the middle of our journey of life, I came to myself
within a dark wood where the straight way was lost. Ah,
how hard it is to tell of that wood. . . .*

DANTE ALIGHIERI

If we think of midlife transition as a psychological journey, then it starts with getting lost. The poet Dante Alighieri wrote the lines above at age thirty-seven, during a time of great personal conflict and self-doubt. Of course, it's not only great poets who have this experience. Dante's words reminded me of something else. When he first came to see me at age forty-one, a client named Steve described feeling "like Jonah swallowed by the whale." While the metaphor is different, he too felt trapped in a dark place, deeply discontented with his work, marriage, and self-image, and groping around blindly for a way out. Steve's personality, akin to the Stimulation Junkie (the type that thrives on change), prompted him to look for a quick fix. Admitting to his feelings, though, was just the first step on a long road.

It's striking how often such images of darkness and confusion occur in descriptions of how people feel early in midlife whether centuries ago as in Dante's work or today. The social forces that shape us may change drastically, but aspects of the inner struggle that emerges around midlife are timeless and universal.

It's as if, in your thirties, you had been striding confidently down a well-lit path, your choices and commitments clearly illuminated, when, suddenly or gradually, the view becomes obscured. Unexpected urges well up from some deep place inside; goals you've been steadily pursuing no longer seem worthwhile, and disappear.

You look back to the person you were at twenty and can't recognize him or her in the person you've become. You tend to blame others around you, or your situation, for problems that arise from feeling out of sync with yourself. Most unsettling of all, you gaze into the future and see an unbearably dull, flat, familiar road stretching endlessly ahead—or else a blank and terrifying *terra incognita*.

The urge to change can start with any single element of your life structure—relationships, work, your place in the community. It rarely remains that narrowly focused, however, and usually widens to encompass more and more issues. Sooner or later we realize that what we're looking for isn't just a new set of individual circumstances. The fundamental quest, the source of all those dark and bewildering feelings, is nothing less than the need to redefine our identity—to figure out who we are and who we want to be as we get ready to embark on the second half of life.

By the time we're midway through adulthood, we've taken on so many roles—the child, the student, the lover, the explorer, the employee, the boss, the friend, often the spouse and the parent—among other emotional roles our unique experience has taught us to play. We may simply have been too busy for years to pause and consider which of these roles are truly important to our well-being, and which may be holding back our growth.

Midlife demands such a pause. It becomes critical to dig down through all those layers in search of our essential being, our authentic self, to make sure that he or she is someone we want to spend the rest of our lives with—or to discover what it will take to become that person.

In the preceding chapter we referred to the process of growing and evolving through adulthood: *individuation.* Jung coined the term and was largely responsible for the idea that human development continues throughout our adult life. He defines individuation as "coming to selfhood," or "the process by which a man becomes the definite, unique being he in fact is." It is the individual becoming separate, but not set apart from the rest of humanity, or "the gradual differentiation of functions and faculties which in themselves are universal." Put another way, it is the challenge of becoming both fully human and fully ourselves.

The work of individuation goes on all the time, but most intensely during transitional times. Because certain events tend to cluster around midlife—the death of parents, our stock–taking about how well we've fulfilled our own and other's expectations, the feeling that we've lived in the world long enough to have our own opinions—midlife is often the first time we truly experience ourselves as separate, integral, independent beings. And it takes getting used to.

## Will the Real You Please Stand Up?

The work of redefining our identity in midlife can be like an archeological dig, taking us back through the roles we've learned to play since childhood. A client named Jill undertook such an exploration in therapy.

Jill's father was a high-achieving scientist in a research firm. From an early age, Jill got good grades and figured that intellectual precociousness was the only way to make an impact on her father because of his intelligence and accomplishments. She denied herself a social life in order to study and was accepted at Stanford in chemistry.

> [I was] still following in Daddy's footsteps. My brothers had taken themselves out of the race for approval, one by dropping out of school and the other by joining the Peace Corps, which was considered a nice little diversion. I figured the "holy grail" was mine for the taking. Boy, was I wrong.
>
> When I decided to apply to graduate school in architecture, my parents were shocked. My mother was sure I wouldn't make it; remember, this was 1970 and women architects were not common. I got no help from them at all, and had the definite feeling they were waiting for me to fall on my face. I was so angry!

Jill used her anger to spur herself on and show her parents they were wrong. She started a company, put in impossible hours, and built her business with her sweat and blood. After ten years it paid off: "We were the leading shop of our size for several years . . . lots of awards, lots of praise." As she approached midlife, though, things started to go sour for Jill, both on the personal and business fronts.

> I look at my life now, and it makes me sick. I'm forty-one, never been married, no children, bored with architecture. And to top things off, the last two years have been a financial disaster—my business is on the verge of bankruptcy. I'm so angry with myself—I thought I had finally figured out who I was, and now being an architect seems meaningless. Besides which, I've failed at it!

She knew her business problems were mostly due to changes in the industry; it was getting harder for small firms to compete. But in the back of her mind was a small voice saying, "I told you so."

> I don't know if it's Daddy's voice chiding me for leaving the academic world or Mother's telling me she knew I couldn't make it. I try to block it out by just working harder, but I'm barely running in place. When I think about making any major change in my life, I get paralyzed by fear. It's preposterous. I know I'm smart and capable. I've got a list of accomplishments a mile long, and all I can think of is the disasters that might happen if I take any chances.

Like many boomers, Jill saw her profession as her primary identity, and it was being severely shaken by her recent business problems. Underlying that identity was a role she'd been playing since childhood: the good, hard-working girl trying to please her parents, grubbing for grades, getting into graduate school, doing her grown-up work ultra-conscientiously. She was smart enough to see that this behavior wasn't working the way it used to, but she wasn't yet able to envision other ways of operating. She needed, at midlife, to call on other aspects of her character to help herself through transition—but first she needed to discover them.

Allowing the suppressed or neglected sides of our personality to emerge is one of the primary tasks of midlife. We'll come back to Jill's story as we examine in more detail the psychological processes the identity quest involves.

## Gearing Up for the Identity Quest

Midlife stories vary widely, but most of those I hear contain one indispensable ingredient: emotional intensity. Yale psychologist Daniel Levinson makes this observation about the intense quality of the feelings we experience during this transition.

> A profound reappraisal of this kind cannot be a cool, intellectual process. It must involve emotional turmoil, despair,

the sense of not knowing where to turn or of being stagnant and unable to move at all. A man in this state often makes false starts. He tentatively tests a variety of new choices, not only out of impulsiveness but, equally, out of a need to explore, to see what is possible, to find out how it feels to engage in a particular love relationship, occupation, or solitary pursuit. Every genuine reappraisal must be agonizing, because it challenges the illusions and vested interests on which the existing structure is based.

In other words, the feelings of midlife must be strong enough to rattle our cages. We may be so heavily invested in maintaining what we've achieved, our core identity so buried under the layering of roles we've taken on, that we need a blast of emotional energy to break us loose and get us moving.

That power is also the great potential of midlife: the same energy that can scatter the building blocks of our identity can, if used constructively, turn transition into a quantum leap in personal growth, a true opportunity for transformation. To make that happen, though, we have to take the plunge into the emotional maelstrom. This means allowing yourself to feel the doubts, confusion, sadness, and fear that come with midlife, as well as the joy, elation, and hope. It means dropping the defenses that dampen your feelings, the good along with the bad. Strong emotions are more than stimulants; they carry information that we need. Ignore the feeling and you miss the message.

The reverse is equally true: if we sweep our strong feelings away in a frenzy of hyperactivity, or take various escape routes to hide from them, we may stop growing at this critical point. Our perspectives will shrink, our fear of aging increase rather than subside, and our connections with the world and other people atrophy rather than multiply. We may simply postpone the "genuine reappraisal" of our lives to a later age when it becomes much more difficult. "If a man goes through a relatively bland period when midlife transition is going on," Levinson says, "it will limit his growth."

"This is not to suggest," as Gail Sheehy says in *Passages*, "that people who suffer the most severe crisis always come through with the most inspired rebirth. But people who allow themselves to be stopped, seized by the real issues, shaken into a reexamination—these are the people who find their validity and thrive."

## THE PERSONALITY FACTOR

Personality and our personal history are key pieces of the psychological background, an outline that guides our perception of midlife. How we perceive events is influenced not just by what is there to be seen but also by what we need to see, what we are afraid of seeing, what we are used to seeing, and what others tell us we should see.

Personality is the collection of deeply embedded traits that comprise our individual character. By the time we reach forty-something, most of us have good working knowledge of our basic personality type: whether we're chiefly gregarious or more solitary, impulsive or cautious, dependent or self-sufficient, or any of countless variations. This self-knowledge is important as we enter the midlife crucible.

Whatever your unique psychological profile, it will be brought out in relief when midlife turns the emotional volume up. Personality traits and conflicts seem to grow from mere hills into mountains—or the pressures of transition may reveal cracks in the foundation of personality you never noticed before. If you tend to be insecure, for example, but suppressed those feelings while riding the success wave in your thirties, don't be surprised to find yourself questioning your worth or competence during midlife. Just keep in mind that remedies that worked in the past—such as burying yourself still deeper in your work—will likely be less effective now.

The full range of personality traits is present in each of us, in varying degrees. We all have some obsessiveness, for example, or some narcissism in our character. When one or more features becomes dominant and overbearing, an imbalance exists; that is, the trait becomes hardened and inflexible, running the person's behavior with little reference to external reality. Transitions are especially taxing, even disabling, for people with character disorders. The following tendencies, if present, rate special attention during midlife.

*Narcissistic personality.* Such people are overly invested in their appearance, which masks an underlying fear of inadequacy. The prospect of aging and the visible loss of physical beauty threatens them at a deeper level than most people. They are prone to magical or ritualistic behavior—such as compulsive exercise or faith in a cosmetic regimen—to keep the beast of aging at bay.

*Obsessive-compulsive personality.* This person's need for order and organization masks a fear of being out of control. Midlife requires a tolerance for ambiguity, which can be hard on this personality type, especially. He may resist change or act impulsively to avoid anxiety.

*Passive-dependent personality.* These people are overly dependent on others and doubtful of their viability as independent beings. They can be very manipulative during midlife, trying to get others to make decisions for them and acting angry if pushed to decide for themselves. They frequently see themselves as victims of midlife.

*Antisocial personality.* This type carries chronic anger around and displays it as disregard for the rules others live by. Accordingly, she is tempted by easy escape mechanisms that provide short-term relief from decision-making. She has little regard for the trauma her behavior may inflict on others, and, in the extreme, actually derives satisfaction from it.

## BALANCING YOUR POLARITIES

Another way to look at the evolution of identity is in terms of polarities—sets of opposing characteristics or ways of behaving that change over time. Each pair represents a kind of continuum of feeling and behavior along which we move between the extremes. Transitions can cause a shift in where we stand. Daniel Levinson describes four major sets of polarities.

*Young/Old.* At any time we may be young in some ways and old in others. Where we stand on this continuum is the primary focus of the midlife transition. We must find new ways to be young or old that reflect our changing values and sense of self. The generativity urge, expressed in mentoring younger people or guiding one's own children, is a typical mode of being older. Paradoxically, giving of ourselves to those coming after can also keep us young. Physical aging, of course, is the primary way in which we feel older, whereas the kinds of risk-taking people feel compelled to do in midlife provide ballast on the young side.

*Masculine/Feminine.* Traits that we associate with each gender coexist in all of us, and as we move through life, we become less typically one or the other. In midlife, men begin to manifest traits most often thought of as female (for example, sensitivity, or the desire to nurture), and women exhibit traits thought of as male, such as decisiveness and aggressiveness—a healthy process that permits the evolution of a more balanced personality. This is one of the most profound changes that occurs in midlife, and one of the most threatening to people with rigid ideas about gender-appropriate behavior and feelings.

Jung recounts the story of a Native American warrior chief "to whom the Great Spirit appeared in a dream. The spirit announced to him that from then on he must sit among the women and children, wear women's clothes, and eat the food of women. He obeyed the dream without suffering a loss of prestige. This vision is a true expression of the psychic revolution of life's noon . . ."

The story has meaning for men today who are feeling the desire to spend more time with their families. Midlife women, on the other hand, are more likely to exercise their potential to move out into the larger world, to assert themselves in a business or community activity.

*Constructive/Destructive.* At various points in our lives we are either putting life structures together or more involved with taking things apart. The latter is definitely characteristic of transitions. Razing the old life structure, or parts of it, is a necessary step on the way to rebuilding a new structure that reflects our interior changes—a kind of psychological urban renewal. The destructive stage of early transition brings forth a lot of anger and negativity, and is threatening and scary to most. It is the time when marriages are most likely to be wrecked, careers trashed, old friendships and pursuits abandoned.

*Detached/Connected.* This polarity describes the degree to which we are connected to the outer world of people and things, or to the inner world of thoughts and feelings. We often describe personalities in similar terms, such as inner-directed versus outer-directed or extroverted versus introverted. The usual movement in midlife is to become more detached and introspective, at least for a time. But for people whose lives have been more solitary, or not so weighted with connections, the opposite may happen: they become more attentive to the world around them, becoming involved in family, volunteer organizations, and social service.

These are not all of life's polarities, of course. Other dimensions in which we may change include active/passive, spontaneous/planned, rational/intuitive. The last is an important polarity to pay attention to in midlife, especially if you tend to make decisions and choices on a logical, empirical basis. In order to find out what's really important to you at this time of life, to get a true fix on the self beneath all the roles and the direction you're headed in, you need to become more attuned to your emotional, intuitive side. You need to listen to messages that may not make rational sense at first.

The overall aim of individuation is the development of a more balanced personality. Until middle adulthood, our experience leads us to emphasize one side of the polarities more heavily: we're taught to "act like a man," be constructive (or, depending on your background, to be destructive), get along with others. Around midlife, though, our inner voice starts talking about the other side of the polarity, and it grows strong enough to be heard through the external messages. We can sense movement within ourselves, though we may not understand where it is taking us. This natural movement is toward a state of integration and balance that we can glimpse at midlife, if we're lucky—maybe for the first time in our lives. We *can* get there from here, as long as we don't get in the way.

## Coming Apart

How does the identity quest operate in midlife? The polarity set of destructive versus constructive is a good model. It starts with coming apart—disassembling the components of self such as work and family life for close scrutiny; shedding expectations, roles, and assumptions that are no longer valid or useful. This is primarily an experience of loss, which brings us into a close encounter with the dark side—midlife depression—and compels us to confront the reality of aging and mortality.

There is no avoiding coming apart if we want to come together again, to experience the renewal and reintegration of
our identity in a vital form—a form in which we know who we
are, what we want, and where we're going. All the psychological processes, or tasks, and the states of feeling that characterize midlife take place in the context of one or the other of these
two larger movements. Let's look at the various aspects of
what happens while we're coming apart.

### DE-ILLUSIONMENT: WHAT AREN'T YOU GOING TO BE WHEN YOU GROW UP?

*De-illusionment* is Daniel Levinson's term for the liberating
process of giving up the illusions of earlier stages of development: childhood, adolescence, or younger adulthood. This
process primarily occurs in the early stages of transition, and
is related to *disillusionment.* However where that term con-
notes disappointment and loss of faith in people and ideas, de-
illusionment is a broader, more encompassing internal event
that promises growth.

In our younger life, we are sustained by certain myths: our
unconscious belief in immortality, our sense of unlimited potential, belief in the world's essential benevolence, and our
personal innocence. Such beliefs enable us to take the bold
steps of breaking away from our parents and making a place
for ourselves in the world.

As we move on through life, however, those myths become
handicaps. If you persist in believing you have all the time in
the world, then you can forever put off living fully, learning
how to be intimate, saving money for the future, or practicing
a healthy lifestyle. If you haven't figured out that you're probably not going to become president of the company, your work
will be constantly shadowed by frustration and a sense of
failure. If you can't acknowledge your own capacity for mal-
ice, greed, laziness, or jealousy, then everything that happens
to you will always be someone else's fault.

De-illusioning ourselves is not an easy process by any means, and it is especially hard if you have fallen far short of what you thought you would achieve by the middle of your life. Dwelling on the gap between your present reality and the idealized image you had at twenty produces little but blame of yourself or others. But even those who have attained their goals sometimes find that the old dreams can't sustain them forever. Remember that we need to stay just outside the comfort zone to keep growing: continued vitality and enthusiasm are contingent on embracing new challenges. Those who "stay with the old, achieved dream," observes Gail Sheehy, "find themselves in their fifties literally squeezing it for lifeblood."

Before the company he worked for was taken over, Ian had felt optimistic about rising to the top of its marketing division. He'd paid his dues, been steadily promoted, felt he was looked on favorably by top management. After the takeover, when he met with the new management, they did a lot of talking about restructuring. The message was subtle, but Ian was able to read between the lines and realize that his future was being sidetracked.

"When my new supervisor called me in, I first thought we were going to talk about expanded possibilities, or that he would want to use what I knew about the business. I'd been there eight years; I thought I had invaluable experience. The real news hit me like a ton of bricks."

Ian's options were to accept being plateaued and soldier on with the company, or start looking elsewhere. Continuing to grow in his job didn't seem to be among them. For quite a while he didn't do anything except feel bewildered, angry, and ashamed. He kept up a good front with his friends, but his wife soon felt the strain of living with someone who was so unhappy.

Several years later—after leaving to go into business for himself, then realizing he preferred a collaborative environment and joining another, smaller company—Ian is still coming to terms with the change in his self-image. "My parents were immigrants, and I had that message pounded into me: that if you got the right education, the right start, there was no ceiling in this country. Anyone could get to the top."

Maybe anyone—but not everyone. De-illusionment carries a double whammy for many baby boomers: we were raised to have high expectations of success but then caught in the wave of competition and corporate consolidation.

The process of de-illusionment goes deeper than adjusting one's self-image based on career success. Some of the myths that we have to shed operate beneath the conscious level: we're not even aware of them. UCLA professor Roger Gould, in his book *Transformations,* refers to a series of *component assumptions* that have to die as we mature. The most general one, from which all the others proceed, is: "There is no evil or death in the world. The sinister has been destroyed." Though we may consciously deny that we believe anything so naive, rooting it out of the unconscious is a different matter. Here are the other component assumptions we must face in the coming-apart phase.

*The illusion of safety can last forever.* As children we believe that our parents have the power to keep us safe from the world. That internalized sense of protection lingers past the time when we acknowledge our parents to be mere humans, because we have invested other things with this magical power—our mates, career status, social position, money. Perhaps the most truly important, and truly terrifying, awareness midlife brings is that ultimately we are alone and unprotected.

*Death can't happen to me or my loved ones.* As we'll discuss in more detail later in this chapter, we can intellectually accept the fact of death while rejecting it as a personal reality. This illusion is responsible for a lot of procrastination and escapist behavior. It can be most troublesome for men, who tend to be more heavily invested in their physical identities.

*It is impossible to live without a protector.* This is a corollary to the illusion of safety, and a common excuse for shying away from risk. It is especially relevant to women who are raised to expect that being a *good girl* or a *good wife* will bring its just rewards. My client Jill, who was introduced near the beginning of chapter four, is someone who suffered from this illusion—despite the contrary evidence of her own life.

*There is no life beyond this family.* This can be an illusion of childhood, which dies as we grow more independent and leave the home. It can also affect those who are parents around midlife, especially mothers whose primary work and purpose has been raising their children, and who now find themselves in an empty nest.

*I am an innocent.* If we were truly innocent, we would live forever—isn't that the lesson of Genesis? Conversely, as long as we retain the illusion of immortality, we can deny our dark side. In midlife, though, the game is up on both fronts: we must acknowledge, if we haven't before, our own complicity in the bad things that happen—our own power to be destructive. People who see themselves as victims or powerless cling to the illusion of innocence, and in consequence can be blind to self-destructive behavior. They may attack others when threatened, or retreat into substance abuse. For adult children of alcoholics or of otherwise dysfunctional families, midlife is often the time when they come to this important realization.

The stripping away of illusions in midlife can be likened to sculpture: as the distinctive human image emerges from the uncut rock, so is our identity clarified and distinguished from all others. Or we can think of the Japanese samurai sword, pounded down to a thin but incredibly strong and flexible blade from a shapeless mass of metal; so the well-tempered self comes out of the midlife forge.

One direct and concrete benefit of the de-illusionment process comes from the fact that maintaining our illusions past the point of usefulness takes enormous energy. Jettisoning them liberates us for more productive uses of our inner resources.

## THE DEATH OF THE HERO

In the coming-apart phase, a powerful metaphor for identity change and maturing of the personality is the death (and rebirth) of the hero. Every culture has its hero myths, as studies such as Sir James Frazer's *The Golden Bough* and Joseph Campbell's *Hero with a Thousand Faces* have shown. In the stories of heroes, people have always seen parallels to the challenges, triumphs, and defeats of ordinary life.

Jung was one of the first to point out the important psychological function the hero serves. On a psychological level, heroes are models for the development of our *ego consciousness*—our awareness of strengths and weaknesses in our character, and the self-knowledge we need to cope with life's major tasks.

In a classical myth such as that of the Greek hero Perseus, the youthful hero, full of vigor and self-confidence, slays a monster or triumphs in some other kind of struggle with the forces of evil. This superhuman achievement can symbolize the individual making the difficult transition from adolescence to adulthood over all obstacles of personal history and circumstances.

But the idealism and confidence that allow the hero to succeed can eventually lead to his downfall, through the sin of pride, in a sacrifice for the common good. In Greek myth, the gods punish those who aspire to be godlike; Oedipus saved the city of Thebes from the Sphinx but doomed himself by breaking the incest taboo. In Jung's interpretation, the gods represent other parts of the psyche keeping the ego in check. All the classical tragedies turn on the hero's fall. In a modern-day variant, Tom Wolfe's novel *The Bonfire of the Vanities*, his bond-trader hero calls himself a "Master of the Universe" and so comes to a nasty end.

Each of us is the hero or heroine of our own myth, a complex amalgam of our aspirations, ideals, dreams, talents, and flaws. We are the sum of all our parts, the best and the worst, the larger-than-life essence of the individual. Individuation can be seen as our personal hero evolving over time. The adolescent hero is rough-cut, trying on different roles but rarely integrating them into a whole. In early adulthood, the hero becomes more focused and directed, his traits more clearly defined. This is the time of dragonslaying: the hero of the twenties and thirties typically expresses his power through identification with work, or for many women, through childbearing.

As we approach midlife, our youthful hero is running out of steam and his mission is questionable. Maybe the dragon has been dispatched, or maybe we've just lost interest in being the leading architect, the most perfect hostess, the attorney with the highest billings. Still, we're loath to part with the mission or set of values that has defined us for so long. We associate it with power, beauty and physical strength, and the optimism of our youth.

Yet the old hero must die if we are to continue growing, even if we haven't yet conceived of its replacement. Hearkening back to the identity confusion of adolescence, the midlife hero needs to try on new costumes and new roles, to find which ones fit best.

In working with my client Jill, we identified several aspects of her heroine. The *rejected child* was buried deep—Jill felt she was an unplanned child and that her mother's attention was directed toward her father—but came to the surface under the stress of a major transition. Then there was the *hardworking girl* striving for Daddy's attention. These two sides of her personality had been running Jill for some time, but it was clear that neither could guide her in making her midlife choices. She had to let them go and look elsewhere to define the new hero she might live by.

There's an inevitable period of mourning over the loss of our youthful hero; this is what midlife depression is largely about. But the hero isn't permanently dead, of course. As in so many myths—from the story of Christ to the return of Persephone from the underworld each spring—our personal hero will be resurrected to carry on through the second half of life. Our work of the later stages of midlife will be to discover the new form, roles, and world relationship that hero will have.

## THE FORTYSOMETHING BLUES

The identity changes we go through in midlife produce strong emotions; those most likely to trouble us are depression and anxiety. Feeling depressed is a natural reaction to loss, and at a time when we're conscious of so many losses, it is not surprising. Note, though, that depression is linked with letting go of the past and thus with the earlier part of transition, the coming apart. Anxiety, on the other hand, is related to the future and all its unknowns—what are we becoming? What will the rest of our lives be like? It can affect us at any time during midlife, but we will talk about it in context of putting our identity back together.

It's easy to feel overwhelmed with cumulative losses at midlife; there seem to be so many! Loss of youth and its attendant dreams, hopes, values, and vigor. Loss of friends, lovers, family members, places left behind. Loss of our unlimited options. And, as we've discussed, the deeper loss of belief that the world is basically nurturing and protective, and that we ourselves are essentially good and adequate and competent.

Our naive expectations about the world and ourselves crumble, eroding the underpinnings of our identity. Until we work through these losses—by which I mean create a new set of viable hypotheses to replace the old ones—we feel terribly vulnerable, and the world can seem very hostile.

Midlife depression is experienced and expressed in many ways: as a lack of energy and purpose in daily life; the sense of moving through a fog, with our path ahead totally obscured; of being trapped in a monotonous, unrewarding life structure with no apparent options for change, like my client Steve. People in midlife talk about feeling numb, or even dead. We may see our interaction with work, family, and friends as ritualistic, a kind of going through the motions. This alienation from the world follows naturally from feeling out of touch with what we sense is our true self: "Who is this person I have become?"

Sometimes normal feelings of being lost or stagnated, of regret for lost youth and opportunities, can produce symptoms of a clinically defined depression. Changes in appetite and sleep patterns (early morning waking, insomnia, fitful or nonrestorative sleep); loss of libido; chronic fatigue; weight loss or gain; restlessness or agitation; increase in alcohol or drug consumption—these may indicate a serious depression that calls for therapy, especially if multiple symptoms occur. But these reactions are rare. In general, midlife depression is *not* clinical. Still, we should take note of and address any such symptoms as significant problems since they can rob us of the energy needed for the identity quest.

Depression is often masked by risk-taking, gambling, sexual, escapades, and anger. Other typical behaviors include withdrawal, irritability, argumentativeness, frequent tearfulness and histrionics. Any of these can be related to a more serious, ongoing depressed state, but in midlife they are more often responses to the pressures of a shifting identity: job burnout, problems with family roles, dissatisfaction with our achievements, and feeling boxed in by commitments.

Jill's struggle to find a way out of her midlife dilemma was handicapped by her lack of energy, which often led her to scuttle plans or dismiss alternatives.

> I'm tired all the time. I'm not eating enough to keep up my energy, and I know I'm not working efficiently. I drag myself to the office, and once I'm there I feel like locking the door and not taking any phone calls. In the evening I go home and crash. It just seems like too much effort to do anything different.

When I brought up the importance of developing her social life, Jill's response was a weak, frustrated laugh. "Just what I need," she said, "more responsibility. You don't seem to understand, there's no energy for what I'm doing already."

Jill's resistance, more than simple fatigue, is typical of people who feel helpless and hopeless. Because they can't see an immediate benefit, any effort seems worthless. This "what for" attitude can be as problematic as any aspect of depression, undermining basic attempts to put life back in order. For Jill, it was rooted in the anger that she had done everything asked of her, yet still wasn't satisfied with important parts of her life. She wanted a family, children, a place in the country, but like many boomer women, she was hesitant about expressing these desires. Her depression protected her by making it impossible for her to attempt a change.

If depression has always been part of the midlife picture, baby boomers are prime targets. Martin Seligmann, in his article "Boomer Blues" in *Psychology Today,* reports that the rate of reported depression in this country has risen greatly in the past few decades.

Why is our generation more likely to experience depression? Seligmann attributes it to two key factors. On one hand is the loss of faith in major institutions like religion, government, and family. It's ironic that baby boomers, who participated so enthusiastically in bringing down these institutions, now find themselves up the creek without a paddle in midlife. Support is a vital resource in any transition, and we've shut off many of the traditional sources. For some people, this sense of alienation becomes so frightening that they make a radical aboutface into the arms of fundamentalist or cult religions, which may be effective in relieving depression, but are just as effective in stifling personal growth.

The other factor is the exaltation of the individual self, which permeates our generation. The exhortation "be all you can be," whether from our parents, a human-potential guru, or a TV commercial, creates tremendous pressure. Says Seligmann, "We blindly accept soaring expectations for the self—as if some idiot raised the ante on what it takes to be a normal human being. What's remarkable is not that we fail on some but that we achieve so many."

Inevitably, we do fail to meet some of our expectations, however unrealistic, and that's inevitably depressing. Women feel this in a very specific way: told that they can "have it all"—a successful career and a close-knit family—they are now programmed to feel bad if they can manage only one of these.

Seligmann's prescription for a mentally healthier future calls for tempering our worship of the individual with "a renewed commitment to the common good." It is an accepted psychological truth that directing attention outside ourselves is an antidote to depression.

The challenge, though, is that midlife demands a fair amount of introspection, which is likely to produce some depression. Don't forget that it is part of the process, a necessary stimulus to personal growth and not in itself pathological.

If, however, symptoms of depression grow strong enough to compromise functioning—if your work performance suffers dramatically or your relationships deteriorate badly—it is a good idea to seek professional help. If you do undertake therapy in midlife (many people who have put off dealing with psychological problems find it a compelling occasion), do not assume that the therapist will make your choices for you. His or her job is to explore with you the intersection of your personality with your life situation on the map of midlife. The work calls for a less-traditional model of psychotherapy, a coach more than a healer, someone who facilitates exploration by stimulating your own thinking.

### COMING TO TERMS WITH DEATH

An internal force that impels us strongly toward change in midlife is our growing awareness of mortality. Many events conspire to bring the reality of death home to us on a personal level. As we reach midlife, the death of elderly parents becomes common. Often it is our first personal encounter with death, and it has an immediate effect on our self-perception; if we're no longer someone's child, we must be—ready or not—our own adult.

Deaths among one's contemporaries become more uncomfortably frequent: who hasn't heard with a shiver about the friend with an inoperable brain tumor, the uterine cancer not caught in time, the heart attack on the squash court? Fortysomething women seem to know a lot of other women who have had breast cancer. Lastly, our own bodies are sending us unignorable signals that they aren't going to last forever.

We don't welcome these messages or accept them easily. But a heightened awareness of death in midlife seems to be a necessary shock to stimulate identity change. It reinforces the urgency to do things "while there's still time" and the importance of living in the present. As a woman I know puts it: "This isn't a rehearsal."

In that quintessential boomer movie, *The Big Chill,* the death of one of a close-knit group of college classmates has a powerful effect on his friends. First it brings them together, and, in the course of a weekend, leads them into crises with their mates, dalliances with each other partners, confrontations over values, at least one personal apotheosis and one career change. It may be a Hollywood snapshot of midlife, but it is recognizably accurate. The deaths of well-known symbols of our generation, John Lennon a decade ago or Abbie Hoffman more recently, can hit us hard, reminding us of how much we and our world have changed since the high-flying sixties.

It need not take a literal death to bring us to the close encounter with mortality. Writer Mark Gerzon, in an article in the *Utne Reader,* describes his experience of this as beginning with a blissful vacation in which he and his wife rediscovered a priceless intimacy. On the journey home, Gerzon was struck by the fragility of any such happiness in a life full of distractions and burdens, and in any long-term relationship where people have the power to hurt each other. He realized that, while he believed in taking responsibility for oneself, "there were a host of people—family, children, friends—against whom I still held grudges for one thing or another, people whom I blamed for contributing to my pain—or the world's."

Gerzon was reminded of the need for forgiveness that comes as death approaches. He recognized that he needed to practice such forgiveness now, in order to free himself and others of blame, to really accept responsibility for his future happiness.

> I also realized that beneath all those biographical grudges had been another deeper and more timeless grudge. I had resented Life for ending in Death. I had resented God for making us mortal. It had seemed unfair, unkind, unjust, and unnecessary.

And so it must seem to all of us, if we truly admit it. Keeping death at a distance is a natural part of the psychology of youth, and breaking through that denial into acceptance is an important part of the de-illusionment process. It teaches us to be both more accepting of ourselves and less willing to accept an unfulfilling life structure. It helps us integrate our internal selves with the external world, by reminding us that we are earthly creatures.

If we do not move past that denial in midlife, the fear of aging and death is likely to get worse as we get older, poisoning our later life, setting us more rigidly into defensive patterns and risk-minimizing behaviors. But if we face the awareness of death squarely and act on it—which means, among other things, not acting as though the future were infinite and not wasting energy blaming God, or others, or ourselves for our humanity—then its intensity subsides after a while. On the other side of midlife, we become less preoccupied with signs of aging, and death recedes into the background.

Baby boomers are lucky in having a physically vigorous future to look forward to. But we must pay attention to our psychic as well as our cardiovascular fitness for the second half of life. Coming to terms with mortality is a vital step in reassembling our identity in a form that can continue to grow, a pivotal event between our coming apart and coming together. As Jung describes the paradox: "Only [s]he remains vitally alive who is ready to die with life."

## Coming Together

Here you are with the pieces of your identity scattered around you like so much earthquake rubble. What are the main psychological processes involved in rebuilding it, and what does this part of midlife feel like? The work and emotional states discussed below are not limited to midlife, but they do characterize the time we might think of as the hero's rebirth.

### GOING INSIDE

"For a young person it is almost a sin, or at least a danger, to be too preoccupied with himself; but for the aging person it is a duty and necessity to devote serious attention to himself. After having lavished its light upon the world, the sun withdraws its rays in order to illuminate itself."

C. G. Jung

Noted social psychologist Bernice L. Neugarten uses the term *interiority* for the midlife process of turning inward, and becoming more introspective. In contrast to earlier life stages, when our energy was directed outward toward establishing our place in the world, our task now is to reevaluate our identity by standards we can only discover by looking inside.

Where do we get the answers to questions like: What do I want to spend my time doing? or, Is this a relationship that satisfies my needs today? In the past, our answers often came from our parents, society, our peers or mates. We thought those answers would suffice, but now the questions are back and we don't trust the old sources of wisdom. We're stronger, we have a better sense of how well we do or do not fit into standard social and familial roles; we know how easy it is to get the answers we think we want from our friends.

Convincing answers can come only from our inner voice at this point, but hearing it above the clamor of our fortysomething lives is a challenge. Spending time contemplating our dreams and fantasies, or just being alone with ourselves, can seem less important than getting that report done or meeting with the kids' teacher. Sometimes we respond to the need for interiority without realizing it. The person who spends hours each week on a bicycle or in a swimming pool (sometimes provoking family resentment) is likely to claim health reasons when an equally real motive is having time to themselves. Sometimes the urge is expressed by emotional withdrawal.

Some people are more conscious of their need and take more dramatic steps, like arranging to go away by themselves, entering therapy for self-exploration, or using meditation techniques. Gail Sheehy tells in *Passages* about a clergyman who felt he had lost sight of himself beneath his role as a helper, the man with the answers. His solution was to take a post as director of a rural retreat center where people came to investigate spiritual issues through group meetings and workshops. "The isolation in nature," writes Sheehy, "suited his need . . . for reflection," and he was able to share his seeking with others.

What we are trying to locate is the change, subtle or otherwise, in the values that guide our actions. These can be very specific, as in: "I used to spend as much of my free time as possible competing in tennis matches. Now I'd rather use it learning to play the piano."

But it can also be experienced as the general value shift that happens to most people in midlife: from ends to means, from product to process, and from quantitative values to qualitative ones. If formerly we were ready to sacrifice satisfaction in the present to gain a future prize, it is now more important for the process itself to be rewarding. And how much we can do becomes less critical than how well we do it.

This change helps us transcend some of the fear of aging and decline. Diminution of performance is inevitable as we age: the runner gets slower, the sales executive has less stamina for travel. The runner in his thirties is numbers-oriented. He'll say, "It was a great run. I did fifteen miles in an hour and thirty-seven minutes." The midlife runner will say something a little different, adding the qualitative dimension: "It was a great run. I did fifteen miles in two hours or so. I really enjoyed how it felt to get out in the woods."

This values change also steers us away from the inevitable frustration of *more*—which is rooted in outside appearances and the judgments of others—and toward the inherently more rewarding variable of *better*. It is about how something feels to the person who's doing it, the person to whom it matters. Maybe it's nature's way of easing us out of competitions that we need to leave behind.

People who have survived near-death experiences are said

to report major changes in their values after the incident, comparable to the changes most people experience in midlife. They become more concerned about taking care of personal realtionships; they have an enhanced appreciation of the natural world and its integrity; they are less preoccupied with material success and status, and more alive to the spiritual side of life. This is the direction we are moved in by the death of our old hero and our encounter with personal death in midlife. These new values that emerge from and reflect our inner journey are the basis of the redefined self.

## THE AGE OF ANXIETY

Much of our effort in early adulthood is geared toward gaining a sense of control of our environment by exploring the unknowns of family, work, and social life and turning them into knowns. Then midlife throws the big curve. For reasons we can't understand, the structure we've set up and nurtured isn't giving back to us anymore. The present is unsatisfactory, and as we begin to contemplate changes, the future suddenly looks like a maze without clues. Our sense of being in control evaporates.

Welcome to anxiety, the emotional state we occupy when we're aware of going through changes but uncertain of where they're taking us. It is abetted in midlife by two factors: our awareness of limited time, which makes our need for direction more urgent, and the knowledge we've gained of the darker side of life. It is virtually impossible to arrive at midlife without some measure of insecurity; by now we know that things *do not* always work out for the best.

Midlife sings the siren's song of new possibilities, but which ones do we choose? How do we make the most of them? What new picture of identity will emerge from the palette of roles we are offered? Can we survive the wrong choices? How do we balance our own needs with those of the people closest to us? How do we still make a living while undergoing this self-change? These questions are hauntingly familiar to midlifers. "Freedom is possibility, and anxiety is the possibility of freedom," said philosopher Sören Kierkegaard. His brave words can ring hollow when we are facing choices that seem critical, in a world that seems unforgiving of any misstep.

Our current social environment is fanning the flames of midlife anxiety to white heat. The accelerating pace of life, the breakdown of institutions and predictable life patterns, the myriad options our history and education have promised baby boomers as our birthright—all contribute their shared stresses. There's even a new term, *information anxiety,* for the pressure we feel to absorb massive input from a global, electronic society in order to act intelligently in our personal and professional lives.

The result is that anxiety disorders have become this country's second most common form of mental illness (after alcohol and substance abuse, which also are often associated with midlife). These disorders include ordinary stress and nervousness as well as the more severe phobias, panic reactions, and anxiety attacks. Where does the typical midlifer fit on this continuum? As with depression, midlife anxiety will only seldom take the form of a true anxiety disorder. More often it is expressed as a mixture of self-doubt, nagging worries about health, work, and family, and a vague sense of disquiet about the future.

The basically healthy midlifer knows that life must go on, and that choices, however uncertain and risky, must be made. What makes them the right choices is the energy and commitment that go into them. It is a seductive illusion that there are only so many "right" choices available, and that our job is merely to find them. This resembles an adult version of hide-and-seek, a game that obscures the complex truth of decision making. Right and wrong are not easily defined; we are charged with the responsibility to make our actions one or the other. In other words, with freedom comes not just the possibility but the obligation to *make* our choices, in the fullest sense of the verb. Commitment is the most potent antidote to anxiety.

My friend (and client) Peter is a worrier, heavily invested in feeling in control, an Anticipator when it came to midlife change. He had wanted for years to do something entrepreneurial, to be the owner of his labor as a computer programmer, but it took a corporate turnover to kick him into it. Before that he told me, "I'm not even sure I want to stay in this profession. I know I'm not supposed to think this way, but what if I make the break and can't cut it? Then everybody will think I made a mistake, or that I was just lucky in my current job."

When the ax fell, Peter used his severance pay to take time off and look over his options, even though several companies made him offers right away. Once he commited himself to the new business, he still had plenty of worries, but they were concrete, not cosmic. Also, the anxiety level in other parts of his life diminished in unexpected ways. His more flexible schedule allowed him more time with his wife and five-year-old daughter; he no longer had to worry about her growing up without him. It also opened the option for his wife to return to school, which she had been wanting to do. Once Peter found that he did not need to be controlling with her, his overall energy level at home and in their marriage seemed to go up as a result.

## MAKING CHOICES WITH PASSION

As we become more aware of changes in our values, new options become very attractive. This is where the work of making choices comes in. Sometimes any option looks good, as long as it's different. However, there is no particular merit in making a choice merely because it represents a new direction—or, for that matter, because it supports an old value. One of the ways people short-circuit transition is by chasing the first impulse that comes along. It's good to keep in mind that impulses are like buses: another one will be along any minute.

While putting off decisions endlessly isn't productive, investing some time in living with various possibilities is. We often spring into action as a means of avoiding anxiety, but midlife isn't the time to shut out inconvenient emotions. The choices we make now will shape the rest of our lives, and we can learn a lot by allowing a state of uncertainty to go on for a while, by experiencing the full range of our emotional reactions to the options before us.

The importance of basing midlife choices on passion holds true even if we're not contemplating any radical change in behavior or life structure. Values and behavior that seem exhausted can be rejuvenated with a dose of midlife energy—the process of subjecting them to scrutiny, weighing them against other options, and letting the emotional fevers burn hot. The choices that emerge will be a sound foundation for your next life structure.

## ENJOYING THE UPSIDE

Lest you think that the emotions of midlife are all dark and grim, you should know that euphoria is also part of the package, especially in the later stages of a transition. There is an excitement that comes with the feeling of being borne along on a tide of change, once we relax and accept it as inevitable. It is as if we have survived the tidal wave of self-criticism and can float along through whatever follows.

Baby boomers are more likely to have a positive experience of midlife, because we can go through it with a network of support other generations didn't have. If we've lost the support of institutions, we've gained from bonding with our generation, from talking with friends and mentors, and from the information and resources available to us. As a generation, we can leave our mark on midlife with a new kind of optimism.

Feelings of composed exhilaration, self-acceptance, of being comfortable in time are a good preview of what life after midlife can be. Take note of and enjoy them whenever they surface during the passage.

### THE HERO REBORN

In therapy, Jill, the architect, learned that the earlier versions of her heroine, the *rejected child* and the *good girl,* weren't going to guide her in making midlife choices. She had to let them go. But we uncovered another side of her: the young woman who chose to go into architecture instead of pursuing a career in chemistry, where her father's position would have served her well. This was a rather shadowy and elusive figure, but also an angry heroine capable of incredible bursts of energy.

It was this heroine, whom we came to call the *rebel,* whom we focused on contacting and whose help we enlisted. As she got better acquainted with her personal myth, she was able to bring the rebel into the consultation room. A dream eventually led Jill to an important awareness.

> It was about cowboys and Indians. The Indians were creatures of the land, very primitive. The cowboys were hardworking, virtuous types, but unable to make it on the land. Starving, they had to turn to the Indians for help. At first the Indians rejected them, still angry about the injustices the cowboys had done to them, but eventually they relented and showed the cowboys some tricks of survival. The dream ended with them working together, though there was still distrust.

When I asked what the dream meant to her, Jill said that she was both the cowboys and the Indians—the part that worked relentlessly and the other side whose strength came out in rebellion. She thought the dream held an important message: that she needed to include both parts in any plans for her future.

> I'd been trying to figure out my next move using just the hard-working cowboy side, as if that would be enough, but something held me back. Now I can see that the Indians needed a voice too. Letting that be heard has melted a lot of the resistance and fear, given me new energy.

Six months later Jill had formed a plan for her midlife career transition. She cut her staff by half, so instead of a small army going against greater forces for jobs, she had a mobile and resourceful guerrilla corps of professionals who could join together to work on specific projects. The new configuration of her company allowed her to compete more effectively, and reduced her overhead. It also freed her from time-consuming administrative choices, and allowed her to pursue a more active social life. She joined a social club that offered a wide range of activities and scheduled events. Getting in touch with a different side of her heroine gave Jill the impetus to change her life structure significantly in midlife.

As Jill's story indicates, the concept of the hero's death and rebirth does not mean that it is necessary to remake your identity completely in midlife. In most cases, people who try to reinvent themselves from scratch are those who haven't really settled into an adult personality before midlife. The reborn hero more closely resembles a new dimension of a familiar reality, a dormant aspect of selfhood that is seeing the light for the first time.

We all have some side of ourself that needs more fertile ground in which to grow. Dante was precise in his choice of a deep wood for an image of midlife. It is often dark, tangled and confusing. Scary beasts (like aging) lurk behind rocks, and it can be hard to see the forest for the trees.

But this is also an environment of great fecundity and diversity, a shelter from the noisy, brightly lit world beyond its borders, and a place of growth and renewal. Here is where our reborn hero is nurtured. He knows his way around in this wood and will be our guide on the rest of the journey.

# 5

## Midlife Management Strategies
## The Ten
## Master Skills

*Experience is the child of Thought, and Thought is the
Child of Action.*

BENJAMIN DISRAELI

We have emphasized the importance of letting go and letting things flow in midlife, not resisting the force of transition, allowing yourself to experience the emotional power
of this passage. That doesn't mean, though, passively letting
yourself be buffeted around by midlife's storms, totally out of
control of what is happening to you. Seeing yourself as a helpless victim of outside forces, psychological handicaps, or the
actions of others is a reliable prescription for depression.

Some people experience the midlife transition almost im-
perceptibly; for others it is a life crisis of major proportions;
most of us fall somewhere between these extremes. The point
is, *how* midlife happens to you isn't just an accident. By understanding our own psyches, the predictable rhythms of transition, and the social forces acting on us, we can control how
midlife plays itself out to a great extent. Instead of blundering
around in the dark, we can bring our own light to illuminate

the path. We can wield the sculptor's tool that is carving our new identity.

Of course there's no such thing as complete control. Factors such as personality type, as we saw in Chapter 3, economic circumstances, health, genetic predisposition, and simple twists of fate all help set the stage and write the script that we eventually live out. Every transition starts with a given set of raw materials.

Taking an active role in managing the process, however, can shape and guide its outcome. Much of midlife's discomfort centers on feelings of being helpless or lost. Forming strategies and setting goals has the immediate benefit of getting us moving; it makes us feel better, even if we wind up a million miles from the plan we started with. Being proactive (the term used in therapy) involves the ability to see one's situation developing, to assess it accurately, make necessary accommodations, incorporate feedback, and employ contingency plans when appropriate. Your strategies can be vague and elastic at first—in fact, the more flexible the better, with details worked out as your direction becomes clearer. Allowing for contingencies is essential. In the words of one Zen master: "Expect nothing. Be ready for everything."

While each of us must develop unique strategies to deal with our situation, there are certain *master skills* essential to midlife management. In this chapter we describe the ten that we feel are most important and most widely useful. Some of them are *global* skills whose basic aim is to assist the process of individuation. They're vital at any time of life but especially during periods of identity restructuring. Others are *transition tools* that help us function on the practical, day-to-day level in our work and family relationships.

Depending on your change-response type—Stimulation Junkie, Change Resister, Anticipator—these skills will be harder or easier to develop, and some will be more important for you than others. No matter what type you are, being conscious of what's happening to you and committed to making the most of midlife are the key ingredients. It starts with believing that you *can* guide your own fate.

In *The Adventures of Don Juan*, the shaman Don Juan tells author Carlos Castaneda that he can fly. Incredulous, Castaneda asks, "What do you mean, do you really fly? Suppose I chained you to a rock, would you fly?" Don Juan replies, "Well, I guess I'd fly with the rock." The message is: There is objective reality, and there is also how we perceive it and react to it, which is at least as important.

### *Skill #1   Make Time for Transition or Stop . . . Look . . . Listen*

Time is the rarest commodity in modern life, and time to devote to self-exploration is usually scarcest of all. Yet, it's crucial in midlife to make time to hear yourself and your needs, and allow time to let the transition unfold at its own pace. We touched on this in the last chapter when discussing interiority, the inward journey we undertake in search of the values that will guide our future lives and the parts of our personality that can realize them. For most of us it takes conscious practice to spend time with ourselves and screen out the distractions that life presents at every turn. It doesn't happen quickly.

When Steve first came to see me, the sources of his discontent were manifold. He began with his frustrations about being an attorney. "I make a lot of money and I'm good at it. But something is missing . . . the thrill or the challenge. I used to feel it, but now it seems all I do is manage cases. I feel dead when I walk through the doors. Sunday nights are especially bad, just thinking about going in on Monday."

Steve went on to describe what was wrong with his marriage, his friendships, his family connections, his hobbies, his body. The deep well of his discontent was poisoning every part of his life, and, at this point, complaining was all he could do with any enthusiasm.

Steve's personality had qualities of both the Stimulation Junkie and the Escape Artist. He wanted change, and he wanted it quick. That wasn't surprising, and he was impulsive by nature, relying on intuition and instinct. These were working just enough to sound the SOS, but the content of the message was obscured by the state he was in. The inner voice that might have told him what he needed was muffled by a shroud of depression and the clamor of his daily life.

His practical argument for a quick fix was that his cash flow couldn't tolerate a prolonged career disruption; unfortunately, his spirit wouldn't tolerate anything except sitting out a full turn. A sabbatical was the tool that worked for Steve. It became clear in our work together that he was too obsessively busy to ask himself the essential questions about who he was and what really mattered to him. Which of his values did he want to keep, and which were reflexive reactions to life in the fast lane? These weren't simple questions, and they demanded that Steve make time for some internal work.

Six months away from the office was a good place to start, and Steve was unusually lucky in being able to arrange it. Not that being away was easy at first. "When I stopped going to the office I tried to keep up the same frenetic level of activity. I was involved in a thousand projects, almost anything to avoid dealing with myself." In time, Steve grew more comfortable with the idea of doing less. Only then did he begin to look at himself closely, to comprehend the changes he'd gone through in the past twenty years. "And that was really a shock. I wasn't the rising star coming out of law school anymore—but who was I now?"

Steve tried to observe the childhood maxim of *stop, look, and listen*—a good rule of thumb for many people. He stopped the hectic pace. He looked around at his family, and at the work he'd been doing. He listened to his heart. "It had been such a long time since I'd asked myself what I really wanted to do. The hard part wasn't just asking—it was listening to and believing the answers when they finally came."

At the end of his sabbatical, Steve returned to his practice with some logistical accommodations: working fewer hours and taking on riskier cases that challenged him. But the real changes were internal. He had rediscovered the importance of feeling passionate about what he did, and realized that he wasn't going to get those feelings from work alone. The total Steve was more than what he did professionally; he began to invest more of himself in family, hobbies, and community. Taking a course in metal sculpture liberated an artistic side that had been suppressed by the success chase.

Midlife transition is not about what you do, though that often serves as a focus for the need to change. It is about who you are. Take the time to explore that question, and the rest tends to fall into place. Few have the luxury of taking an extended leave to do the inner work required, but sabbaticals can take many forms: a daily walk, a trip up the coast, or some quiet time each day spent reflecting on some basic questions. What matters to me? How do I feel about this or that? Where am I going, and who is going with me?

There are good reasons why you are feeling the way you do. Remember that you are the product of a lifetime of experience, of many turns and bumps in the road. If you plan to change the route you are on, you must give it time. Transition is a process, not an event.

### Skill #2  Be Here Now
### or The Importance of Being Present

In the popular song "Glory Days," Bruce Springsteen recalls a high school buddy who was the star pitcher on the baseball team. In adult life he remained fixated on those glory days, unable to grow out of the past. Likewise, many of us know the former prom queen who can't help looking back on adolescence as the best time of her life.

For all of us, especially the generation that grew up in the turbulent sixties, the glory days are heady stuff. Their allure is especially seductive in times of change, when an uncertain future looms, and when the passage of time blurs the sharp outlines of the past, making it easier to see it as we need to rather than as it was.

It is no accident that a tremendous nostalgia boom is hitting America right now. It represents the energy of millions of baby boomers reacting to their arrival at midlife. The sixties are being romanticized as a time of passion and commitment such as we will perhaps not know again in our lives; Paul McCartney can pack stadiums by singing Beatles songs that take us back there.

Trying to recapture the past is futile. Our memories of that era are seen through the brightly colored lens of youth, through veils of illusion that have since been stripped away. But the temptation remains, and as a generation we are more entranced by youth than most. This makes the midlife adjustment that much more wrenching.

As individuals we are tempted to look longingly toward the past whenever we grow uncomfortable in our relationships and our self-image. In Chapter 3 we described the Nostalgia Buff, who stubbornly keeps trying to recycle old solutions that clearly won't work in the present. We saw people like Jeff, who thought his marital problems would be solved if his wife became pregnant again, when what she wanted was to go back to school. As with any persistent form of denial, you only fool yourself.

Living in the future can be seductive, too. To quench our thirst for resolution and get midlife's discomfort over with, we head for the fountain of *someday . . . maybe*. If we believe in a magical future, we can postpone work that needs to be done about our health, our relationships, our career.

It's natural to feel the pull of past or future during transition. We salve anxiety with memories of the past and boost ourselves out of depression through dreams of the future. Both are psychic resources that give us a sense of the flow of our lives. Who we were and who we will be are part of who we are becoming. Any effective strategy for change must incorporate the experience of the past and the exciting promise of the future, but neither can be a permanent asylum from change. We must stay firmly in touch with the present: what roles fit or don't fit *now*? What do we need *now*? What do we have to work with *now*? A satisfying future can be built only on satisfactory answers to those questions. As Kierkegaard said, "Life can only be understood backward, but it must be lived forward."

## *Skill #3   Break New Ground*
## *or You Can't Make an Omelet Without Breaking Eggs*

In the decade or so prior to midlife, most of us have focused our field of operation and learning on a fairly narrow band. To achieve maximum efficiency in any one endeavor, such as getting ahead in a career or raising children, a close focus is usually an advantage.

By the time we reach midlife, we have invested a lot of energy in one or two places and have a pretty clear picture of where that has taken us. Sure, there's always something more to learn in a given field, and some people can progress in one direction for a very long time before reaching a plateau. But it is common to feel that you've taken your best shot at any one endeavor by now. The results are in: the kids are formed, for better or worse; the career has settled into a pattern.

Some liken this process to running out of gas, as though

human energy were a finite commodity. I prefer to see it as a natural, predictable need to redirect our energy in midlife—to expand our focus, to learn and explore in new directions. This ensures that the well of enthusiasm and energy will never run dry.

It is ironic that many people in the midst of the midlife transition experience a sort of psychic shutdown, closing themselves off from new stimulation. They seem to be saying that they can't handle anything new until they have a new base of identity to work from. But that's putting the cart before the horse: it's just at this time that we most need fresh information and experiences from which to shape the postmidlife self. It takes some tolerance of discomfort and may occasionally produce stimulation overload, but learning new skills, new ways of thinking, and taking manageable risks is the stuff from which successful midlife transitions are made.

New avenues of learning can branch off in many directions. A very macho client of mine decided in midlife to take cooking lessons. I suspected that he really did it to meet women—he had been single since an early marriage ended in divorce—but he insisted there were other reasons. He was considering the possibility that he might never meet the woman of his dreams, and was getting sick of eating frozen dinners. Learning to cook might seem like a trivial skill to some, but the content of the learning is less important than the process. Exposing yourself to new challenges can jump-start an engine whose battery has gone dead. And if you're lucky, you may stumble on something that really lights your fire and becomes a keystone of your future life structure.

Besides, the experience of being a beginner teaches a lesson that every toddler learns. After you fall, you get up. By the time we reach midlife, most of us are deathly afraid of failing at anything. Each failure feels like a little ego death, proof that we're not really grown up after all. But fear of falling inhibits growth at just the time when continuing to grow is so critical.

For this reason, experimentation in an area outside your primary role, a field where you don't have so much ego invested, can be liberating and strengthening.

Another client made such a discovery. A marketing executive, she turned to freelance work at thirty-seven after leaving a staff job. Single, she'd poured most of herself into work and wasn't getting enough back from it anymore; she came to see that her loss of enthusiasm was partly why her last job didn't fly.

Since business was slow at first, she followed up on a long-postponed wish to join a choral group, an activity she'd enjoyed in high school and college. With encouragement from this new support group, she developed her voice, began taking some solo parts, and helped start a small theater-music company where she could move more into the spotlight. Her professional work was behind the scenes, helping others communicate their ideas, and music became a way to express herself more directly. Surprised that she was largely untroubled by the stage fright she remembered from youth, she soon realized why. "At this point in my life, I can get up there and say, 'This is who I am: like it or not.' Besides, it's not what I do for a living. I'm doing it because I love it."

## Skill #4   Learn to Tolerate Discomfort
## or Don't Just Do Something, Stand There

Midlife is often driven by an urgent need to change one's life structure, the feeling that what we have is no longer valuable or stimulating. That belief is reasonable: few life structures can go on indefinitely without major revision. But before you trash them in a clean sweep, look closely at your structures to see how much vitality they still have.

It is easy to project the anger and loss we feel about time

passing, the helplessness about being stuck, onto situations and people in our lives. Mates and careers are the most common scapegoats, but targets of projection also include one's location, body image, old friendships, relationships with parents and/or children, hobbies, and so on.

Usually, these are innocent bystanders, or even part of the solution rather than part of the problem. In the midst of emotional turmoil, our need to see things in a certain way can overwhelm their reality. Once we've recovered from the emotional shock wave of early midlife, things can look quite different. This advice applies in spades to the Stimulation Junkie and the Escape Artist. The impulse to keep on the move or to run away is practically synonymous with midlife.

Tom, a client approaching his middle forties, had begun to pull away from his marriage. He had a supportive wife, a nine-year-old daughter, and a stable career as owner of a retail store, but he couldn't fight off the nagging idea that he should be getting more out of life. The product of a repressive upbringing, he was ashamed to discuss his feelings with anyone, including his wife. There must be something wrong with me, he figured, to want out of a situation that many would envy.

Finding him increasingly withdrawn and unreachable, his wife began expressing her loneliness to an attentive male co-worker. At first it wasn't a sexual relationship, but it was intimate in ways that transcend sexuality. Her friend listened and responded, validating her feelings. This was what she wasn't getting from Tom, and was infinitely more satisfying to her than the sexual liaison, which indeed developed.

At the same time, Tom was sabotaging his store. He devalued his business, calling it a "no-brainer" and assuming that anyone could run a successful retail operation. His negativity infected his staff, who became lazy and indifferent to customers, while Tom acted out his discontent in bad merchandising decisions. The business began to fail, confirming his thought that retailing was a poor avenue for his efforts. Everything came to a head in Tom's forty-sixth year when his wife moved out, taking their daughter with her. Around the same time, his creditors informed him that he was tapped out financially; the store closed a few months later.

Trying to pick up the shattered pieces of his life structure in therapy, Tom at first valiantly defended what had happened, claiming good riddance to both the marriage and the store. This defense lasted about three months, during which he acted almost euphoric about what he felt was his midlife liberation. Then the depression set in, triggered not coincidentally by the experience of starting to date again and his decision to open a new store. Both reminded him of the former cornerstones of his life structure and his own role in their demise. In retrospect, he saw that each had been viable and vital, but had become scapegoats for his angry rejection of aging. A year later, he's still trying to put the pieces back together.

Admittedly, it's easy to counsel patience and caution and harder to practice them when you're feeling the desperate urge to *do something*! The skill involved is that of being able to tolerate discomfort, to live with the tension of a conflict and resist the impulse to resolve it immediately. Your strong feelings contain messages, but usually their meaning needs time to emerge. To help you look before you leap, first-aid tactics like support systems, therapy, and stress management come into play. Breaking time down into smaller units also helps: *One day at a time* is trite but true and infinitely more manageable than a concept like *the rest of my life.*

Remember that the option to end a relationship or close a business comes around more than once. If you feel an urgent need to get on with it, slow down and ask yourself why it has to happen right now. Might this urge be symptomatic of a wish to stop time, or to do something before you feel it's too late? Have you tried everything you can think of to revitalize the situation? Be sure of your answers to these questions before you take an irrevocable step. In truth, we're often better at tolerating uncertainty than we think; the fear of discomfort can be worse than the discomfort itself.

## Skill #5  Synchronize Values, Skills, and Situation or Act Your Stage

Everyone approaching midlife needs to do a reality check to make sure they are not hanging onto self-images, values, and skills that are outdated; this is the most basic work of transition. As Jung pointed out, "The . . . neurotic disturbances of adult years all have one thing in common: they want to carry the psychology of the youthful phase over the threshold of the so-called years of discretion." Just because we've broken the chains of the *act your age* dictum, it shouldn't encourage us to cling to youthful behavior and values as a defense against aging. It may work for a while, but when it stops working, you're left without other resources.

Start by identifying skills and values you want to cultivate or weed out. The skills required in midlife include prioritizing, dreaming, and making concessions. The skill of sharing, being a team member, becomes more useful than being a great solo performer. The ability to self-disclose and be more emotionally open gains importance, especially for many men.

Some values, like honesty, are deeply rooted and will serve us for a lifetime. But others are age-appropriate, matching the developmental stage we're in. The typical midlifer finds the value of family beginning to reassert itself after the twenties and early thirties, when family bonds were looser. Failing to recognize or denying this shift in values can lead to alienation and internal conflict.

The value we have placed in hard work is likely to change for today's midlifers, as our baby boomer faith in "just rewards" is eroded by current economic realities. Another fundamental value shift is in decreasing emphasis on the body and increasing attention on the spirit. Some may feel a need to reestablish connections with the faith they grew up in, or to find a new arena for spiritual practice. It's no accident that

Joseph Campbell's chats with Bill Moyers about crosscultural spirituality had such an impact on the midlife audience when they aired on PBS a few years ago.

Changes like those mentioned above tend to creep up on us almost unnoticed. This was the case with my client Jack, a forty-seven-year-old consultant with three children, aged ten, eight, and five. He spent much of each year on the road, working with some of the top Fortune 500 companies. His traveling was accepted by his family; they had learned to work around it. But Jack was becoming less willing to leave his wife and kids for up to ten days.

At first he couldn't place the source of his conflict and, as is common, projected his feelings of alienation onto his spouse. In our early sessions, he talked about the pressure he was getting from her to cut back his traveling. Only after establishing this defensive position and becoming convinced that I agreed with him did he express any feelings of sadness or loss about missing so much time with his family. When I commented on this and noted that his wife seemed to have made her peace with his schedule, he confessed with real emotion that maintaining his schedule was costing him a lot.

"I think what hurts the most," he said, "is that the situation seems so easy for my wife. She and the kids have become a self-contained unit. I don't know where to enter the system. I'm an outsider, and it's so frustrating. Maybe I pick fights with her to get some interaction going. Maybe that's my way of saying Daddy's home." Indeed that was Jack's tactic. It was threatening to him that his family had moved on and seemed willing to settle for so little from him. Their independence made him feel unimportant.

Clearly, Jack's values and skills had changed in midlife. In his thirties he had cultivated the ability to be independent and detached, in order to maintain his travel schedule. Now he was feeling the need to be more connected but wasn't sure how to accomplish it. He couldn't communicate his true feelings to his wife until he had absorbed this insight; things started to improve after that.

Sometimes the only signs of changing values are a vague discomfort or some behavior we don't understand, like Jack picking fights with his wife. Recognizing the source of the discomfort usually takes time and deliberate introspection.

## Skill #6   Use Your Intuition
### or Go to Sleep and Pay Attention

Where does the strategy that will guide us through midlife come from? How do you locate and define the dream that will become your mission in the later stages?

Taking control of transition doesn't mean imposing a logical solution on every problem, though that might seem the obvious choice in a crisis. The answers that will endure, the visions we seek to guide us into the second half of life, are more often found in the bubbling, creative ferment of the unconscious. The raw material that is the fuel of dreams comes from intuition, which Webster's Dictionary defines as: "the power or faculty of attaining to direct knowledge or cognition without rational thought and inference." In other words, intuition operates independent of rational thought, manifesting itself in feelings, dreams, fantasies, visions, and images.

Intuition provides much of the *feeling* component of transition. It is the hope, the exhilaration, and the energy of inspiration that can propel us through the difficult spots. Any strategy not founded in intuition will be devoid of soul. It may allow you to function adequately during midlife, but it won't have the sustaining power to guide your postmidlife future.

In truth, the real issue is how we avoid *not* hearing our intuition, how we put the critical censor of consciousness on vacation. The unconscious speaks all the time, but its voice is easily drowned out by the noisy business of getting through our days. We've learned how to ignore this voice in order to get on with things; now we must retune our inner ear to receive it.

Intuitive messages can guide decisions about almost any dimension of life, including work, where you live, and relationships. A woman I knew in Aspen had moved out to the west coast, yet found herself having recurring dreams about Colorado. Without any conscious thoughts of moving back there, she went for a visit and promptly bumped into an excellent job opportunity. Only at this point did she realize that she hadn't been happy since leaving, and that the dreams had pointed her in the right direction.

We've all had experiences with, or heard stories of, people "accidentally" betraying their true feelings about an emotional conflict they were reluctant to face. I heard a blatant example of this recently from a man in midlife with a failing marriage and a lover. He'd written a love poem to his paramour and left it in his briefcase, along with a gift he'd bought his wife out of guilt. Then, rather than presenting her with the gift, he told his wife that he had something for her in his briefcase, why didn't she go find it herself? Naturally, she found more than just the gift!

Mining our unconscious for clues is an essential transition skill that can grow rusty with disuse. Sharpen it by disciplining yourself to keep a journal, record your dreams, or write your autobiography. The important thing about any such effort is to do it regularly but not to impose any rules about content or style; the more unstructured the better. You can note thoughts, feelings, dreams, or events, but don't feel the need to be obsessive about detail. The idea is to observe and carry on a dialogue with yourself; there's no one correct way to do it.

Artistic efforts, however technically unskilled, are a means of contacting unconscious drives. Take note of the "accidental" choice of a book or musical recording, the unplanned impulse to see a certain movie or attend a lecture. Such "accidents of creation" are directed by intuition. Pay special attention to ideas about the future that seem unrealistic; they are often creative solutions in the rough that can be developed as you proceed.

Another useful exercise is to imagine the shape of your ideal life one year from today, then work backward to formulate a series of goals that will take you there. Setting goals is a logical process, but the imagining part comes first.

Once you've made time to hear your unconscious, it's important to pay close attention to its messages, give them credence, and incorporate them into your strategy. Listen to your heart.

## Skill #7  Cultivate Your Support System
### or Talk Is Cheaper Than Therapy

Your support system is the people you can talk to about your midlife experience: what you're feeling, your plans, hopes, and dreams. Developing and maintaining it is a critical coping skill at any time, but especially now, because so much of the work of transition takes place internally; it is easy to feel isolated. One client told me:

> As I started to slide into this period, I felt so alone. I felt like I was on the sidelines watching the parade go by. I could talk about what I was feeling and some people even seemed to understand. They would nod and say they knew what I was talking about, maybe even that they were going through the same thing.
>
> But I always felt dissatisfied after those conversations, as if I had eaten a meal but was still hungry. At the worst, it was like I was speaking a foreign language. I felt at bottom that I was a pain to these people—that all they wanted was for me to go away and solve the problem myself.

This woman may have been relying too much on others to make choices for her, which should not be the purpose of talking. On the most basic level, talking can be simply a way of getting your feelings out. This helps relieve pressure and prevents your emotions from being a burden. Moreover, to express your situation comprehensibly to someone else, you must first analyze it for yourself. Talking makes the abstract concrete; you hear yourself with a more objective ear.

The feedback you get can be helpful, too. The experiences others share is a resource that shouldn't be overlooked since, by comparing yours with theirs, you gain perspective. Keep a few points in mind, though. First, and most obvious, your situation is unique and no one else has all the answers for you. Second, and perhaps less obvious, we shape the feedback we get from others by editing the information we present to them. If we know in advance what we want to hear, it's easy to manipulate feedback by offering only certain kinds of information, such as all the positive aspects of a move and none of the negative ones. If you want an objective response, be as balanced as possible in describing the situation.

Finally, it's important to know the biases of the person supplying the feedback because everyone sees the world through the template of his own experience. Even if the advice you get seems to reveal more about the advisor than about yourself, you might still be able to use it. Keep in mind, also, that it is especially difficult for someone close to you to be objective. He or she will respond primarily to your discomfort and suggest nearly anything in an attempt to make you feel better.

Our social world is made up of many different relationships, and our midlife support network should reflect that diversity: family, friends, men, women, older and younger people. We can get useful feedback from peers, mentors, models, coaches—even those we ourselves are mentoring, such as students. It is very useful to get a variety of viewpoints on your situation. You'll find that the *you* in relation to all these people will change somewhat, yet will show consistency too. Study that core of consistency to locate your strongest feelings.

Men generally find it harder than women to cultivate support systems. Raised by the stiff-upper-lip standard, they either repress their emotions and hesitate to confess to discomfort—or they tend to get all their support from one person, usually a wife or girlfriend. Fortunately, there is a countervailing tendency in midlife to become more expressive and connected, though it is often a struggle for men to accept this change, conditioned as they are to see those qualities as signs of weakness. (And, as our competitive gender sees it, weakness invites defeat.)

This may be the single most important skill for men to develop in midlife. A client, discussing how out of touch he had been with his emotions, made this comparison: "Women have gauges, so they can track their pressure building up or their fuel running low. But men have idiot lights; we don't notice how we're doing until all hell is about to break loose."

There is great comfort in knowing that others go through a similar process and similar pain; such knowledge can make you braver and more resourceful. The networks of sharing built by people going through midlife are the framework for a successful resolution. Ian (whom we met in Chapter 1) had a terrible time asking for support after a corporate takeover forced him out of his niche. Only to his wife did he let down his defenses; to his friends he denied that anything was wrong. "Men don't tell that stuff. We may brag when we get a promotion, but we deny like hell when it turns sour. Looking back, I can see that keeping it inside only added to the weight."

Finally, at a dinner party, Ian's feelings of being "used up" just spilled out. And he found that everyone at the table had similar feelings. The conversation began to revolve around the internal changes people were experiencing. Their life situations were different, but all felt the need for some empowering purpose to reinvigorate their lives.

Having broken the ice, Ian talked to others, paying special attention to people who had taken risks and left secure paths. Dave, a former corporate marketing vice president, now in his fifties, had a thriving consulting business, but had been through the same *what if?* fears Ian had: What if I don't make it, what if I can't survive outside the corporate structure, and so on.

Buoyed by such examples, Ian decided to leave the company. Even though he eventually went back to work for another firm, his breakthrough in seeking support was what gave him the courage to take the leap. One of the great benefits of talking through your midlife transition is that it lets you articulate possibilities and thereby take them seriously. "It wasn't until I went public with my feelings that I could really entertain some different options for the second part of my life," said Ian.

Certain people can be the keystone of your support system: a mentor, coach, or role model—like Dave was for Ian. While such people help facilitate your transition by encouraging trial-and-error and offering feedback, remember that no one has your personal prescription. A mentor empowers by example, not instruction; a hero provides inspiration, but doesn't solicit imitation.

A therapist can be part of your support system, but since midlife isn't in itself pathological, traditional psychotherapy is often irrelevant. Rather than enter the standard healer-patient relationship, the person who feels stuck in midlife may be better off with a therapist who is really more of a coach, someone who encourages self-discovery by stimulation.

This role isn't one that comes naturally to many therapists, so don't hesitate to interview several candidates, or to spring for the cost of preliminary consultations. Ask yourself whether the therapist is communicating in language you can relate to or is trying to fit you into an arcane system of healing. How comfortable do you feel revealing yourself to this person? Does any difference in age or sex between you and the therapist present a barrier? In therapy, are you focusing on what matters to you, or are you being led into less relevant territory? Beware of the *bait and switch,* a tendency of some therapists to ditch the subject you want to talk about in favor of a subject they're more interested in; for example, you want to deal with identity problems, and he wants to dwell on your mother. Style of therapy is also an issue: some therapists mainly provide a safe space in which you can talk things through; others are more actively participatory and directive.

## Skill #8   Use Landmark Events in Meaningful Ways or A Birthday is a Terrible Thing to Waste

Landmark events are those unignorable markers of the passage of time—birthdays, holidays, new decades, anniversaries—or decisive changes in our life situation, such as marriage or divorce, beginning or ending a job, a cross-country move. They are natural occasions for reflecting on who we are, how we have changed, what lies ahead. Deliberately marking such events in meaningful ways is an opportunity to reinforce the work of successful transition.

Sometimes these events provoke knee-jerk denial and resistance; hence, the tired humor about turning forty or celebrating the tenth or twentieth wedding anniversary. Milestones like these do become bittersweet as we grow older, unequivocal reminders of the limits of a lifespan. This feeling intensifies as we age and perceive time passing ever more swiftly.

It makes sense to celebrate reminders of aging with constructive action rather than futile resistance. Choosing to let a birthday or other landmark pass unmarked deprives appropriate feelings of a necessary outlet. Why not use these natural pauses to rest, observe the vista, chart or correct our course, and then move on? Failing to do so is wasting a resource. This applies especially to those culturally potent decade birthdays.

Julie, a friend who is approaching forty, told me about her plans to observe this birthday. The ten-year segments had been highly significant for her, she noted. On her twentieth birthday she'd moved out of her parents' home. By thirty, since she was married and had had her first child, she celebrated by running in a marathon, a statement to herself and her family that she was capable of choosing a goal and meeting it, while balancing a full plate of demands.

A lot of her friends were turning forty with big parties, she said, but that didn't appeal to her. "To tell the truth, they seem like such a facade, such an effort. Either it's a big blow-out, with everyone pretending they haven't really lost anything in the struggle with aging, or like a mini-funeral."

Julie had something quite different in mind: she and her husband and daughter were taking a trip to Africa. She'd always wanted to go on a photo safari, and besides, "At forty it seems like you're entering a new land, anyway, so why not do it literally in a new place?"

Perhaps the most significant feature of the trip was that Julie would be paying for it herself, with money she'd been setting aside from her paycheck systematically over a year. "I never said anything to anybody because it was a very personal fantasy." More than that, the way she realized her fantasy announced a new vision of herself as someone who had arrived at a higher level of independence.

Rituals are punctuations that give our lives shape and coherence. Beginnings and endings should be noted and defined. The decision to leave a job or a relationship, for example, is best accompanied by a clear termination date and an effort to close the books. As an unusual example, I heard of a couple who gathered their friends for an anniversary party, then used it as an occasion to announce their impending divorce instead. If characterized by rancor it would have been in bad taste, but they were parting on relatively amicable terms and wanted an occasion to communicate their situation and feelings to the people they were close to. Their guests came away surprised at how well the event served its purpose and appreciative of the couple's thoughtfulness.

In such ways, ritual serves as a public notice of our intention, soliciting the endorsement and support of others. And in the choppy waters of midlife transition, the support of friends and family can make the difference between sinking and swimming.

## Skill #9   Learn to Transcend Your Body
### or Less is Less but Often Better

One of the most fundamental demands of midlife is that we learn to accept our physical aging. But, more than passively accept it, we must learn to actively transcend it. Two complementary skills are involved, the first of which is to diversify and develop the aspects of ourself that we value. To maintain a sense of wholeness, we must make a conscious effort to broaden the base of our self-esteem. Joseph Campbell, in a TV discussion with Bill Moyers, said that in midlife we must learn to appreciate our intellectual, social and spiritual capacities; otherwise we can only see ourselves "like a car, with pieces gradually falling off."

This is never an easy process, the difficulty varying with the degree to which we are exclusively invested in our physical identity. The earliest feedback in our lives is in response to our physical selves: the little girl is told she is cute or pretty, and learns that her self-worth derives from these traits; the little boy is strong, or fast, or agile. As we grow, we develop other traits like loyalty, responsibility and tenacity based on feedback. But our sense of ourself as a physical being underlies it all.

This is not to downplay the joy we can get from our bodies, which leads to the second skill involved in body transcendence—body maintenance. Learn to care for yourself in an educated way. Those inclined to be athletic especially need to learn new modes of exercise and training. The attitude of *more is better* must give way to an approach based on self-knowledge and feedback. Such people engage in a monumental amount of denial: many midlife athletes exist in a state of chronic fatigue by trying to stay young. Ironically, their struggles only exacerbate the feeling they are trying to escape—of being old and tired.

Gerry was referred to me after an automobile accident that injured his back. I already knew Gerry from the health club we both belonged to and had watched him work-out on several occasions; at forty-two, he was ferociously fit. Then the accident, and accompanying back pain, changed his life by severely curtailing his activities. He couldn't work for awhile, which was causing great financial strain, and he was moody and irritable—as anyone in pain might be.

What most frustrated and depressed him, however, was not being able to work out and compete. His identification with his physical prowess was almost complete. I suggested a number of activities to distract him from this obsession but nothing worked, and his mood continued to plummet. A relationship he valued ended when his girlfriend could no longer put up with his self-inflicted misery.

After several months of fruitless probing at his defenses we came to the heart of the issue. Gerry admitted that he was threatened down to his soul about getting older; his physical routine was like a magic ritual against the demons of aging. Without it, he'd lost his center, and he had not developed other resources to fall back on.

For Gerry, this insight wasn't enough. After a couple of months, he couldn't stay away from the club any longer and went back to his workouts. I cautioned him to take it easy, but

I might have been speaking Martian. A month later I was called to the hospital where Gerry had been readmitted with an acute flare-up of back pain following a workout. To compound the problem, he'd been taking huge doses of painkillers to mask his symptoms. Even after surgery, which he could have avoided by changing his habits, and despite the most explicit warnings of doctors and physical therapists, he continued to focus only on how soon he could get back to the gym.

Gerry is an extreme example, but we all face this challenge in some form. Body maintenance in midlife is not an all-or-nothing proposition, it's an arena of negotiation and compromise. If anything, we need to pay more attention to it, not take it so much for granted. A sensible approach neither concedes nor denies the aging process, but incorporates it as another variable in the constantly changing chemistry of self.

The issue of health—body maintenance to foster well-being and performance—intersects with the psychology of how we appear to others. For many people, traditionally women, appearance is the identity component most threatened by midlife. The quantum growth of cosmetic surgery is indicative of how important this is to the baby boom generation—and not only among its women. Men underwent as many as 16 percent of the 600,000 cosmetic surgeries performed in 1986, not including the millions of hair transplants and related minor procedures.

The decision to have cosmetic surgery is not, in itself, significant with regard to body transcendence. Getting a facelift may be a indication that one hasn't accepted the fact of aging—but not necessarily. Real acceptance or denial is internal, and cosmetic surgery is quite literally superficial: What matters is what you expect from it. If you acknowledge that the surgery, at best, is a temporary expedient and not a foundation for postmidlife happiness, it can be a harmless indulgence. Conversely, there's no value in looking one's age for the sake of authenticity alone. In either case, the true work of midlife goes on beneath the skin.

## *Skill #10   Learn to Transcend Your Ego*
## *or Passing the Torch without Getting Burned*

This skill is about learning to engage in relationships that are gratifying for reasons that include, but go beyond their obvious benefit to ourselves—what we can call mentoring relationships. Erik Erikson wrote about the need for generativity, but this is more than just the production and nurturing of a new generation. It's the challenge of guiding those who follow us, of passing on some of our wisdom and experience: the desire to leave a legacy.

As a generation, the baby boom is likely to find this a difficult task. We have leaned toward narcissism and a feeling that we were the only generation that mattered. That's not hard to understand, given our lifelong immersion in a culture dominated by our numbers, and the media spotlight focused on us from birth—a first for any generation. But in midlife we have to learn to share the spotlight.

It's possible to pass the torch without feeling diminished or suffering loss. Again, we come back to issues of age-appropriate sources of self-esteem, to diversification and role models. If we accept the impulse to nurture others as an appropriate midlife activity, then giving up center stage becomes a natural and satisfying act. If we have diversified skills and a good base of support, we can be generous with our energy. Finally, if we ourselves have experienced good parenting and/or mentoring, we have a model of what ego transcendence looks like, and how it can work for the benefit of all concerned.

The word *mentor* comes from the Greek god Mentor, who was entrusted by his friend Odysseus with the education of the king's son, Telemachus. The position of a mentor is one of trust and honor. The appreciation of the person receiving our guidance is one trade-off for giving up some of the applause; another benefit is in satisfying our urge for immortality, as midlife confronts us with the limits of our lifespan.

Mentoring is implicit in parenting, so those without children may need to actively seek out mentoring relationships for the opportunity they offer to leave behind something of ourselves.

Some reject the role of mentor out of denial of aging, or because they fear it means they have reached the limits of success and can go no farther. This isn't necessarily so, but it does mean they move over to another ladder and accept the idea of being senior with someone else being in the junior position. This can happen in the context of work, the community, the family, in government, or the arts.

Gail Sheehy referred in *Passages* to a study of junior and senior analysts at a psychiatric institute. The former (average age thirty-eight) saw their important issues in terms of relationships: problems with marital partners, career competition with younger people, or consciousness of physical decline in comparison with others. The senior group (average age fifty-three) focused on themselves as separate beings and their potential for personalized solutions and pleasures. Having restabilized after midlife, they were less competitive and more self-sufficient in relationships. This change was described as a movement from *us-ness* to *me-ness*.

A prerequisite of ego transcendence is giving up or changing relationships with our own mentors. This can be painful, because we idealize mentors and resist seeing them as flawed. But in midlife, we come to see the human frailties and faults of both individuals and the relationships; this is part of the larger processes of de-illusionment and individuation. Being a good mentor demands a strong sense of one's identity as a separate and valuable individual, so that mentoring efforts are not sabotaged by an urge to steal the thunder—or by excessive subjugation of the self. A balance must be struck between altruism and egotism. Also important is the realization that any mentoring relationship has its own dynamic, based on a comfortable distance between mentor and student, which varies over the course of time. Sooner or later the mentor will be out-grown and trying to maintain too much intimacy at this stage will cause problems.

A further payoff of mentoring is that it reinforces the *young* side in the young/old polarity of identity—it is a constructive way of staying young and keeping in touch with the next gen-eration. Recently, I consulted with a professional ballet com-pany that was developing a retirement program for its danc-ers. Louise, the director of the program and a former dancer herself, was now forty-nine; she had been forced to retire from performing at age twenty-eight because of a knee injury. That was a difficult time for Louise, and she had actually left the world of dance to pursue other means of making a living. But her love of dance endured, and when an administrative position with her former company opened up, she leaped at the chance.

Louise was married but had no children. "These are all my children," she told me. "I've been lucky to have seen so many wonderful kids come through our company. The relationships have been very important to me—and, I hope, to them."

It wasn't easy at first. "I was really jealous of these kids with their future in front of them. I felt there was still a lot missing from my life because I couldn't perform. I hated to admit it, even denied it to myself for a long time, but I felt old and awk-ward around the dancers." Eventually, though, she made peace with her new role and found a way to connect with the younger dancers that didn't make her feel over the hill.

Louise took special satisfaction from the programs she de-signed to help other dancers deal with retirement. "Dancers' careers are often short, and many of them never realize their dreams. The selection process is very competitive. It's inevita-ble that many of them leave, seeing the end of their career as a failure." She tried to help them by pointing out other skills they could develop, and simply by offering emotional support and empathy. "Dancers think they are in this alone, that only other dancers know what they're up against. I try to show them that there *is* life after dance, and maybe just seeing that I'm okay helps them believe it. It works both ways—I know I get as much as I give."

For Louise, as for many physical performers, midlife came early and suddenly. For most of us the transition from rising star to mentor isn't marked by anything as dramatic as a career-ending injury. But in the way she adapted to her new role, Louise is a fine example of ego transcendence.

## Putting the Skills to Work

The aim of these early chapters has been to equip you with an understanding of the special considerations our generation will bring to the midlife passage, what to expect in general from the transition process, the psychology of our changing identity, and the coping skills that can pave the way to a successful resolution.

Now we'll turn to the specific arenas of life where we need to apply our understanding and skills—our physical selves, our closest relationships, and our work. Most of these master skills, as you will see, will reappear as we look at each of these issues. Take the time to understand them now, though. The sooner you begin to integrate them into your transition process, the easier it will be to apply them in any specific situation.

# 6

## Staying Alive

### Our Bodies at Fortysomething

*No matter how you tell yourself*
*It's what we all go through,*
*Those lines are pretty hard to take*
*When they're staring back at you.*
BONNIE RAITT

I've always been athletically inclined, an enthusiast about both professional and participatory sports. For me, a very big part of midlife has been coming to terms with the changing capacities and demands of my body.

An incident I had on the squash court last year brought the issue into sharp focus. I was warming up before a semifinals match with a much younger opponent. He asked how old I was, and I replied, a bit self-consciously, "Forty-two." "That's more than twice as old as I am," he said without thinking. "I'm nineteen." As I was wondering how to respond and, more, why we were having this conversation at all, he continued with a grin, "You know what? I'm going to let you win this match. At your age, who knows how many you have left? Me, I've got a whole career ahead of me."

Well, I did win that match. I would have died before losing, after what the kid said, but he looked like he was trying too.

Win or lose, though, he was right. While I was playing at the top of my game that season, he was far from reaching the peak of his, and he's beaten me every time we've met in a tournament since. This year, though, in a gesture of self-acceptance, I've stopped playing in the open division and taken up residence in the thirty-five-plus category. I figure you have to pick your shots.

More importantly, the squash court became my laboratory for learning to deal with midlife in the flesh. My body was changing, and I needed to pace myself differently; I recovered more slowly from injuries. I learned that the mental game was as important as the muscular one. I learned that the body needs rest as well as stress to remain strong, and that too much stimulation can lead to chronic exhaustion.

Our sense of identity is more closely tied to our physical selves than we often realize. Some are more heavily invested in their appearance and physical competence than others, but whether you regard your body as a high-performance machine or a commuter vehicle, midlife demands that you develop a new relationship with it.

A keen awareness of physical aging—changes in performance, appearance, and health—is the single most powerful ingredient of midlife. Reminders are everywhere; we begin to avoid driving at night because of eyestrain; we can't stay up late and party; we can't get to sleep after an extra-hard workout. Gray hairs and facial lines seem to multiply as we gaze into the mirror—or the hairs disappear at an alarming rate. Extra pounds take more effort to shed. That sporadic twinge in the lower back becomes a familiar companion.

Men and women share some of the physiological issues of aging, but each sex has special concerns. Men who are athletic, especially, notice declines in peak performance and endurance; they can't rebound as quickly after a few hard sets of tennis or a long run. Hair loss is a common complaint among those genetically disposed to it. Some loss of sexual performance, as measured by the frequency of erections and the intensity of ejaculations, is inevitable. How men react to this is at least as much a psychological as a physical issue, since we tend to evaluate sexuality by these quantitative standards and so feel our male identity threatened. A major task for men in midlife, then, is to broaden their view of what constitutes physical well-being and a satisfying sex life.

How biological factors affect women depends largely on how their lives have been patterned so far. For women who haven't yet had children, the awareness of limits to their childbearing years becomes a dominant issue. It is sometimes said that women go through *biological midlife* twice: once in their mid-thirties, when the issue of children becomes urgent, and again in their mid-fifties, when menopause completes the gradual loss of fertility. (It could as easily be argued that midlife for women spans this entire period, peaking at certain points.)

Most women are highly conscious of the ways aging skin and muscles affect their looks, as the booming cosmetics industry attests. In general, though, women experience less sense of physical decline than men, tending to retain more vigor and endurance through the middle years. Their sense of self is less closely tied to physical strength, and, as is often noted, their sex drive suffers no diminution in midlife.

Male or female, fit or flabby, at some point you wake up to the fact that you can't take your body for granted anymore. Like any other pain, the twinges of turning forty have a message for us, but it *isn't* that we have to stop thinking of ourselves as physical beings, now that we're *over the hill*. The success of over-forty athletes such as runner Bill Rodgers, basketball great Kareem Abdul-Jabbar, golfer Jack Nicklaus, fifty-year-old Wilt Chamberlain in his new volleyball career, tennis star Billie Jean King, and dancer Margot Fonteyn (among many other women) are ample evidence that midlife is no arbitrary cut-off point for performance. To the contrary, the message is that it's time to pay more attention to our bodies—that a long and vigorous life requires conscious physical maintenance.

This chapter will summarize the most current knowledge about why and how we age, what happens to the body and what we can do about it. We'll examine common misconceptions about aging, the latest trends in research on controlling it, and the vital interface of psychology and physiology. And we'll point you in the right directions for taking charge of your body in midlife through health and fitness.

## The Biology of Aging

The lifespan of a member of the human species has not increased significantly for thousands of years. Since the days of the Romans, the upper limit of life has been stuck at around 115 years. What *has* changed is the average life *expectancy*. Medical advances and improved living conditions have allowed vastly more people to reach or approach the limit of what appears to be a fixed lifespan. As Groucho Marx said, "Anyone can get old; all you have to do is live long enough."

The fundamental cause of death in later years is the body's greater vulnerability to disease or accident, due to a gradual decline in its peak functioning from about age thirty on. While death may be attributed to cardiovascular disease or cancer—either of which can arise from environmental causes—those illnessess are able to take hold because of normal age-related degeneration of the immune system or of arterial walls.

What causes the machinery to run down? Scientists have advanced many theories, beginning with the idea that our bodies simply wear out. This theory ignores the fact that our cells reproduce, however, and today the more popular theory is that aging is programmed into our genes. There are various permutations on this idea, and researchers are working to find the specific location and mechanism of this clock of aging.

Others have suggested that our cellular reproduction becomes less precise as we age, like a photocopy that becomes blurred and unreadable by the twentieth generation. Some think that our immune systems may gradually go haywire and begin attacking healthy cells as well as pernicious invaders, or that the indispensable pituitary gland at some point turns on us and begins to produce an aging hormone.

A currently fashionable explanation focuses on the role of *free radicals*, unstable chemicals produced during metabolism, that link up with other molecules in the body and disrupt their DNA. People familiar with this theory may chide you for switching to unsaturated fats as a health measure, pointing out that these increase oxidation in the cells and create more free radicals in the process.

Research in human growth hormones has recently produced some exciting results. A study published in the *New England Journal of Medicine* in mid-1990 found that six months of treatment with a recombinant version of the natural growth hormone reversed the effects of aging in a group of men aged sixty-one to eighty-one. By many measures, including body composition, skin, and bone mass, their bodies were nearly twenty years younger after the treatment. The study suggests that decreased hormone production may cause aging symptoms such as fat increases and shrinking muscles and organs, but the longterm effects of such treatment are not known.

The ultimate aim of this research is to help more people attain the full potential lifespan of our species and, perhaps, to crack that fixed upper limit—a modern-day version of Ponce de Leon's quest for the Fountain of Youth. Many believe that the key to prolonging life lies in our genetic programming.

So far, though, the genetic codes remain uncracked, and science has found only two, possibly three, proven ways of extending life. First is restricting one's diet fairly stringently, both in the kind of foods and quantity of calories consumed. Next is avoiding exposure to toxic agents in the environment—a tricky proposition and much influenced by genetic vulnerability to such factors. Some believe that lowering body temperature, either with techniques like those practiced by certain long-lived Indian yogis or with drugs, can be significant, especially in combination with a restricted diet.

## BIOLOGICAL VERSUS CHRONOLOGICAL AGE

While genetically programmed aging will catch up with us all sooner or later, the timing can vary quite widely. Science seems to have confirmed an old adage by proving that people who look young for their age are actually biologically younger.

To determine biological age, the National Institute on Aging developed the Borkan-Norris profile, which evaluates twenty-four functions including vision, hearing, heart performance, and reaction speed. Studies showed that physical appearance corresponded to biological age as gauged by this profile, whatever the chronological age.

Being biologically young for one's age is partly a matter of genetic luck, but health and lifestyle factors do appear to influence biological age considerably. Of people tested, those with older biological scores were in worse mental or physical health, and were heavier and less active. The biologically younger group tended to be athletic, highly educated, and married. While these studies were of men, the findings should be essentially the same for women.

## GOOD NEWS FOR BABY BOOMERS

Despite recent encouraging developments, as yet we have no control over the fact of aging. But we do have, today, considerable control over *how* we age, and it starts here, at midlife. At this pivotal juncture, making choices on behalf of good health and longevity will bring tangible rewards in the way you look and feel right now. They will also be the basis for decades of vitality yet to be lived.

Even without taking any healthier measures individually, we can anticipate longer and healthier lives than any previous generation. Medical advances are partly responsible, but more significant for midlifers is the extent to which we can overcome aging through self-care and fitness. A growing amount of evidence indicates that the length and quality of our later life depend largely on health patterns established in midlife. So even if your youthful health habits weren't ideal, improving them at fortysomething can make a huge difference to your future. If you can avoid the chronic diseases that develop in the middle years—heart conditions, gastro-intestinal disorders, and many forms of cancer—your chances of living into your eighties or nineties increase every year.

Exercise is obviously a key factor, and it needn't be at a competitive level. One of many recent studies showed that age-adjusted death rates dropped sharply between a group of subjects who were almost totally sedentary and another whose lifestyle included very moderate exercise, such as walking a half hour to an hour each day.

We have also learned how to better distinguish the biology of aging from the psychology of aging. Many of the problems of old age—feelings of helplessness, isolation, or depression— are rooted not in physical but in psychological losses, which can affect anyone, regardless of age.

And we have learned to distinguish normal age-related changes from changes due to illness. Conditions once thought to be inevitable byproducts of growing old—osteoporosis, hardening of the arteries, or excessive wrinkling—more often result from inactivity, poor nutrition, cell damage, or disease.

Baby boomers thus have more motivation for health maintenance than any earlier generation, as well as more resources to practice it. Many of us discovered in our twenties or thirties the benefits of a sensible diet and exercise in how we look and feel, and, as with other trends, we've made it accepted in the larger culture. Since they are rewarding, these habits become self-perpetuating; boomers will tend to continue to be physically active and concerned with self-care in their midlives and beyond. This alone will produce a tremendous change in the culture's experience and perception of midlife: from a time of rapid decline to, instead, a slight adjustment in a vigorous life.

Looking ahead, we can anticipate more good news from the scientific community. Based on what we already know about the aging process, there are likely to be some breakthroughs during our lifetimes. Some recent discoveries about controlling aging of the heart, lungs, and skin are described below.

## From the Outside In:
## Skin and Hair, Muscles and Bones

To some degree, we are all invested in the face and body we present to the world. The aging symptoms that get our attention first are usually those that affect our appearance: skin that is no longer smooth and resilient, hair that is graying or going the changing shape of our figure. There's nothing wrong with taking a certain amount of pride in appearance, and many of our efforts to enhance this are good for our health too. But this is a crucial time to sort out how much of our self-worth derives from outward beauty versus inner strengths and adjust the balance if it's off-center. Midlifers must face this issue squarely, or we set ourselves up for future pain.

### SKIN DEEP

Our skin is the front line of aging. No one knows this better than the cosmetics industry, which plays on baby boomer vanity to the tune of billions of dollars each year. Women have been and remain the primary targets of cosmetics purveyors, but men are starting to close the gap—a recent issue of *Vanity Fair* featured five full pages of advertising for men's skincare products and fragrances.

As the body ages, the supportive middle layer of skin—the dermis—thins, and, with it, the supply of protein fibers, elastin, and collagen that give the skin its firmness and elasticity. The dermis also contains oil glands, which decrease in production after adolescence (and more sharply after menopause), leaving the skin more prone to dryness.

Dermatologists have steadfastly maintained that the usefulness of cosmetics, however fancy their pricetag, is limited to moisturizing skin and protecting it from the elements with sunscreens. Products advertised as exfoliants or "cell renewal" treatments can speed the replacement of cells in the epidermis—but even the new skin cells of a forty-five-year-old aren't the same as those of a twenty-five-year-old.

The dermis is not permeable to molecules of collagen, elastin, or Vitamin E from external applications. Apparently some of the newer, more sophisticated products may be able to cross the skin barrier to some extent, creating headaches for the FDA, which doesn't know whether to classify them as cosmetics or drugs. Public response to the drug Retin-A, once its anti-aging properties were substantiated, has been tremendous.

Wrinkled, sagging, or spotted skin—the most obvious badges of aging—may be more attributable to sun damage than to growing older. Too much exposure to direct sunlight exacerbates the above effects, especially in people of northern European descent. Ultraviolet radiation damages the protein fibers and is the most direct cause of wrinkles. In fact, dermatologists estimate that as much as 70 percent of what we consider the effects of aging on skin may actually be due to sun damage.

Excessive or rapid weight gain or loss has negative effects on skin, causing it to lose its natural elasticity. Chronically obese women and men tend to look older because of the development of jowls and loose neck skin. If a woman loses excess weight before age thirty-five, her skin should be resilient enough to spring back into shape, but Dr. Barbara Edelstein, author of *The Woman Doctor's Diet for Women,* cautions that rapidly losing more than 10 percent of one's total body weight is bad for the skin at any age.

Smoking constricts small blood vessels, thereby reducing oxygen supply to skin tissues, and also damages collagen. According to Dr. Arthur Balin, former president of the American Aging Association, this can cause a thirty-year-old smoker to be more wrinkled than a forty-five-year-old nonsmoker.

Therefore, some of the prescriptions for more youthful-looking skin are obvious: use sunscreens, avoid radical weight changes, don't smoke. We also know that aerobic exercise benefits the skin as well as other systems; it delivers blood rapidly to the skin, bringing nutrients and removing cellular wastes. Some researchers believe that exercise may encourage deposits of collagen and elastin, which are produced at a decreasing rate as we age. And a balanced, nutritious diet, with vitamin supplements if needed, is essential to healthy skin.

For consumers to sort out the truth in cosmetics advertising is highly problematic; in general, it is best not to rely on creams for anything except moisturizing and protection. Retin-A is clearly effective in making wrinkles less pronounced, though its other effects can include skin irritation and increased sensitivity to sun exposure.

Whether or not cosmetic surgery of any kind is a good idea for you depends largely on your motives. As long as you accept the medical risks involved and do what you can to minimize them, the decision to have plastic surgery should reflect realistic personal expectations. It may give you a little more confidence with which to face the world; it won't keep you young forever or reconstruct a deeply damaged case of self-esteem. As with other aspects of aging, the most effective remedies for the skin are not externally applied but come from the inside out: good nutrition, aerobic fitness, and a healthy attitude.

## OFF THE TOP OF YOUR HEAD

I have thinning hair, and sometimes, when I see myself, it takes me by surprise—I stare at it and comfort myself by thinking, well, I'm not bald. . . yet. But I wonder about men who wear toupees, or who compensate for their bald pates by growing their hair long on one side and then wrapping it around the top. To me it seems that, by trying to deny something so obvious, they draw even more attention to it. They might as well wear a neon sign saying "Self-conscious about being bald!"

Hair loss is an age-related problem that mostly affects men. Thinning usually begins at the temples and moves toward the back of the head. Nearly 40 percent of forty-year-old men are affected by male pattern baldness, and after age sixty, overall thinning is almost universal due to a decline in new hair growth. Female pattern baldness can begin around age thirty, reducing hair growth in the crown area in about 25 percent of women.

Science has been helpful here, with good results from Minidoxil, the hair-restoring drug developed by Upjohn. New research shows that this drug (often marketed as Rogaine) may be more effective when used in combination with Retin-A. A still newer drug is Cyoctol, which disrupts the action of the male hormone androgen, believed to be responsible for baldness. At the University of Miami, researchers are deciphering the genetic factors that control hair growth; a genetically engineered hair tonic is predicted within the next decade.

## COMING ON STRONG: THE MUSCULOSKELETAL SYSTEM

Our standard of attractiveness, especially for women, has changed dramatically in the last decade, since Jane Fonda and female bodybuilder Lisa Lyons made muscles acceptable. Magazine models, once skin and bones, are now more athletic. Men, too, are paying more attention to their musculature; shirtmakers are catering to the trend toward bigger shoulders and narrower waists.

"At first I felt embarrassed about standing around in a gym 'pumping iron' with the guys," confessed my client Francine. "But nothing was more embarrassing than realizing I was starting to get those pouchy upper arms that I always associated with old ladies."

Getting older has been associated with increases in body fat and decreases in muscle mass and bone density. In the average sedentary person, physical strength usually peaks around age twenty, then declines about 30 percent over the years into old age. The weakening of muscle and connective tissue leads to skeletal weakening, which makes us more vulnerable to accidents and normal wear and tear.

Even moderate exercise can contribute to greater bone and muscle mass, more strength, and leaner bodies. Medical experts used to think that older muscle lost the capacity to grow and be strengthened, but in a study at Tufts University, a group of elderly people who lifted weights for twelve weeks increased their muscle mass by 20 percent and their strength by 400 percent. Exercise helps to minimize the effects of osteoporosis, the progressive weakening and deterioration of bones, because it increases bone mass as well as muscle. Tennis players, for example, have larger and stronger bones in their playing arms.

Besides maintaining muscle and bone mass, exercise helps keep muscles and connective tissues flexible, preventing strains that can injure joints. You're also less likely to have back problems if you do abdominal strengthening.

Diet is important in preventing osteoporosis, especially in women, and vitamin D and calcium are the key ingredients. As we age, we don't absorb calcium as well from our food;

consequently, after age thirty-five, we lose about one percent of bone mass per year. Most adults eat only about half the calcium they need—a recommended 1,000 milligrams a day for men and premenopausal women. After menopause, lowered estrogen slows calcium absorption even more, and the loss of bone mass can rise to three percent per year unless offset by more calcium in the diet.

One hope for osteoporosis sufferers is the recent development of local bone-growth factors. Scientists are working to isolate these growth-factor genes, and drugs to stimulate the production of new bone mass may be available within ten years.

Arthritis can make its first appearance around fortysomething; fortunately, better treatments are close at hand due to the recent discovery of the protein that controls joint inflammation.

## Midlife and the Senses

We tend to be affected powerfully by any change in the capacity of our senses. Changes in vision are often the very first sign of reaching midlife, appearing long before the first gray hair or serious wrinkle. A forty-two-year-old friend, Vicki, says, "I denied I needed reading glasses until I couldn't read a menu or thread a needle!"

Visual acuity tends to decline gradually from the middle twenties through the fifties, after which it declines a bit faster. Presbyopia, the gradual loss of the eye's focusing ability, is caused by increasing rigidity of the lens, which brings on the need for reading glasses or bifocals. The diameter of the pupil also shrinks as we age, so less light reaches the retina of the eye. This makes it harder for us to adjust to changes in light levels. Walking from a brightly lit space into a darkened one, like a movie theater, can cause momentary blindness. Driving at night is more of a challenge, and very bright sun makes us squint more.

The senses of hearing, smell, and taste all diminish with age. Hearing loss, often a debilitating handicap late in life, actually begins quite early: a thirty-year-old can't hear as well as a child. Hearing loss accelerates after age fifty and is usually worse in men than in women. Baby boomers with a history of exposure to electronically amplified music are undoubtedly at more hearing loss risk (witness guitarist Pete Townsend of The Who), and amplified sound through portable-stereo headphones can be especially harmful if played at high volume.

## The Beat Goes On: Heart and Lungs

Tom was only forty-three when he was rushed to the emergency room in the throes of a massive heart attack. He had been under a lot of stress in the preceding year. His father had died suddenly, leaving him to carry on the family business alone. It seemed like one bad thing would happen after another: he would have problems with his wife and kids, his mother's medical bills, or his betting on football.

> My health habits weren't commendable either. My family always liked big meals, and I'm talking meat, potatoes, gravy, rolls and butter, salt pork in the vegetables, and dessert at lunch and dinner. Plenty of beer. I had played football in college and a little tennis on the weekends, but that was about it for exercise.

Four days after his triple bypass surgery, a psychologist from Cardiac Rehabilitation suggested that Tom join their program after he was discharged. Tom could hardly believe this was happening to him at such a young age, but he decided to give the program, which involved exercise, weight loss, and group therapy, a try. Now he believes it turned his life around.

Before the heart attack he weighed 240 pounds, though at his height (6' 4") that didn't seem very unusual to him. In a year, he had reduced his cholesterol levels drastically and dropped fifty pounds. He began by walking, and within two years was running twenty to thirty miles a week. At his last examination, Tom's cardiologist told him that there was no atherosclerosis in his arteries. Tom's never felt better. Stress-management classes taught him how to control his type-A behavior, and he found that taking care of his body was part of improving his self-esteem.

Complete recovery from a midlife heart attack like Tom's is not rare today. Most people have an exaggerated idea about how much heart function declines with age. The passing of time does make the heart and blood vessels more vulnerable to disease. Heart disease is a leading cause of death today, largely due to the absence of infectious diseases that allowed fewer people to grow old in earlier times. There is a gradual reduction after age twenty in the maximum heart rate during exercise; this is most often manifested as fatigue during strenuous activity. And it is true that increased arterial wall stiffness and other changes in the cardiovascular system normally occurs as one ages. But in someone with a normal, healthy heart, such changes do not typically lead to cardiac dysfunction.

You'd have to be living under a rock not to know that staying active has a major impact on cardiovascular function. Consider your maximum oxygen consumption—the measure of how efficiently your body uses oxygen, expressed as the $VO_2$ *max quotient*. Oxygen exchange in the tissues affects the body's health in many areas: skin, hair, bone formation, metabolism, weight, and sex hormones. Until recently, $VO_2$ max was thought to decline at the depressing rate of nine percent every ten years after age twenty-five. But new research shows that regular exercise slows the loss of $VO_2$ max considerably.

All this means that many of the symptoms we associate with heart *disease*—chiefly fatigue and shortness of breath—are really related to heart *fitness*, a matter well within our control.

The lungs work in tandem with the heart to achieve $VO_2$ max, and lung efficiency affects the volume of blood pumped with each heart stroke. After about age twenty-five, the volume of air that can be inhaled and expelled by the lungs decreases by an average of one percent each year as the lungs lose elasticity. Regular exercise can't stop lungs from aging, but it can maximize the efficiency of oxygen exchange in the lungs, as well as toning the muscles of the ribcage and diaphragm, which move air in and out.

Staying fit can, in some cases, prevent or delay the onset of heart disease, but in some cases it's genetic. Your doctor can tell you if you are predisposed to it and recommend compensatory measures.

## Mind Over Matter: The Brain and Memory

Midlife is a little early to be worried about the so-called *brain drain*—and, in any case, the assumption that our brains function less well with increasing age is simplistic and inaccurate. It is based largely on the fact that older people have performed less well in standardized intelligence tests, but recent studies have shown that such tests are distinctly biased in favor of younger people who are in, or have recently been in, school and are well practiced at being tested.

Moreover, it's important to distinguish between the two modes of intelligence that such tests measure. The first is *crystallized* or acquired knowledge, which actually increases as we age, provided we remain mentally active and engaged with the world. The second type, *fluid intelligence*, essentially represents the brain's speed at solving abstract problems and analyzing new information. Here there is an age-related decline, which may become noticeable around midlife in certain situations. The physical basis for the loss of fluid intelligence seems to be a biochemical slowdown: the neurons don't transmit signals as quickly.

It's common knowledge that we lose brain cells as we age. More recently, though, a remarkable compensating mechanism has been discovered. Apparently, in the brains of older people the neurons grow more interconnecting branches, or dendrites—these interconnections, rather than the sheer number of cells, are the crucial element in learning and memory.

Long-term memory—the sum total of things we can recall from our past—tends to erode somewhat as we age, but not, as people often assume, because of brain-cell loss or breakdown of the basic memory function. More likely, the problem is accessing information in the memory, due to the slowdown of fluid intelligence, or poor memorization and learning techniques, which can apply at any age. Usually the reason we can't retrieve something from memory is because it wasn't learned well before filing. Researchers are currently searching for *cognition activators*, drugs that enhance the flow of neurotransmitting chemicals that have grown sluggish with age.

Again, fortysomething is a bit soon to be concerned about serious memory loss, but practicing memory-enhancing techniques may promote welcome feelings of self-control and self-confidence in midlife. Looking ahead, the evidence is overwhelming that *brain fitness,* like physical fitness, is directly linked to mental exercising: dealing with new challenges, learning, staying interested in what you do. Countless examples of older people in creative fields—composers, painters, writers—prove the point, probably as well as people you know in your own family. So the learning and experimentation we do in midlife, the new paths explored and risks successfully taken, will lay the groundwork for a stimulating, mind-sustaining environment in later life.

## Compromising Positions: Sexuality in Midlife

The generation currently entering midlife were the shock troops of the sexual revolution, campaigning to liberate repressed society under the banner of free sex. Our history of associating sex with unencumbered pleasure, with freedom and youthful energy and even world-changing optimism, gives special poignancy to the physical and psychological changes in sexuality that come with midlife.

While we've heard much about the dark side of sex in recent years, the sexual legacy of the sixties includes the benefits of greater openness between partners and more latitude for women to seek pleasure. In any case, it is deeply rooted in us and, largely as a result of our success in bringing sex out of the closet and into the light, we are today surrounded by it inescapably: in movies, magazines, TV, billboards, and everyday conversation sprinkled with once-banned words.

But sex as a selling tool is far from sex as most of us experience it in real life. Sexual expectations based on popular fantasies can set us up for frustration, especially in the pressurized environment of midlife. Against this background, let's look at the sexual issues baby boomer men and women are dealing with in midlife, before we go on to detail the physiological particulars for each.

*Female gratification and the new man.* These represent the joint legacy of the sexual revolution and the women's movement. Among today's midlifers there is a vastly greater acceptance of a woman's right to sexual pleasure than in any prior generation.

This phenomenon has been confusing for men trained to more traditional sex roles and is sometimes blamed for men feeling a loss of masculine identity or virility. With regard to sex in midlife and later, however, it holds promise for improved sexual relations. Since women derive satisfaction from many lovemaking techniques including but not limited to intercourse, the specter of declining potency may become less threatening to midlife men.

*Episodic sex drive.* Both men and women report that their sex drive kicks into gear on a more episodic basis as they get older. Instead of being primed for sex at a certain time every day, or capable of being stimulated by almost any erotic suggestion, sexual desire seems to visit and depart at longer intervals, though it may be no less intense when present. Creating a specific setting or occasion for sensory stimulation and relaxation, such as a vacation, is often necessary to permit desire to surface through the turmoil of busy, diffused lives.

*The DINS dilemma.* The lifestyle of many midlife couples today is not terribly accommodating of a vital sex life. The DINS (Double Income No Sex) dilemma, as it's been called, often stems from chronic workaholism and hectic social lives, but whatever the sources, the result is that people are just too tired to be interested in sex. A couple I worked with, Susan and Rick, are fairly typical, as is Susan's comment: "I'm exhausted all the time. I have no energy left for Rick. I know he feels ignored, but by the time I get home from work, get the baby fed, and do whatever needs doing around the house, I can't think of anything but sleep. I love him, but when he sends out signals that he'd like to make love, sometimes I just pretend I don't notice."

*Delayed parenting.* In contrast to earlier generations, many baby boomers are becoming parents in the late thirties and forties. Lowered interest in sex among new mothers in the first year after birth is one result, but factor young children into the double-career equation, and sex tends to drop even further down the list of priorities.

A survey conducted by *Parenting* magazine found that the frequency of sexual relations was lower among respondents when compared with another survey of mainly childless couples: 33 percent of the former said they had sex one to three times a week, and 46 percent of the latter.

*Rise in alternative sexual practices.* Call it safe sex, soft-core sex, or "outercourse," many people are experimenting with various forms of nonpenetrative, even nonejaculatory sex. The motives can be medical, spiritual, romantic, or political— some couples want to bring back the thrill of courtship; others agree to refrain from intercourse temporarily in favor of sexual activities that don't depend on male potency.

*The no-sex option.* There are more single midlifers today, so this is becoming more significant. Fear of sexually transmitted diseases is undoubtedly one reason, as well as the same kind of scheduling pressures couples feel. (Finding time for sex can be even more of a problem for singles, since one's partner isn't right at hand.) And many people feel that it's simply harder, as one gets older, to find someone who rings all your bells.

While many of these socio-sexual trends of midlife are common to baby boomer men and women, we are quite different when it comes to physical and psychological sexuality. Men tend to be more performance-oriented, and their concerns center on diminishing strength and potency, while for women the issues of desirability and fertility become paramount. In either case, the changes that come with aging can threaten the essence of our gender-based identity.

In *Passages,* Gail Sheehy describes the male/female sexual life cycle as a diamond-shaped configuration. In this model, adult men and women are most sexually similar at age eighteen and after age sixty. Between eighteen and sixty—the points of the diamond—they gradually move apart, and are at their most distant sexual polarities at around age forty. The disparity at midlife boils down to this: that while women's sexual desire and orgasmic potential increases through their thirties and forties, male sexual performance—when measured as sheer potency—is declining.

Sex lives are as varied as personalities, and age is just one of many influences on both. Moving through midlife is unlikely to cause a revolution in one's sexual personality—either for better or for worse—but the physical changes that come with age usually do cause us to evolve as sexual beings. Here are some of the most widely documented changes in male and female sexuality.

### MEN: PLEASURE BEYOND POTENCY

Both Kinsey and Masters and Johnson found that the frequency of a man's erections and orgasms begins to slow after his late teens. Other studies report that a regular, decade-by-decade decline in performance so measured continues past age fifty. These statistics are all too drearily familiar—and this emphasis on quantitative performance is partly responsible for the common belief that men enjoy sex less as they grow older, while women are enjoying it more. Kinsey's data, collected in 1943, defined male satisfaction as ejaculation and nothing more. But most adult males today would reject that assumption, recognizing the pleasure of prolonged lovemaking as a better standard of satisfaction.

Around their forties, most men do notice a gradual decline in the frequency, spontaneity, and fullness of their erections.

Ejaculations become less intense, and the length of time between orgasm and the ability to have another erection—the *refractory period*—increases. On the other hand, older men can often sustain intercourse longer without ejaculating, a decided plus for both sexes. The degree to which these changes occur varies widely among individuals. What seems consistent is that those who have been sexually active and enthusiastic in youth will most likely continue that way.

The man whose sense of self is being tested on many fronts in midlife will naturally experience any diminishment in his sexual capacity as another threat—especially as he observes his wife or partner coming into her erotic prime around the same time. A single episode of impotency can shake his confidence enough to kick off a negative feedback cycle: his anxiety that it may happen again often ensures that it does.

Men who feel their sexual identity threatened may react by withdrawing from their spouse or partner, sometimes burying themselves in work as a way to avoid sex and have an excuse for being too tired—or they may use hostility toward their partner as a diversion. Some take the path of seeking adventures with other women, often someone younger and/or more superficially attractive than their regular partner. This may wake up a flagging libido, or may send it further into hiding out of guilt or performance anxiety.

Given their reluctance to reveal any weakness, the last thing most men are likely to do is talk through such problems with friends, or seek counsel from a doctor or sex therapist. This is unfortunate, as more information on the issue may give them an answer to their dilemma, and at the very least some much-needed perspective.

Many midlife men may find themselves in a situation like my client Alex. Thirty-nine, married seven years with one child, and very focused on his work, he admits to a significant loss of his sex drive. Essentially, he desires sex with his wife only in special circumstances, such as during a vacation. Occasionally he'll have a fantasy about some woman he meets, but never follows it through. He realizes that sex has assumed a minor role in his life, and feels nostalgic about the good old days of raw sex with college dates, yet he can't reconcile those memories with the present reality.

In this scenario, a man's changing sexuality interacts with a whole complex of factors: the familiarity of a long-term partner, domestic routines that don't encourage sexual excitement, the seductive grip of one's youthful past. At an earlier time of life, the sheer physical thrill of getting erect and having an orgasm can compensate for many flaws in a relationship, especially if the thrill of conquest is also involved. New-woman fantasies are usually attempts to recapture that feeling, and are a retreat from intimacy. Vacations are a time-honored way of rediscovering romance, but they occur too infrequently. What is needed is deliberate effort by both parties to maintain the sexual connection and, on the man's part, to explore beyond the levels of physical pleasure that once contented him.

In confronting the facts of male sexuality in midlife, the point isn't to scare or even to console anyone. But since the facts are inescapable, midlife men need to deemphasize quantitative measures of performance such as how hard, how long, how many times, in order to avoid frustration. We need to broaden our understanding of sexual satisfaction. We might see this particular value shift as part of the death of our youthful hero. Jungian analyst James Hillman points out that sexual pleasure for men in our culture is limited by our "image of lovemaking as heroic performance" and our lack of a deeply imaginative sexual vocabulary. Compare our hard-edged terms for sex, he suggests, with "the marvelous language of foreign erotica: jade stalk, palace gates, ambrosia!"

Midlife is an ideal time for men to stretch their sexual boundaries, to experiment with new styles and techniques of lovemaking, and to be more verbally communicative with their partners. We can make the change in our sexual capacities, an opportunity for growth in intimacy, which will benefit both ourselves and our partners.

## WOMEN: THE SEXUAL BLOOM

Age brings no physiological impairment to sexual satisfaction for women, until menopause, and little change thereafter. Older women are just as capable as young women of reaching orgasm, and often more so. Self-confidence and a positive self-image have much to do with women's capacity to enjoy sex, and growing older often enhances these qualities, while lessening the inhibitions that suppress pleasure earlier in life.

Anything that negatively affects a woman's self-image, such as weight gain, chronic illness, or simply not taking care of her physical being, can inhibit sexual pleasure. In particular, the physical changes that come with menopause (occurring around age fifty) and pre-menopause (the period of about fifteen years prior, sometimes called the *climacteric*) can threaten a woman's sense of herself as a sexual being—which traditionally has been linked with childbearing capacity.

A woman's reproductive system begins to function less regularly at around age thirty-five. For many women, the symptoms of PMS (pre-menstrual syndrome) intensify through the late thirties unless self-care measures are taken to counteract them. The decline in reproductive capacity culminates with menopause; the physiological effects associated with a sharp drop in the hormone estrogen include the thinning of the vaginal walls, general shrinking of the female sexual organs, and a decrease in vaginal lubrication. These can make intercourse uncomfortable unless compensated for, but in most cases the psychological impact of menopause is more important.

The physical changes don't necessarily cause women to become indifferent to sex, as is often believed. According to a National Institute on Aging study, three-quarters of the women reported little or no difference in sexual satisfaction after menopause. Staying sexually active minimizes the physiological losses; as with men, the rule seems to be *use it or lose it.*

In any case, it's relatively easy for women to compensate for physical changes after menopause. The psychological essentials of feeling desirable and creating time and space for sex are far more challenging.

For women, generally more than men, it's important that lifestyle and atmosphere are conducive to feeling sexy. Many women have a hard time focusing on sex amid life's many distractions: taking care of kids, husband, home, and increasingly, a job. Stress can hinder sexual response by upsetting the delicate balance of our sympathetic and parasympathetic nervous systems (the stimulating versus the inhibitory signals). Even so, married women are more likely than singles to have active sex lives after forty: a partner is step one in the process of feeling desirable.

In our sex lives, more than any other aspect of our lives, it's nearly impossible to untangle the physical and the psychological issues. We'll revisit them in the context of relationships in the next chapter. For baby boomers, sex, like other key midlife issues, is a double-edged sword. Having been sexual pioneers, with Thou shalt be entitled to great sex on our personal Bill of Rights, we're likely to feel the pangs of any sexual losses more sharply than past generations. On the other hand, our sexual sophistication should help us through these trying times, equipping us to talk comfortably with our partners, to experiment with techniques, and to seek counsel when appropriate.

## Midlife Stress: What It Means For Our Bodies

Stress accompanies any change, and a profound personal transition such as midlife is replete with it. This has always been true but never more than today, when society's accelerating pace has made stress a household word in less than a decade. Stress can both energize us to peak performance, or it can seriously interfere with our physical, mental, and emotional well-being. It provokes physiological responses that can be life-threatening if unchecked.

Much of the information in this section applies to stress at any time of life. But midlife, especially for today's baby boomers, can focus stress like a lens. As well as coping with the general pressures of modern life, midlifers often must deal with unique and multiple age-related stresses involving identity change, shifts and strains in relationships, turning points in careers, and physical changes. Our careers may demand peak production while our bodies become less able to sustain long hours and high output. With children growing up and parents growing old, our "sandwich generation" feels family pressures from both sides.

As Norman Cousins remarks, "The greatest tragedy in life is not the fact of death, but the little deaths we experience." Midlife is full of these little deaths: divorce, children leaving home, giving up a job or a career, or confronting illness all force us to question ourselves and our place in the world. Most stressful of all, perhaps, are the internal changes midlife brings—the parting with our youthful illusions. Indeed, the proverbial midlife crisis may be the body's way of defending itself against chronic, ongoing stress that is rooted in adolescence and early adulthood. Like blowing a pressure valve, we can go a little crazy in midlife without total loss of control, and with society's permission.

One way to describe stress is the everyday wear and tear on your body as it responds to the world. Its sources can be environmental (smokers at the office), physical (jogging that extra mile), or emotional (bickering with a loved one). Dr. Hans Selye, a pioneer researcher in the field, states that "stress is the nonspecific response of the body to any demand made upon it." In other words, stress is not synonymous with nervous tension, nor is it always a negative influence.

The degree of stress we experience in midlife, and whether it has a positive or negative effect, depends largely on how we perceive and react to the situation. If we respond to stress as a challenge, it can be a positive stimulus to growth. Negative stress is the condition in which a demand is perceived as a threat; over time it can lead to feelings of frustration and help-lessness, and to avoidance behavior.

It's also useful to distinguish between acute, episodic stress and chronic, ongoing stress. This distinction relates to the way our bodies are programmed to respond to danger—the classic *fight or flight* reflex inherited from our ancestors. As a species, we are much better designed to cope with acute stress—jumping out of the street to avoid a car, for instance—than with chronic stress, such as feeling career burnout in midlife. Prolonged chronic stress can exhaust mental and physical re-serves and increase susceptibility to disease. Researchers be-lieve that people who cope poorly with stress are much more likely to become ill than people with good coping skills.

## COPING WITH MIDLIFE STRESS

You can't escape all of life's stresses, in midlife or at any other time, nor can you completely turn off your body's fight or flight response. But, to a great extent, you can control how stress affects you. The most basic issue to consider is the one of attitude and perception—how can you make stress more a positive than a negative influence in your life?

Stress management isn't something separate from your larger life goals. It's connected to your basic attitude and ori-entation. Midlife men and women who cope well with stress feel a sense of purpose and meaning in their lives, and actively engage in tasks that appear achievable and relevant to their energies.

An early step on the road to managing chronic stress is self-awareness. People manifest stress in different ways. Those able to express themselves emotionally may show it through irritability or temper; others, who are more intellectual, in how it affects their thinking. Many people who don't express stress behaviorally may be vulnerable physically: it could show up in headaches, muscle tension, or gastro-intestinal problems. Classic psychosomatic theory says that one system is always the weak link under stress: it may be the nervous system, the immune system, the skin, the heart, or the digestive system. This kind of self-analysis should be part of everyone's midlife inventory.

The ability to respond appropriately to stress and the ability to relax are equally important in maintaining health. Ideally, you should be able to respond to life's challenges quickly and with total attention, then let yourself relax completely. Intense arousal and deep relaxation are optimal responses, and a balance of both is essential.

Unfortunately, most of us in the baby boom generation are more accustomed to stress than to relaxation. We tend to be Stimulation Junkies. When you lose the ability to return to a state of relaxation, the stress response is maintained longer than is useful, putting the body in a chronic and unhealthy state of overstimulation. Fortunately, the brain centers that control your biochemical responses to stress can be mobilized in the opposite direction. Activating the relaxation response can return blood pressure, respiration, and circulation back to normal, as well as normalizing emotional and mental processes. The recuperative effect of relaxation keeps you from being overwhelmed by cumulative pressures.

There are both functional and dysfunctional ways of inducing relaxation. Functional strategies used by most midlifers typically include exercise, hobbies, diversions such as trips, and talking about problems with trusted friends. These are effective in varying degrees, but don't generally produce a state of deep relaxation. To achieve this, specific techniques such as meditation, relaxation exercises, or sometimes hypnosis are called for. (You can explore these options through

books, classes, or counselors.) Common dysfunctional methods include denial of stress or stress-related problems, withdrawal, smoking, and abuse of alcohol, drugs, or food.

Learning to recognize and avoid stress is part of midlife
stress management. It's also important to develop a philosophical stance, a set of beliefs about yourself and the world,
that can serve as a buffer between you and stress. These don't
have to be weighty concepts, just simple reminders of simple
truths that you earnestly believe apply to your life, such as: "I
am who I am," "Money doesn't buy happiness," or "The other
guy has problems too."

On a recent ski trip I bought a baseball cap that's become
my talisman against stress. It's decorated with three Chinese
symbols that translate loosely as: "Things decay," "The river
runs," "Everything is okay." Together they sum up the popular
phrase, "Shit happens." Or, as cardiologist Robert Eliot put it,
"If you can't fight and you can't flee, flow."

## An Expanded Vision of Midlife Health

"Age is a case of mind over matter.
If you don't mind it, it doesn't matter."

Mark Twain

There are many options available to us today for mitigating
the passage of time on our bodies. We can pursue scientifically
developed exercise programs and precisely calibrated nutri-
tional regimens. We have access to incredibly sophisticated
medical care and drugs to control disease and disabilities. We
can get our hair colored, thickened, or replaced; our teeth
whitened or straightened; our eyes refocused; our fertility enhanced; our stress biofeedbacked; and, if we can afford it, our
features and flab surgically overhauled.

But these are only incremental improvements in a finite set
of circumstances. Unless we give equal attention to recalibrat-

ing our attitude toward our body and its capabilities, crafting or grafting a great chassis in midlife won't guarantee happiness any more than having money will. As we've said before, it's a matter of perception: we needn't look further for proof than to the anorexic who truly believes she is fat.

What does this mean? It means finding out what it takes for you to feel good, and doing it. Whether it's getting more sleep, or running ten fewer miles each week (or ten more), getting a massage regularly, or discovering a new way to stimulate your partner or yourself sexually. It means, rather than struggling to maintain levels of performance you once attained, finding a level you can sustain into the future.

When discussing stress, we alluded to the possibility that midlife may be an adaptive response to the cumulative stresses of career and/or family-building during one's thirties. It's nature's way of telling us to lighten up, take the edge off our competitiveness in the interest of longevity and peace of mind.

There was an ad for Gatorade on the tube not long ago. It opens with vintage home movies from the fifties and sixties of high school and college athletes, with a voiceover reminding viewers of the days when they were competitors. The ad then shifts to current shots of middle-aged guys playing tag football, softball, pickup basketball. You may not be competing the way you used to, the voiceover says, but your body still needs Gatorade.

The ad affected me on two levels. First, I saw an image of myself in both sequences. In the old films I was the skinny, gawky adolescent playing basketball for South Shore High School in Chicago. And there I was, too, in the after pictures, heavier, slower, less agile.

The second thing that struck me was the contrasting expressions of the very young and not-so-young men in the films. In the first segment, the faces were fiercely intense; competitive drive oozed from their pores. The older guys were laughing, laid back, *playful.* I could recognize that in myself, too, and accept it. Whatever we do to take care of our bodies in midlife has to have some of that quality, an underlying awareness that any activity is just one aspect of a rich and well-rounded life at fortysomething. Instead of being a life-or-death matter, playing the game is a matter of staying fully alive.

# 7

# Significant Others

## Family and Relationships
## in Midlife

*When I get older, losing my hair*
*Many years from now*
*Will you still be sending me a valentine*
*Birthday greetings, bottle of wine?*
*When I stay out 'til quarter of three*
*Will you lock the door?*
*Will you still need me, will you still feed me*
*When I'm sixty-four?*
JOHN LENNON–PAUL MCCARTNEY

Remember Ozzie and Harriet? Ward and June Cleaver? "The Donna Reed Show," "Lassie," "Father Knows Best"? Baby boomers were weaned on endless TV images of the perfect, breadwinner/homemaker, 2.3 children, suburban nuclear family. Never mind how distant our own families were from this ideal, the image remains potent. It takes on special poignancy as we approach fortysomething: either we feel that we should be comfortably settled into our married-with-children mode by now, or we see midlife as our last chance to achieve it.

But if you look at your own life, and those of your fortysomething friends, you're likely to see something quite different than the TV family of our childhood. You'll see midlife couples having their first child in their forties; you'll see others the same age coping with adolescent children; and you'll see the merging of families through remarriages. You'll see fathers who stay at home while mothers work, and families in which both parents work away from the home. You'll see childless marriages, unmarried couples with and without children, single parents, gay and lesbian parents, and singles whose families are their friends. More than ever before, as Gloria Steinem aptly phrased it, "family is content, not form."

The venerated institution of the family is in the throes of radical change, and baby boomers have had no small part in bringing it about. These changes have important implications for people in midlife. Families can either be a source of support during transition, a major stress factor, or both. Figuring out roles and relationships that are themselves social experiments—or at least not what our social training led us to expect—can undercut the support and bump up the stress. Also, our family situation is often the catalyst for midlife transition, a focal point of the need for change. But even if the process is triggered by something else, it's inevitable that midlife will have an impact on our family in some way, and that family will influence the choices we make.

Relationships and families follow a pattern of development and go through transitions, just as individuals do. They have lives of their own that need attention and reevaluation as much as the individual self does. The same principles hold true for both: the more we nurture them, the more likely they are to keep growing and flourishing—and vice versa. The better we understand what happens in our relations to others, the more insight we can gain into our personal development.

## All in the (Traditional) Family

There are many definitions of family (Webster's Dictionary gives twenty-two), starting with the very basic view taken by the Census Bureau: A family is "two or more persons related by birth, marriage, or adoption who reside in the same household." But a more useful approach is to look at what a family is supposed to provide its members. A State of California task force came up with a handy overview of the family's functions: A family should maintain the physical health and safety of its members, help shape a belief system of goals and values, teach social skills, and create a place for recuperation from external stresses. The final requirement is the most important service that the family can provide the midlife member (though shelter from stress can certainly benefit physical health as well).

In the traditional scheme of things, the person who required such recuperation and nurturing was usually the husband/father. Most of us remember being told as children to "Hush!" because "Dad's had a hard day at the office." Long before midlife was widely understood to be a stressful time, the fortysomething family man was cosseted and catered to by his household (or wanted to be). When the idea of midlife crisis did enter the popular consciousness, it was still chiefly a male phenomenon—a temporary aberration to be indulged, not taken seriously, by his family. Not only was Mom supposedly immune to midlife crisis, she was expected to be the chief nurturer.

Though we may still wax nostalgic over Ozzie and Harriet, we now see more clearly the dark side of the fifties-style nuclear family. Its typical dysfunctions, which have emerged in therapists' offices and the twelve-step programs, include a reluctance to acknowledge and confront family problems, retreats into alcoholism or chronic infidelity, alienation of men from their spouses and children, distrustful children, and frustrated women whose abilities needed an outlet.

The traditional families we grew up in did a pretty good job of looking after the physical needs of their members, and diligently transmitted social skills within an accepted narrow range. They were set up to be stress shelters for the male head of the house. They probably did serve as islands of stability for men going through midcareer transition, as well as tolerating to his other midlife symptoms: the moodiness, the short-lived affair, the sudden urge to bundle the whole family off for a two-month camping trip. But there wasn't much understanding of the midlife experience, or real communication within the family about it. Worse, the possibility that a woman might need such support was totally ignored, or her symptoms dismissed as menopausal.

## THE NEW OUTLINES OF FAMILY LIFE

In the 1960s, as the baby boom tapered off, the breadwinner/homemaker model began to change. Several factors were involved: the average age of first marriages increased, the birth rate decreased, and the divorce rate began to climb. Then, in the 1970s, two events coincided that sent women back to work in droves: the women's movement kicked into high gear and the economy suffered a recession. The mythical nuclear family, so profoundly imprinted on the first wave of baby boomers, entered a period of serious transition.

The restlessness and identity overhaul that accompany midlife have always caused strain in longterm marriages, but today's couples apparently face unprecedented difficulties in staying together. A recent *Newsweek* survey gives some daunting statistics. The divorce rate has doubled since 1965, and it is projected that half of all first marriages today will end in divorce. Six out of ten second marriages are likely to fail. While divorce will never be painless, it now poses no legal hurdles and has lost its social stigma. A declining birth rate since the baby boom means that more midlife couples are childless, or have fewer children—often the only thing holding a midlife marriage together. We may be on the way to an era where serial monogamy (one spouse after the other) is the norm, but meanwhile the rate of changing partners can cause confusion for people raised with the expectation that marriage is till death do us part.

High rates of divorce and remarriages have made the mixed family a major contemporary phenomenon. One third of all children born in the last ten years will probably live in a step-family by age eighteen. One out of four children today is being raised by a single parent.

Today's children remain dependent on their midlife parents further into early adulthood, and increased longevity makes midlifers increasingly responsible for the care of aging parents. The competing demands of work, children, and aging parents on middle-aged couples has given rise to the term *the sandwich generation.*

The emotional, financial, and social impact of so much upheaval and readjustment is enormous. It's convenient to blame social ills—families that barely see each other, adolescents who resort to delinquency or drugs, or who become obsessed with materialism—on the demise of the fifties-style nuclear family. In reality, those problems have longer and more complex roots, going back to the erosion of extended families and tribal societies, and our more recent exposure to mass media and advertising.

But the breakdown of the old model does have consequences for baby boomers. Having created a situation where the Ozzie and Harriet example is an impossible goal, we still feel that somehow we're doing things wrong. As we struggle to learn how to make the new family structures work, we will find little comfort in such an anachronism.

## Today's Families: Where Do You Fit?

How a person develops within a family structure is a subplot to his overall progress through life's stages. According to the old script, we're supposed to leave home in early adulthood, get a job, get married and set up a household, have children, educate them, see our aging parents out of the world, and become supportive grandparents to the next generation.

Within this familiar plot line are endless dramas and struggles. We separate from our parents, accommodate another's needs in an intimate relationship, make the emotional and financial commitment to raise children, and make adjustments in the family for each child.

The evolution of a family structure is sufficiently complex when it unfolds along such traditional lines. Today it's even more convoluted because of the variation in family structures. Midlifers today may find themselves in any of the following family situations. (A section for single midlifers can be found later in this chapter.)

### THE LONGTERMER

When two people have been together for a long time, that in itself can often be the catalyst for crisis. Problems may arise when partners start to change roles, or when one partner focuses their midlife restlessness on the marriage: I wonder if I'm still attractive to women? or, I've only had three lovers in my whole life—it's now or never.

Ann and Richard met while both were graduate students in psychology and had been married for eighteen years. Richard had pursued a successful academic career at an Ivy League school. Now in his early forties, he was due for a sabbatical and was excited about taking a year off and traveling.

Ann received her master's and worked for a while as a school counselor, then quit to raise their two children. When the kids were teenagers, she took a job at a local school but found the work boring. She decided to return to academics and get her doctorate, was accepted, and was due to start in the fall—just when Richard's sabbatical was due to begin. She told me:

> I never resented Richard for getting to do what he wanted while I stayed home with the kids. I really felt that what I was doing was valuable and worthwhile. But now that he's telling me to put off the chance to do what I want, I'm furious. It makes me question how much value he puts on my life.

Richard responds:

> I know that finishing graduate school is important to Ann. But she has lots of time to do that. I'm exhausted from finishing a huge research project. It's taken everything I had, and I need this time away. I wish she would understand that.

On the surface, their disagreement seemed to be merely over timing. But stronger forces were at work underneath. Ann was seeking to reengage with the world just when Richard was trying to disengage. He'd slain all the dragons he needed to, while her challenges still lay ahead.

Ann did postpone her doctoral work and went traveling with Richard. After they returned and she started school, she came in for an update. They had gotten along fine on the trip, she said, but since then things had changed for the worse.

> I don't know if I'm still feeling resentment or what, but there's a deadness inside me about Richard. School is everything I'd hoped; I feel alive and stimulated there. At home, Richard is a bore. He's teaching again but has no enthusiasm. I feel for him, but I can't help him.

Not long after, Ann and Richard separated. Their compromise about the sabbatical trip wasn't the primary cause, only a symptom of their differences at this time in their lives and their marriage. Neither was wrong or right, but they were definitely heading in opposite directions. The marriage came to seem irrelevant.

The breakup of a longterm partnership is a traumatic contributor to midlife stress. But this is only one possible scenario for such relationships; longterm mates who weather the crisis can provide the strongest mutual support for dealing with other midlife issues, like career changes, problems with kids or aging parents. They know each other's needs well and, if unhindered by resentment, can really help smooth the way.

### THE LATECOMER

The many baby boomers who have waited until their thirties or forties to get married and/or have children face a very different midlife experience than the longtermers who followed a more traditional path. For some, the demands of an intimate relationship and the responsibilities of raising young children may be at odds with the midlife urge to experiment and take risks. For others, like Stimulation Junkies finally ready for a little stability, the timing can be perfect.

The feminist consciousness that inspired so many boomer women in young adulthood is certainly a major factor in the trend toward delayed family-making. A friend of mine, Helen, was married at forty and three years later had her first child.

> Like a lot of my friends, I put off getting married. I didn't like much of what I saw in my parents' marriage. And my work was always there to reinforce my ambivalence.
>
> It must have been the right time in our lives for Steve and me, because from day one it was clear the relationship had stability. I never would have made the decision to get pregnant if he hadn't been as eager as he was.

My friends thought I was crazy, and my family wondered why I hadn't been more careful with birth control. I had to laugh—did they really think after all this time that it was an accident? The fact is, I wasn't emotionally ready to be a mother until now.

Helen's worries about postponed parenthood were the usual ones: Would they have enough energy? Would their social life disappear? Would they feel self-conscious about being older parents?

In Lamaze class I felt like I had dropped in on a college orientation meeting. I also wonder about how to maintain connections with our friends. Most of them have raised their families and are relatively free, while we're pretty limited in what we can do. The bottom line, though, is that we did a good thing. There seems to be more substance to our marriage than before, and I know we'll do a good job raising our daughter.

The trend to motherhood over forty has gotten a lot of press, focused on such celebrities as Bette Midler and Cybil Shepherd who have joined the older *primagravidas* (first-time pregnancy). The media coverage of this topic seems to lurch between hysterical admiration and alarmism, tending to obscure the useful facts.

A recent study of older mothers found that, compared to younger mothers, they have less energy, and more physical complaints, need more sleep, and require more support from their spouses, friends, or hired help. On the other hand, older mothers are more comfortable with themselves, and the self-knowledge and self-acceptance that often accompanies aging makes them more patient with their children. They are more relaxed, flexible, humorous, and understanding.

Late parenthood makes sense for a lot of baby boomer men, too. Many have not felt sufficiently grown up to undertake the

role of husband and father, or, lacking social pressure to contribute to the population, have simply concentrated on career
and self-fulfillment. For them, midlife is congenial to the practical aspects of fatherhood. They are, by now, established in
their work, and their financial resources are greater than in
younger days.

## WORKING MATES

In 1976, the number of two-income families in the United
States surpassed those with only one provider. A whopping
two-thirds of all mothers are currently in the workforce
(nearly double the figure in the 1950s) and more than half of
all mothers of infants are working. Most women today work
outside the home for either economic reasons, self-fulfillment,
or both.

The dual-career phenomenon is probably the most profound recent change in family life, and has been the subject of
endless discussion, analysis, and controversy. In midlife, there
is the obvious risk of working couples growing apart, taking
care of business but not of each other, unless they consciously
try to stay intimate. Working parents, clearly, also feel torn between the demands of family and career. While men may be
taking a more active role in domestic work, women still perceive this sharing to be unequal. And it's inevitable that the
strains on both partners will produce some fallout at midlife.

The situation of Rick (forty-five), Susan (a decade younger), and their two-year-old daughter, Leah, is fairly typical.
Rick came to see me because he was thinking about a career
change. Initially, his symptoms seemed those of basic burnout: he felt bored, frustrated, stuck. But as we explored further, the focus shifted more and more to his marriage. The
family routine was pressure-packed, reinforcing his feeling of
burnout at every level. Susan's day began with dropping Leah
off at daycare, then commuting one-hour to work. She was
rarely home before 7:00 P.M. Rick picked the baby up from

daycare, since he left work a bit earlier. Once home, Susan fed the baby, and she and Rick ate dinner, which left about half an hour before they crashed in bed.

Rich had begun to feel that neither his work nor his family life was as rewarding as it should be.

> I feel like I'm on a treadmill that keeps spinning faster. I can't remember the last time I simply sat around and did nothing. We have no time for each other, and when we do squeeze in some time, I feel guilty that Leah isn't getting enough attention.

Like a lot of boomer men, Rick couldn't help feeling nostalgic for an image of family life that hinged on a wife devoting herself full-time to homemaking. At the same time he acknowledged that this wasn't financially fair or practical in their case.

Susan was equally exhausted by the demands of their life and regretted being unresponsive to Rick's needs, but, for her, Leah came first. She also believed that she was doing more around the house than Rick was and resented it. Too caught up in her obligations to envision any change, she worried: "We're running on parallel but very separate tracks. I just hope they intersect somewhere down the line, or there won't be much reason to be together."

There was no quick solution for Rick and Susan. Readjusting priorities sounds easy on paper, but not when everything seems equally important. The having-it-all mentality heightens the stress of dual-career parenting for baby boomers: we feel we're missing out if we can't maintain a career, a social life, and romance in the marriage while doing all the right things by our kids too. One thing that helped Rick and Susan was arranging to have a sitter with Leah one afternoon every weekend. This let them get out together and spend some time discussing their options.

Women, who have made the more dramatic leap away from

traditional roles, are especially vulnerable to guilt-based reactions like the *Supermom* syndrome. For midlife women, the key to success in a dual-career family appears to be the support their spouses provide. The husband should have a positive attitude toward his wife's work and be actively involved in household and child care. Changes in the workplace to accommodate working mothers, such as expanded maternity leave, flex time, and daycare arrangements, have been slow, but they're coming.

In spite of all its strains, the two-career relationship also has unique strengths. Men and women who have competed on relatively equal footing, in both school and the working world, have a fuller understanding of what their mates are experiencing in midlife than did traditional couples. They can empathize with problems in the office, schedules that suddenly change, and career-related identity crises. Men are much more familiar with domestic responsibilities, a trend explored in the movie *Mr. Mom.* Midlife brings out the need in men for more connectedness, for the chance to nurture, and a dual-career family can make it easier for men to indulge these feelings.

## SEPARATEES AND SINGLE PARENTS

Most divorced baby boomers will eventually remarry, but if they don't, what are the issues of family life in midlife for them?

Guilt over a failed relationship or marriage is likely to be keener in the emotionally charged atmosphere of midlife transition, and it can be a prime cause of depression. If the relationship began in your youth, its loss will be hard to disassociate from the painful sense of lost youth. One's self-image suffers a serious blow at a time when you most want to be playing from strength; questions like, Am I really capable of sustaining a relationship? can be haunting. And inevitably there is anxiety over future prospects: Will there be another chance for happiness with a mate? If children are involved, the emotional stakes are even higher.

Many midlife women, and some men, are finding themselves the head of a single-parent family after divorce. Whether it's a temporary arrangement on the road to remarriage or a longterm situation, single parenting brings its own set of considerable challenges. Resources and support systems are the keys.

For some women, becoming a single parent coincides with returning to the job market. Michelle, a latecomer to marriage and childbearing, found herself in this situation. In her late twenties and early thirties she'd been successful in real estate sales: hard-driving, ambitious, resourceful, known in her office as a good "closer" who rarely lost a prospect.

Getting married in her mid-thirties seems to have been a pro forma rather than a deeply felt decision; in any case, the match came apart when her little girl, Lucy, was only six months old. Her ex-husband lived nearby and would help occasionally, but he was not reliable. Michelle found it easier to rely on herself. When she went back to real estate, though, things were different in a way she couldn't understand, but was troubled by.

> I was always so together, so focused . . . the first one in the office and the last to leave. Now I feel so different. It's not that I don't care; I do—but not as much. I feel like there's something wrong with me because I don't get as much done, or I don't go after a sale as aggressively as I used to. But I just don't seem to have the same edge.

Michelle admitted that even if her old competitive fire had been as high, she wouldn't be able to satisfy it. She was running a home, raising a child, and she'd just found out that her mother had cancer.

Eventually, she began to think that losing some of her old competitiveness was not entirely negative. She discovered that the focus of her values had expanded, and we tried to find ways to make her diversified responsibilities acceptable and rewarding to her, and to see the change as an adaptation, not a failure. Eventually, Michelle realized that her self-esteem had become more broadly based—that she didn't need to be a superstar in any one area. One of the natural benefits of midlife is that becoming more of a team player and less a stand-out celebrity feels okay.

The midlife urge to break out of a rut, risk a career change, or move to a new location may need to be stifled by the demands of single parenting. You risk projecting frustration onto the people closest at hand—usually the children.

On the plus side, a single parent contemplating such life changes need not consider the desires and fears of a partner. I know a single mother in her forties whose career demands that she live and work for months at a time in Asia. Her young daughter has benefitted from both a cosmopolitan education, and firm family roots in this country.

### SECOND-TIMERS AND STEP-PARENTS

Statistics show that most divorced boomers will remarry, and that most marriages result in one or more children. These *return engagements* will lead the way in reworking our sense of what a family should be.

Second marriages, like all others, vary tremendously in motives and prospects for success. Some who remarry in midlife choose a new partner who seems entirely unlike the rejected former mate out of the flawed belief that the old marriage was the root of their midlife problems. A new marriage derived from escapist fantasies or a need to recapture youth is built on equally shaky ground. The much-parodied matings of older men with younger women often fall into this category.

Successful second-timers know what they and their relationships need, and the limits of what is possible. As a client,
Janice, put it: "Now, in my second marriage, I try to reassure
Don, but sometimes I get frustrated. We'll have a fight . . . but
then we resolve it. One thing I learned from my first marriage
is that I can't feel responsible for someone's moods."

Parents who remarry in midlife must remember that every
stepfamily is created out of loss. They cannot recreate the
original family or put it back together again, which is usually
the child's fondest wish. Feelings of anger or guilt between the
new stepparent and children are an inevitable part of the adjustment process. Finally, remarriages usually go through a
fantasy stage of unreasonably high expectations: the new family will right all the old wrongs, a new supermom or superdad
will enter the scene and work miracles. Since the new mom or
dad may be going through midlife transition as well as a new
marriage, such expectations are all the more futile.

Larry was forty when he met Sarah. Both had been married
before. Sarah had a twelve-year-old son and Larry had two
children who lived with his ex-wife. After dating for nearly a
year, Sarah invited Larry to move in. Larry felt ready for such
a move; he liked the idea of stability to balance other changes
going on in his life. He had also spent quite a bit of time with
Sarah's son, Josh, and thought the connection between them
would grow quickly.

> Some things about the way Sarah and Josh related annoyed
> me, like her lack of discipline and his talking back to her,
> but I didn't think it would be a major problem. As time went
> on, though, I found myself becoming more intolerant. She
> and Josh had been together for ten years without an older
> male around: they'd worked out a way of relating, even if it
> wasn't perfect. Anything I could offer was coming from the
> outside. It made me irritable and frustrated.
>
> I realized after some counseling that my deeper feeling
> was a fear of losing Sarah—of not being important to her. I

had this notion that she needed me to discipline Josh. If I couldn't, she'd have no use for me. Now that I've learned to stand back a little, it's much better. Josh and I negotiate when we need to, and there's less tension between Sarah and me.

Success for a mixed family comes from a commitment from every member of the system. One of the ground rules recommended by family therapists is for the couple to concentrate on being a couple first, and to present a united front to the children.

## Facing the Issues of Your Midlife Relationship

The core issue for most midlife couples is that of growth versus stagnation. Extramarital affairs aside, the *third party* in a midlife marriage is usually the evolving self, which often feels confined. How do you explore your need for personal growth without upsetting the dynamic of the marriage? How do you breathe new life into a relationship that seems to have stopped growing?

There is no way to avoid these questions, and the only way to deal with them successfully is through conscious attention to the relationship. Midlife partners almost need a new obsession with each other. You need to study closely who the other person is becoming, how you both feel about it, and how it affects your interaction.

In some ways, our parents had it easier. They could just hunker down and wait for the storm to pass. The negative aspects of this mentality is that, often, people grew farther apart privately while staying together publicly. Baby boomers, who have higher expectations for satisfaction from their relationships, won't settle for a respectably lifeless marriage. When today's midlifers feel stifled or ignored or exploited, or simply find themselves growing in different directions, they are much more likely to take action, as the divorce statistics show. Our narcissism can make the challenge of paying attention to our partner still more difficult. Some marriages fail at midlife because of the urgency boomers feel about making changes before it's too late. But our need for growth can also result in relationships that are stronger for adapting to it.

### THE GREAT GENDER ROLE SHIFT

One primary force driving the issue of growth in midlife relationships is a process that Gail Sheehy refers to in *Passages* as the "Switch-40s." Around fortysomething, both men and women begin displaying qualities normally associated with the opposite gender. Men tend to become more nurturing and dependent, qualities supposedly suppressed in the service of achievement; women tend to become more autonomous, aggressive, and achievement-oriented. There is a biological component that accompanies this shift: production of the male hormone testosterone decreases in men, while estrogen production is declining in women.

Jung describes these changes in sexual roles during midlife as a necessary step on the path of individuation. In order to develop a whole personality, a man must embrace his feminine qualities and a women her masculine side.

The gender role shift carries predictable risks to the relationship. In many traditional marriages, both parties felt bewildered by urges that seemed to threaten the very basis of their partnership. If a man denied his changing feelings, and many did, they might reemerge as depression, or alcohol abuse, career sabotage, or an affair with someone who *understands what I'm going through*. Ironically, if he tried to address these feelings, perhaps by considering early retirement, or organizing the family for outings, his wife often feared the usurpation of her role, or the loss of a provider.

For women, who received little support (if not outright resistance) to their attempts to grow beyond the family, they often retreated into their own activities, and tolerated their husband's criticism.

Since this gender shift is now better understood, baby boomers have had a somewhat easier time adapting to it. The women's movement helped; women have more models for midlife achievement in business, the arts, and politics. Men have more societal reaffirmation for valuing their softer side; actor Alan Alda and others made the sensitive male image humorous and attractive.

Lila is a divorced mother in her late forties. Her daughter, fourteen, lives with her, and her nineteen-year-old son with her ex-husband in another city. As a teacher returning to her school district as a consultant, she came to see me with concerns about her career reentry.

> I'm not sure about the person I'm becoming. I know that staying home and being Mom isn't where my heart is, and I feel a little guilty about that. My daughter is getting less of my attention than my son did, although she seems to be doing okay.
>
> I'm amazed at how much I've changed. Even when I was just out of grad school, teaching for the first time, I didn't have the same drive I do now. I'd like to get married again, and stay connected to my friends and family. I'm almost worried that if I get too self-sufficient no one will need me. It's a challenge to see myself as competent and also lovable. But I'm so excited about being back at work, there's no way I would go back to my old life.

Conversely, the gender switch can operate in the reverse for some of today's women. Those who have had high-powered careers early in adulthood, like my client Michelle, whose story we heard in the last chapter, follow a more typically male pattern, and become more family-oriented in midlife.

For myself, the gender switch has been very important. It's

especially apparent in the area of competitive athletics, where training for whatever sport I'm competing in has always taken a lot of my time—up to eighteen hours a week wasn't unusual. When my son, Chase, was born two years ago, the time crunch I always insisted would never happen to me, did. I'd seen various training partners fall victim to the dreaded "F" word (family), and vowed I'd never have my wings clipped. So, for a year I fought the good fight, managing to balance a modicum of family responsibility with my commitment to bicycle racing. But there was a lot of conflict—I felt neither was getting enough of me.

The past year, through, has been very different. Now I feel as though cycling is cutting too much into my family time. Why did it happen? My values have gone through a radical, if gradual, change. Over the past three years, the pieces of my life structure have been tossed into the air; now that they've settled to earth, family has emerged a winner and athletics a loser, relatively speaking.

However risky the process may be, midlife marriages need not collapse because the partners' roles are evolving. In fact, as each person grows toward wholeness, their bonds can be strengthened. The risk is greatest when there is no movement, and one or both partners start to stagnate.

## GROWING APART

Couples who enter marriage counseling at midlife are often suffering more from boredom than from any traumatic event in the relationship. Some marriages that seem good are in reality unexamined and uneventful rather than stimulating and truly intimate. Partners who have avoided real communication for years, discover they are distant from or uninterested in what the other is feeling and doing. Longtermers, especially, tend to take intimacy for granted, though its absence may simply be obscured by the pressures of work and child-rearing. When those pressures ease, as they often do around midlife, the surprising result can be marital blahs instead of bliss.

John and Charlotte are fairly typical of this growing apart: in this scenario, the man feels the need for change and his wife resists it. John says:

> I don't think Charlotte has any idea what I'm going through. I hate my work; I'm sick of the responsibility. It seems like every day is a battleground. Her only concern seems to be to patch me up and send me out there again. She seems really selfish to me. I feel as if time is running out and I have some big decisions to make.
>
> I look at other women and fantasize about starting over. The younger ones especially attract me—I know it's a cliche, but I feel like I could be a "hero" to them. They don't have such high demands, and they'd be so much easier to deal with.

Charlotte expressed fear about what was happening.

> I sense John's rejection of me, and I'm afraid that it's a physical thing. But I'm not going to try to compete with someone fifteen years younger. I won't be reduced to that. He's rejecting everything in his life, really. I know he's miserable at work and resents all the demands. But I can't be a mother and make it all go away, which is what I think he expects. It's a hard time for me, too.
>
> My friends tell me to be patient and supportive, to prop him up. I try, but it seems to make him resent me more. And when I hear that rejection in his voice, something in me tightens up and I withdraw. If he's thinking of leaving me, I wish he'd just get on with it.

John and Charlotte tried counseling for six months, but didn't use it constructively. They were very clear about what was making them angry, but neither had much empathy for the other's situation. Eventually they did separate.

In some cases, the nurturing qualities that may have tially attracted a man to a woman seem inadequate when reaches midlife; he may seek someone more emotionally an financially independent. *Fortune* magazine described this phenomenon in an article about the second wives of powerful executives. The piece clearly struck some sensitive nerves: it received harsh criticism and the ultimate backhanded compliment: a parody in the "Doonesbury" comic strip in which Mark Slackmeyer's capitalist-swine father discards his wife and gets engaged to a young woman with her own business.

In another scenario, the man leaves his wife because she is growing stronger and more assertive, and seeks the opposite kind of mate: usually younger, nonthreatening, admiring, and compliant.

Often, however, it's women who feel stifled within the confines of a marriage, and whose need for growth becomes the chief threat to the established structure. The movie *Kramer vs. Kramer* portrayed this situation, the Meryl Streep character moving out to pursue her career and leaving the toddler to the tender mercies of Dustin Hoffman.

Of course, many couples do grow irremediably apart in midlife. Sometimes their best efforts to save the relationship are for naught. But fleeing a marriage is all too often the easy way out of an uncomfortable situation. My partner is inhibiting my growth, the excuse goes, or no longer satisfies my needs because he or she has changed. More often, the person seeking a way out has lost faith in the possibility of intimacy, is unwilling to undertake the mutual work of reestablishing it, or hasn't looked inward for the true sources of his discontent—sometimes all of these.

### THE PROJECTION PITFALL

Among the greatest risks in any intimate relationship is the tendency to transfer blame for anything that goes wrong in one's life to the handiest person: your partner. It's been noted

...e ideal, complete self, we often choose
...ies qualities we feel we are missing: She's
...ock—so dependable. Or, I was attracted to
...confidence. Conversely, it becomes just as easy
...r mates the flaws we don't like to admit in ourselves.
...anger at his wife of ten years, Lisa, was a good exam-
...r projection. Jack had risen quickly as an architect. Now
...e was entering his forties and was a principal in his firm, but
it wasn't doing well and he felt stalled. Both the company and
Jack needed a shot in the arm, but he didn't have the energy
for it.

When Jack felt stressed, he would displace it onto Lisa. He
attributed his inability to change his situation to traits he
found in her.

> The problem with Lisa is that she gets stuck too easily. She's
> passive—she won't do the work needed to break through to
> new ground. She's too accepting of how things are to see
> new ways of operating. How can I be expected to face prob-
> lems at work without some inspiration at home?

While, as with most projections, there was a kernel of truth
to what Jack saw in Lisa, he really feared inadequacy in himself. In fact, Lisa could have given him considerable support if
he'd been able to stop punishing her for his own shortcomings,
but for a long time that insight was beyond him.

This kind of scenario leads many married people into a
lover's arms during midlife (as it did Jack). Projection often
leads to fault-finding, and soon it becomes easy to rationalize
leaving your partner, especially if you meet someone else who
fulfills your needs, however unexamined those needs are. A
man may also justify his behavior by saying that his wife has
enjoyed freedom and leisure while he was engaged in a stressful, competitive career or surviving the boredom of an unrewarding job.

The midlife woman in a traditional marriage, frustrated with staying home and sacrificing herself on the altar of family, sometimes projects her lack of fulfillment onto her husband. If he were bolder, more assertive, they might have been more successful. From her point of view, her husband has had all the opportunities for success, freedom, and recognition that she longs for. It's all too easy at midlife for either partner to perceive the other as having something valuable that is missing from his or her life, and to blame the partner for this deprivation.

## INFIDELITY AND DIVORCE

Men and women responding to their need to grow in midlife may turn to a third party who seems to answer that need better than their mates. Men typically seek greater self-awareness and fulfillment in personal relationships—sometimes unconsciously. In getting to know themselves as emotional beings, men may discover creative pursuits or the neglected joys of family life. Or they may engage in sexual experimentation, or pursue love affairs.

Midlife women typically search for a more complete identity through returning to school, acquiring money and/or influence, and restarting or bolstering a career. Seeking validation in the world outside the home, they are also more likely to have an affair.

If either a man or a woman is haunted by the sense of time running out, if either abruptly realizes that they have spent much of their lives doing what others wanted them to do, then either one is a likely candidate to follow wherever a forbidden impulse leads. Midlife affairs are streets of fire where everyone gets burned: an overwhelming 90 percent of divorces in longstanding marriages are related to infidelity.

Except in the case of the chronic philanderer, however, infidelity is usually a symptom of midlife unease rather than the cause of the problem. Depending on their personality and their marriage, midlifers may risk an affair out of anxiety over physical aging, a last-chance wish to prove their attractiveness, a desire to experiment in ways they feel might be unacceptable to their spouse, or simply the urge to inject some drama into a stagnating life structure.

When Ann and Richard, the divorced couple from academia discussed previously, were in the last stages of their marriage, Ann had a brief affair with one of her professors at graduate school, a man younger than she. It was an accidental affair—an unplanned, disorienting sexual encounter in which the chief emotions are usually anxiety and guilt. Ann was shocked by herself at the time—she'd never considered herself vulnerable to that temptation—but in hindsight realized she was a prime candidate.

> I was probably getting back at Richard unconsciously for insisting on having his way about the sabbatical trip. Being back in school was the first time I'd been out on my own since the kids were grown, and Richard was so grim and spiritless after the trip. I suppose it was just part of my general craving for excitement and adventure, though I soon realized I couldn't cope with the level of anxiety I felt.

In Ann's case, the affair occurred while the separation was already in progress, though it may have helped speed the divorce.

Whatever the causes and circumstances of a midlife affair, what counts is whether the partners want to put it in the past and get on with repairing their relationship. Having to confess an affair demands some soul-searching, and is an opportunity for personal growth.

The person being betrayed should try to behave sanely until the issues are resolved. While he should avoid taking the blame for his mate's actions, he should also consider his role in them and recognize that he'll probably have to make some changes too. And as any counselor or relationship manual will advise, it's important to work on reviving romance.

Once the worst is over, the marriage may emerge stronger. The alternative is usually divorce, which can produce profound emotional dislocation at midlife, or any other time. Its effects on children are well-documented, and guilt on their behalf is only one of the repercussions. The difficulty of adjusting to the loss of a longterm relationship is compounded by the additional losses of "couple friends," former in-laws, and one's personal identity as a spouse. Strain on the financial resources of both parties also contributes to the overall costs of divorce.

These losses can have a devastating effect on self-esteem, especially during midlife transition when it is being tested anyway. A great many people internalize divorce as personal failure. Working up the courage to reenter the dating scene can take a long time, and a further trauma occurs on finding that the rules have changed dramatically. Successful reorientation after a midlife divorce may be somewhat easier for those with above-average financial resources, strong kinship bonds, close personal friends, and a high educational background.

### GROWING TOGETHER

Respecting a midlife mate's need to grow and change is an exercise that calls for daily practice, like aerobic conditioning. This can be especially challenging for the mate who is not going through transition, but the effort will benefit both.

The survival of the relationship may hinge on letting a partner venture outside familiar roles without feeling personally threatened. If a wife's hobby of photography comes to the point of her having gallery shows, or a husband wants to take the kids off on a camping weekend by himself, it's not a sign of rejection.

As we've said, the midlife identity struggle is similar in some ways to adolescence, and trying to impose control may provoke the rebellion response. Personality types come into play strongly: if your style is to be a Change Resister or a Nostalgia Buff and your partner is a Stimulation Junkie or an Escape Artist, you're likely to have conflict on many levels.

In coping with a midlife partner, a useful tactic is to focus on your own life instead of theirs. The benefits are many: not only do you lessen dependency on your mate, but you'll become more interesting to them as well. At the same time, let your partner know that you take their transition seriously, and respect what they're going through.

For a little inspiration on the task of growing together, here is psychologist Roger Gould's eloquent description of the rewards of a successfully renegotiated midlife marriage.

> The old conspiracies are abandoned. In their place is a relationship based on empathetic acceptance of our authentic partner, who is not a myth, not a god, not a mother, not a father, not a protector, not a censor. Instead there is just another human being with a full range of passions, rational ability, strengths and weaknesses, trying to figure out how to conduct a meaningful life with real friendship and companionship.

## The Loner: Family Issues for Midlife Singles

For never-married or long-divorced people, midlife is a time to take an honest look at the reasons you are single, take inventory of what you do and don't like about it, and perhaps make peace with the possibility that you may live most of your life unattached in the traditional sense.

It can be very difficult to sort out how you truly feel about being single. If you feel alienated from the social mainstream, that you've failed a key test of growing up, or simply lonely, how much of those feelings comes from within? How much is a reaction to the expectations we were raised with and the judgments of others? While it's important to consider this, the answer is moot to some extent: we respond to the feelings, whatever their source.

Despite the vast social changes of the past few decades, there is still tremendous pressure to mate and raise children. Single women, especially, feel the heat. The growth of feminist consciousness shaped the lives of millions of contemporary women, who took to heart Gloria Steinem's claim that "A woman without a man is like a fish without a bicycle." The idea that a woman doesn't really need a man helped many women to forge independent identities.

But if a woman no longer *needs* a man in the traditional sense, to shelter and provide for her, she may still *want* very much to be with a man. A great many women feel torn by these contradictory messages. Midlife may be the first time they can honestly confront their desire to form a permanent bond and many feel they have waited too long.

One *Newsweek* article compared the likelihood of midlife women getting married to the odds of being "attacked by terrorists," and sent thousands of single women into dating services and psychotherapists' offices.

Stephanie was one of these.

> I'm almost embarrassed to admit how much I want to settle down with a man. I've tried all the alternatives: cohabitation, communes in the seventies, a good collection of friends who treated me like family. I've been the third wheel in too many situations to name. I even have old lovers who swear that if they ever get divorced, I'll be the first one they call. Thanks a lot.
>
> I don't mean to put any of these options down, but let's face it, they're substitutes for a family of my own. It doesn't

even have to be my own children; I'd be happy being a step-mom. I want some security, to grow old with someone. When most of my friends were getting married and having babies, my career was still my main focus. But now I'm ready for something else. The problem is that I don't see many men who attract me. Are all the good ones taken, like they say? Or is it me? I've grown to be pretty damn independent and inflexible.

Single men, too, often wake up in midlife to the realization that family has slowly or suddenly become a priority. Changes, both biological and emotional, are bringing out their softer side in most cases, and the confrontation with aging makes the prospect of growing old alone less attractive.

For many single men, midlife is a time to abandon the fantasy of the perfect woman that has kept them on the move. A thirty-nine-year-old mechanic named Doug came to see me as the date of his first marriage neared, still troubled by that old feeling.

I decided about two years ago that I wanted to be married by the time I was forty, and when I met Kelly it seemed as though we were completely in sync. We'd only known each other three months when we decided to get married, and the excitement carried me along for a while.

But now I'm not so sure. Kelly's great, but I just don't know if I love her the way you're supposed to love somebody when you're going to spend the rest of your lives together. I've always moved from one relationship to the next fairly quickly. I think I would leave the woman as soon as I saw some flaw. I guess I wanted them to be perfect, and they all seemed that way in the beginning.

So here I am with Kelly, who isn't perfect. Do I need perfect? I don't know. But I do know I feel different than I did a decade ago. This feeling of being in love is different—less of a roller-coaster, a smoother ride.

Singles who are truly happy being single are probably in the minority. Certainly they must be strong-minded to hold their course against the social tide. The most acute pressure often comes from a midlifer's own parents, if they are still alive. A forty-year-old client named Ruth rarely sees her mother, because it would be too upsetting for the older woman to witness what her unmarried daughter's life must be like. "She just assumes I'm terribly lonely, and that gets my hackles up every time. Even our phone calls are tense with her unspoken thoughts. At some point she always gets around to the main thing on her mind: Are you going out with any men?

Remember that in expressing their dissatisfaction with our lives, our parents are revealing their own fears about having raised us poorly. Every single midlifer must work out his or her own feelings about remaining single or starting a family, and act positively on those decisions. If you decide to accept it, you may need to put greater effort into nurturing your networks, make sure that career and other activities are as rewarding as possible, and give yourself the opportunity to act as a mentor.

If you really want to change your status, you may need to put pride aside and explore new options for meeting people: dating services or clubs, activities where the opposite gender predominates, or urging friends to keep you in mind as a fix-up prospect.

Singles, not preoccupied with families of their own, often find that their birth families become the focus for some midlife changes. Whereas the long struggle to separate emotionally from one's parents is eased by becoming a parent oneself, it can be harder for single midlifers and their aging parents to break out of the old dynamic.

On the other hand, the personal growth that midlife baby boomers undergo can lead to breakthroughs and reconciliations in difficult relationships with their parents. As one client said, "I find it easier now to sidestep a confrontation now when my Mom pushes my buttons about being single. I may not be thrilled about it myself, but getting angry at her doesn't help—it just made me feel guilty and immature. And each time I can let it pass, I feel that much stronger."

Single baby boomers have become creative at filling the need for family interaction: close networks of friends gather for holidays, celebrations, and crises; bonds form with temporary partners and *their* families; and their own extended families are rediscovered. The rewards of getting to know one's siblings, cousins, and other relations in adulthood can be considerable—and surprisingly accessible in this age of cheap transcontinental travel. The traditional family reunion seems to be enjoying a modest revival, whether as a regularly scheduled, annual event drawing lots of participants or more informal gatherings.

The options being explored by midlife singles are in some ways the most truly representative of changes in the family. The keynotes in making such options work are flexibility, diversity, tolerance, and openness—all equally indispensable to families that we create rather than inherit. And since the trend for boomers and later generations is clearly toward multiple and mixed families, those qualities will be universally needed in the family life of the future.

### THE SANDWICH GENERATION

Most fortysomething baby boomers are facing responsibility for aging parents as well as for their own children. Not only is the percentage of older people increasing, but people will be older for much *longer,* adding to the strain on their families.

Midlife women, who traditionally maintain stronger connections among family members, are most likely to feel the pressures of caring for the older generation (often while their own children are still living at home). The demands of work may enable a son, psychologically, to give less time to aging parents, but daughters are still expected to put family first and are more prone to feel guilt if they do not—especially if they are single. Older parents tend to live with an unmarried child more than with married children of either sex, and are twice as likely to live with an unmarried daughter as with a son. For many women, caring for dependent parents is a reentry job that requires no resume.

The psychological effects of caring for dependent parents can have a large impact on family stability. For midlifers already facing small daily reminders of their mortality, close involvement with infirm parents can evoke large doses of fear, guilt, anger, and sorrow. Such feelings are an inevitable part of midlife, and people who still have major unresolved issues with their parents may find that these are stumbling blocks to transition. Here are a few observations that may help to make caring for dependent parents less of an emotional drain.

The demand to spend excessive amounts of time with an aging parent can be a result of the *empty nest* syndrome, the need to feel important to someone after the children have left home. It can also be prompted by guilt over an old conflict between parent and child, or an attempt to fill a marital void. Fewer visits with more quality time may be less stressful for both parent and midlifer.

If maintaining a workable relationship with an aging parent is extremely difficult, consider joining a support group as a way to relieve the stress and share experiences with people in similar positions. You could also hire a social worker who specializes in geriatrics to act as a go-between.

Dealing at close range with elderly parents should be an instructional part of the midlife growth process, useful in helping us prepare for our own aging. We can learn what we admire and what we would do differently. Just as our parents taught us how to live, they can also teach us how to live with our own aging.

## The New Family

In so many ways, the baby boom is in the process of redefining the nature of family. This process is far from over, but we can summarize the major themes that have emerged so far.

Most boomers desire to bond with a mate and have the experience of child-raising, though staying single is a more acceptable option than ever before. As high divorce and remarriage rates confirm, staying bonded is the tricky part. Mixed families of step- and half-siblings will become more the norm. Parenting out of wedlock is reasonably common (especially at the low and high ends of the socio-economic spectrum), and people of both sexes are having children at an older age.

Even more significant, perhaps, is the extent to which baby boomers are relying on their friends rather than blood families for support, in daily life and midlife. This phenomenon is due in part to our mobility—most of us no longer live within a day's drive of our parents—and also to the strong bonds we formed with our friends in youth.

Social analyst Ken Dychtwald predicts that "the child-centered nuclear family will increasingly be replaced by the *matrix* family, an adult-centered unit that spans generations and is bound together by friendship and circumstances as well as by blood and obligation." Such a modern-day version of the pre-industrial extended family could encompass multiple households as well as friendship and kinship networks.

Midlife poses serious challenges to family and relationships, whichever form these assume. On the other hand, the midlife urge for experimentation and connection can result in better communication and more openness. Diverse family styles allow more opportunity for individual growth within the protection of the family system. We can look forward to more tolerance and understanding of changing roles and of the challenges involved in making families work in the real world, and less guilt about not fitting the model of an ideal family.

# 8

# What Am I Working For?

## The Career
## Challenge Again

*We are what we pretend to be, so we must be
careful about what we pretend to be.*
                                        KURT VONNEGUT, JR.

I got a midlife wake-up call on my way to work one day. I commute into San Francisco on the Golden Gate Bridge, and I crossed the span that morning with a sense of reluctance and boredom about my work.

Looking at my situation objectively, it was hard to pinpoint the problem. The work was intrinsically interesting and worthwhile. My clients were satisfied; I had respect from the people I worked with and a fair amount of material success. Yet I still felt exhausted anticipating the day ahead, its complex responsibilities, the frustration I had carried home last night, and would again tonight, of seeking solutions to sometimes insoluble problems. I started fantasizing about a job where I could just do my work and go home.

At just that point in my reverie, I rolled up to the toll plaza. Observing the toll-takers perform their quick ritual, I was suddenly consumed with envy. What wouldn't I have given to switch places with one of them—a quick "hello, have a nice day" and on to the next car. And a beautiful view, besides.

I know the heavens were smiling when I walked into my office a few minutes later to meet a new client. He was short and dark, in his mid-forties, I guessed—and he was wearing the uniform of a Golden Gate Bridge toll taker.

The full irony of the coincidence unfolded over the next hour. Tony was forty-two and had been working on the bridge for seven years. Before that he had been a butcher but hated working inside all day; when his cousin had mentioned an opening for a toll taker, he applied and was assigned a slot. For a few years, it had been great—just as I'd pictured in my fantasy. But lately Tony had been feeling doubtful.

> It's the same thing, day after day. I take the money, wave people through. Sometimes you get a nut. Sometimes people are rude, or nice, or you get a funny line. But believe me, that's the exception. Most of the time it's the same, hour after hour, day after day. People hardly notice you. It's like you don't exist.
>
> What gets to me most is looking at people in their cars and imagining what they do. They look like important people—doctors, lawyers, accountants—but even if they're not, at least their job changes. They do different things and get involved with people. That's what I want—not to just watch them flash past me on their way somewhere.

So what kind of career change was Tony contemplating to get more involved with people? Psychology! He was thinking about going back to school—felt it might be his last chance to make a big change. He'd been a good student, and thought he had a knack for understanding people. He wanted to explore it with some formal training and work as a counselor with kids. He wanted to make a difference in people's lives, and had arranged to see me to get some reinforcement and guidance for his dream.

While my professional self was answering Tony as best I could, privately I was marveling at the forces that had brought us to the same place from such different perspectives. Each of us was looking over the fence at greener grass. I could identify with his concern about making a change while there was still time, and about what people around him would think.

How much of our discontent was due to the nature of our work, and how much could be laid at the door of basic midlife restlessness? It was important for both of us to sort this out, and I asked him to look at his feelings carefully. Being dissatisfied with one's work is probably, along with marital discontent, the most common symptom of midlife's urge toward change. We tend to think that the problem lies in what we are doing, and that the solution is to switch jobs, or fields. While that's not *necessarily* untrue—a job or career change can be enormously revitalizing—it's not a magic formula.

Work is a major component of most life structures, consuming a great deal of our time and energy. It also serves as a shorthand method of defining ourselves in relation to the world; because it does, we tend as adults to submerge our identity in it. What I do is what I am. That statement may work as an adequate definition of self in our twenties and thirties, but as we approach midlife, it begins to have a hollow ring. We start hearing instead an insistent question: Is this *all* I am?

In this chapter we'll look at the role work plays in our lives, and the kinds of rewards that baby boomers in particular seek from it. We'll review the rhythms of the traditional career cycle, and see how they have been thrown out of phase by social and economic changes, intensifying the midcareer crisis. We'll see what leads some midlifers into workaholism and burnout, and others to explore new options. Most of the chapter applies equally to women and men, since baby boom women have tended to pursue careers, but there is also a section directed at women who are reentering the working world around midlife.

How you resolve your work situation in midlife is affected by many of the factors we've discussed previously, such as how your personality responds to change, what kind of support systems you have, how healthy you are, and how healthy your relationships are. Several of the master skills discussed in Chapter 5 will be useful in managing the midcareer challenge.

## Baby Boomers and Work

A friend of mine named Jack runs a successful clothing store and does well by most standards. He works hard, putting in six-day weeks and ten-hour days. But he has a fantasy that he talks about all the time.

> If I had enough money, if I won the lottery or something, I'd move to Hawaii and open up a hot dog stand. I'd do it in a second. Open up a little hot dog stand by the beach. Sell my hot dogs. Work the hours I want to. Wouldn't worry about a thing.

The part about moving to Hawaii isn't very original; lots of forty-seven-year-olds who have worked hard all their lives share the fantasy of a tropical paradise. What strikes me as unusual about Jack's vision is that he sees himself running a hot dog stand. Why bother, assuming he had all the money he needed?

Jack's fantasy embodies a fundamental truth of human psychology: work seems to be essential to our psychological well being. What we do is a cornerstone of our identity. Even if we don't need to work to support ourselves, producing something by our labors satisfies deeply rooted psychic needs. Psychologists often group these under the headings of *ego needs,* which include feelings of self-esteem, mastery, control, status, and understanding of the world; *affiliation needs,* our desire for group support and connection with others; *play needs,* such as adventure and competition; and *existential needs*—for meaning and significance in what we do.

We choose our work because of the needs it satisfies. Some look to their work to fulfill a wide range of needs—especially if other areas of life are impoverished. Others look outside work for most nonmaterial rewards. Which of our needs take precedence depends on our personality, background, and stage of development: for people without strong family or friendship ties, for example, the sense of belonging to a group at work may be most important. In young and early middle adulthood, ego needs tend to dominate; we're looking to make a place for ourselves, to master a field of endeavor, to have our achievements acknowledged.

In midlife, our needs change. Affiliation and play needs usually assert themselves more strongly. The need to find meaning in one's work may become more of an issue. The generativity urge—the desire for a measure of immortality— often comes up in the work setting.

## THE CAREER LIFE CYCLE

As our needs change, our working lives also go through a cycle of several stages, just as our individual selves and relationships do. We move from an adolescence populated by dreams and fantasies into young adulthood, where the career person seeks entry into a new fraternity, continue through years of growing knowledge and deepening experience, and arrive at a time of reassessment around midlife.

Career development experts use different terms to describe these stages. Douglas Hall of Boston University refers to five phases, beginning with *exploration,* in which you choose a field and get acquainted with it. In the *trial* phase, you are acquiring and developing skills. Next comes *establishment,* a period of deepening those skills and taking on increased responsibility and authority, gaining what another expert calls *full membership* in a career. Then follows a period of *maintenance,* a time of consolidating one's position and making small adjustments in long-range planning.

The last phase described by Hall is *disengagement,* when one starts to ease away from full career involvement in a move that eventually leads to retirement. This is usually a gradual process, as one begins to take on more of a mentoring role and increased leadership responsibilities. Later, one learns to make peace with more limited levels of power and control, and to compensate for this loss with alternative rewards of avocations, family, and social activities.

Before the disengagement period begins, most people experience some sort of *midcareer crisis*—a major reassessment of progress, especially as compared to expectations. At this time, the role of work in one's life is reevaluated: how important work is in relation to other components of the structure such as family and avocations. The symptoms of midcareer crisis are familiar variants on midlife symptoms generally: a sense of boredom and staleness about the work you do, unfavorable comparisons between youthful goals and present reality, the urge to break out conflicting with fear of the unknown.

This traditional portrait of a career cycle is based on a few key premises. It assumes that one embarks full tilt on a career early in adulthood and remains in that career throughout one's working life. It is also patterned chiefly on the experience of men in business or professional fields. From what we already know about how baby boomers behave, it shouldn't be surprising that this pattern is currently undergoing renovation.

## JOB SATISFACTION: THE NEW WORK ETHIC

For the previous generation, the guiding principles of work were security and minimizing risks. The factors that kept our fathers relatively settled for life in their jobs included the

Protestant/capitalist work ethic built into the American myth, reaction to the Depression, the rise of big-brother corporate structures, and early marriages and fatherhood. By and large, work fulfilled their needs: it took care of material security and affiliation needs, and in the booming economy of the fifties and sixties, it offered plenty of opportunity to meet ego needs of achievement and progress.

While they may have felt some dissatisfaction, they perceived limited options for making major changes. Moving to a new company was a big event; changing careers entirely was rare. And they didn't feel the existential need for job satisfaction as strongly as baby boomers do. As a friend's father once told her, "Who said work was supposed to be fun?"

However, baby boomers expect more from work than a desk and a paycheck. Work is much more than a job to us, in the sense that a job is something you do that's separate from who you are. We identify with our labor; a career is integral to our self-image. Fulfillment through work isn't a concept invented by baby boomers; we are simply the first generation in modern times to whom it has been widely available. The idea that work should be meaningful was encouraged by our extended liberal educations, economic security, and coming of age in the socially conscious sixties. It may have gotten submerged for a decade or so in the success chase, but at midlife it is likely to surface again, as the excitement of the chase wanes and material needs have largely been met (or else seem less attainable than ever).

Social analyst Daniel Yankelovich sees the boomer drive for job satisfaction as part of a larger change in society's collective consciousness. In *The New Rules,* he describes a shift in the *giving/getting* balance: from the prior generation's emphasis on deferred gratification and self-denial to the current demand that day-to-day life—including work—be rewarding and significant.

Abraham Maslow, the dean of humanist psychology, describes the importance of work in the development of identity.

The only happy people I know are the ones who are working at something they consider important . . . [their motivation] is expressed in their devotion to, and identification with, some great and important job . . . Self-actualizing work is simultaneously a seeking and fulfilling of the self and also an achieving of the selflessness which is the ultimate expression of real self.

Maslow's ideal of work as an expression both of the self and selflessness is supported by statistics. Apparently, when job satisfaction is present, the employer and society benefit as well as the worker. A Gallup poll showed that Americans whose work gave them a sense of identity worked harder, longer, and more contentedly than those who merely worked for a living. In another recent study, 70 percent of those polled said they would continue working even if they didn't have to, but only 39 percent said they would continue in the same job. This seems to reinforce both the intrinsic need to work and the increasing demand for job satisfaction.

### AMBIVALENCE AND ALIENATION

At the same time, it is also important to note that the baby boomers who identify so much with their careers also bring a strong feeling of ambivalence to their work. In the sixties sitcom "The Many Loves of Dobie Gillis," Bob Denver's beatnik character, Maynard G. Krebs, would react with extreme alarm whenever the work came up: "Work??!!" Krebs was a caricature of the pre-WW II generation's image of us as hedonistic and unmotivated, but there's undeniably a little of him in most boomers.

In many cases, we had the luxury of putting off work for a long time—through college, maybe graduate school, a trip abroad, Peace Corps stints, or a succession of uncommitted jobs such as restaurant work or unskilled labor. In any case, a large number of us discovered the joys of extended leisure that only much more privileged classes had been able to experience in the past, and we liked it. So, while we've largely buckled down and joined the workforce in a committed way, we're not prepared to sacrifice our leisure pursuits entirely until retirement: hence the pressure for longer vacations, shorter work weeks, unpaid leaves of absence, flex time, and sabbaticals—all of which are becoming accepted practices in corporate working rhythms.

But our ambivalence goes deeper than just a desire for pleasure. Some people in this generation feel fundamentally alienated from work and question its ultimate moral value—at least work in the centralized, pyramidal form it has taken since the Industrial Revolution. While we don't have the space here to explore this complex subject exhaustively, it does seem clear that many in the postwar generation question the modern work ethic, either intellectually or instinctively, and display contradictory attitudes toward work. On one hand, we are competitive and achievement-oriented. We appreciate a high standard of living, identify with our careers to the extent that we often use them as surrogates for family life. On the other, we strive toward the ideal of a balanced life in which work is only one of many satisfying elements, and are resentful if work impinges too heavily on our pleasures.

## GETTING SATISFACTION: CHANGING NEEDS, CHANGING JOBS

Each of us has a self-concept that is the product of our abilities, experience, interests, values, and personality traits. To the extent that we can bring these into our work situation, it will be considered to be satisfying. But, because our experience and values are constantly changing, we must regularly evaluate whether or not our work continues to be satisfying. Men whose jobs formerly met ego needs such as power and status, for example, may find in their forties that play needs and group connections become more compelling, but are not accommodated by their work. Women, on the other hand, often discover the values of mastery, control and power later in life, and seek careers that provide them.

We are more likely than our parents to recognize and act on such value shifts, changing jobs and careers at an unprecedented rate. We see ourselves as having more options in choosing careers, and far more freedom to abandon an established career path for a new one. This is especially true for women who in a generation have seen their career options expand from very few choices to a virtually unlimited menu.

As a result, the traditional career cycle has become a crazy-quilt pattern. Some people race through a career in their twenties and hit midcareer crisis in the early thirties. They may then make a choice that precludes any further crises, or start the cycle all over again; many will experience multiple midcareer turning points. Other boomers, slower to establish themselves in a career, may not come to a reassessment until well after midlife.

In short, we are quickly becoming a society in which multiple careers are the norm. Estimates of the number of jobs an individual will have over a lifetime range from four to six. A 1988 Gallup poll found that one-quarter of Americans between twenty-six and forty were planning to change jobs or careers within three years.

Alison, an attorney who had returned to law school at forty-two, is a dramatic example of how career patterns have changed. She told me a story about others in her field:

> I overheard a conversation at a courthouse between two attorneys in their mid-thirties; I recognized one of them from school. He started to tell the other guy that he doesn't know how much longer he can continue in the profession; how abusive the judges are, how hard he has to work, how disillusioned he feels.

The other attorney is nodding in agreement, and he says, "I know what you mean. I think maybe I'll do this for another three years, five max, and then find something else." Now, I know they aren't making this up. And these aren't weirdos, by any means. They may be extreme, but it seems like people are changing their careers like they change a suit of clothes.

The need for fulfillment and the unlimited-option mentality are mutually reinforcing. The quest for satisfaction impels baby boomers to move on if they feel they're not getting it from their job, and the sense that new careers are available at almost any time in life discourages settling for *good enough.* This remains true in midlife, though it may start to conflict with fears that we're getting too old for big changes.

## Midcareer Crisis in a Changing Workplace

Let's look briefly at how trends in the working world today dovetail with baby boomer attitudes. John Naisbitt, the author of *Megatrends,* popularized the idea that we are moving from an industrial age, a time of producing things, into the information age—an era when ideas and knowledge are the currency of exchange. *The Futurist* estimates that by the year 2000, 95 percent of all jobs will be in the service and information management industries.

For baby boomers, this is a significant factor in loosening the roles, rules, and boundaries that kept our parents in place during midlife. We are entering an era where it is not only possible, but mandatory, to reinvent oneself continually. Adaptability is the keynote to success in such an environment. The notion that you learn a skill and practice it for the rest of your life is no longer valid.

A related development is the shift from large institutional hierarchies to smaller, more adaptive networks that tend to be loosely structured, formed around a single purpose, and oriented toward innovation. Today's workplace increasingly reflects the network mentality: more collaborative than hierarchical, a place where systems and roles are temporary and expedient. The typical comparison is of an old-line corporation like IBM with its upstart competitor, Apple. Even IBM is now recognizing the advantages of the network approach and encouraging the formation of smaller units within its corporate whole.

Compared with monolithic organizations, the boundaries of networks are more permeable. Role definitions—how you function within the network—are more fluid. They are thus, in many ways, the perfect home for the midlife baby boomer, encouraging mobility and congenial to the urge for change.

## THE PLATEAUING TRAP

If you aren't feeling pulled toward midcareer change by the promise of greater fulfillment, you may be pushed by today's corporate reality. Change Resisters especially, who prefer to settle into a career and coast along in security are likely to feel the effects of this.

In the fifties there were plenty of jobs to go around. In the sixties the demographic squeeze began, with ten candidates for every available position. That figure rose to twenty in the 1970s, and the 1980s brought a flood tide of nearly thirty candidates for each job—even more in some industries. We're seeing the bulge of the baby boom trying to get through a shrinking door, resulting in a buyer's market that has made job security and predictable advancement rare.

Exacerbating the number crunch is the housecleaning that has been taking place in American business in recent years. Takeovers and mergers have created an unstable and harshly competitive corporate environment. Call it workforce reduction, downscaling, flattening out the hierarchy, or knocking out the middle managers, the bottom line is the same: jobs and promotions are being eliminated. Companies no longer buy talent, they rent it. People become expendable as companies strive to get lean and mean. For many, the midcareer crisis alarm sounds when the company delivers this unwelcome message.

The phenomenon of *plateauing*—getting stuck in the lower or middle ranks of management because there is stiffer competition for fewer spots at the top—is a fact of life for boomers, especially those in the second wave. Rather than continuing to move up the ranks through one's forties and fifties, many are finding that, by around age forty, they've progressed as far as they're likely to in a given company. Sometimes the best they can hope for is a lateral move; even if they consider moving to another company in their field, the competition for the top spots is just as intense.

What Lisa Grunwald in *Esquire* calls "the fierce tyranny of the pyramid" has been operating for a long time, but people are reaching the upper limit earlier these days. This comes as a cold shock for the upwardly mobile baby boomer who assumed that up had no upper limit. As Landon Jones remarks in his book, *Great Expectations,* "A generation that had expected to be chiefs will have to be braves. . . . In effect, the entire generation will be like a large group of people being moved from a big room into a smaller room." The psychological impact of plateauing on boomers—people raised with the highest expectations of success, a tendency to see their potential as limitless, and a strong identification with their work—is immense.

Often the harshest blow isn't the stalled growth in one's earning power, but the ego threat to one's identity, which is so often tightly wrapped up in career progress. Consider the case of Janice, who at forty-three came to see me during a work transition. Six months earlier, she had left her job of regional sales manager for a San Francisco radio station after being passed over several times for promotion to national sales manager.

I'm not sure what to make of the company's decision. That's part of the problem—nobody ever told me what I was doing wrong. All I ever got was praise and positive reviews.

The first time it happened, I assumed it was because I had only been regional sales manager for a year, and they thought I had more learning to do. The second time, I felt they should have known I could do the job and I wondered if it might be because I was female. But I'd been there for some time and hadn't seen any signs of discrimination, so I put it out of my mind and just worked harder to convince them I was top material.

Janice thought her motivation may have slipped a little after the second time. The resentment started to creep into her work, and she held back from giving the proverbial 110 percent. Focusing on what she could get away with instead of what she could accomplish seemed like a way of getting even, but ironically contributed to the situation she was trying to change.

When the national sales manager left last year, I thought, "Well, they can't possibly pass me over a third time." And they did. I was hurt, furious, and discouraged; I went directly to the network heads and asked them what the story was. Their answer didn't help much: they liked what I was doing but felt I wasn't the best qualified person for the national position. It didn't make sense to me that they could like my work and not promote me.

But the reality eventually sank in. I had job security; they were willing to let me go on in my job forever. And it wasn't the money—I was getting good yearly raises. I was just used to getting promoted regularly. Like a shark, you know: you have to keep moving to stay alive.

Janice remembers the day she decided to leave the station. Her son was home with the flu, and she planned to go in to work late. Just after eight, the national sales manager called her at home for some information.

> "I started to panic. What if I don't go in? Will they be angry and not promote me? Then I started to laugh; how could I be so naive? They weren't going to promote me anyway, so what was I killing myself for?"

In the six months since leaving her job, Janice realized that a lot of her unhappiness was caused from being hooked on promotions. A Stimulation Junkie with a strong need for approval, she basically liked what she did but had become obsessed with moving up, to the exclusion of other rewards. Now, looking at jobs with other stations, she wanted to see if she could enjoy the work for its own sake, rather than for the payoffs of more money, more power, more control.

Janice's story is typical of what happens to ambitious people who get plateaued. Some of her resentment about being passed over came from feeling that she was falling short of her own expectations and some came from negatively comparing herself with others—both part of her midlife assessment. Given Janice's personality, she probably needed to leave her old employer. Sometimes the ego rejection of being plateaued can be alleviated by a lateral move to a new situation.

## DOWNWARD MOBILITY

It's the age of the *MADMUP*: the Middle Aged Downwardly Mobile Urban Professional. Despite the media focus on rapidly rising yuppies, baby-boom families have experienced a decline in real earning power, even though the two-income family is now the norm. Incomes have not kept pace with the cost of living, and the cost of the most basic family investment—housing—has gone off the scale. It takes two working baby boomers to finance the standard of living and the level of savings that their parents managed with one salary.

Is it any wonder, then, that boomers in midlife are questioning the value of their work and looking to standards other than material success against which to measure satisfaction? Or that they are so willing to consider job changes, alternative lifestyles, and entrepreneurial risks? If you think of work as a balance between costs and benefits, it's clear that benefits are currently lagging behind. This makes the hold many jobs have on their owners tenuous. Frequently the normal turbulence of midlife transition is more than enough to break it loose.

Louise, a forty-three-year-old computer programmer, tells a familiar story.

> My husband and our two boys and I went home for the holidays last year. Looking around my parents' big house, I realized that they had put all the pieces of family and home together long before John and I did, and with just my father working. I'm beginning to wonder if we'll ever catch up, even though we both work.
>
> I've never loved computer programming; I really do it for the money. But I'm working as hard as my parents did, and getting less out of it—John too. So both of us have started looking for ways to cut back, to get more out of what we do with our time. We aren't going to make the kind of money that buys freedom, and we don't want our kids to look back on their childhoods and wonder where we were.

Both Louise and Janice's stories illustrate what has happened to the old idea of company loyalty in the new workplace. In our parents' time, it was a fairly simple matter of workers demonstrating loyalty in exchange for job security and steady advancement. The *me first* mentality that prevails today is in part a defense against an insecure corporate environment, but also reflects the baby boom's greater demands for job satisfaction.

## THE MOMMY/DADDY TRACK

The so-called *mommy track,* a much-ballyhooed phenomenon of the late 1980s, is another byproduct of baby boomers hitting midlife. It is a response by many women who, after pursuing careers earlier in life, are choosing maternity as they approach midlife. The term was introduced in an article by Felice Schwartz in a 1989 *Harvard Business Review* article, in which she reports that corporations are instituting a *de facto* tracking system that allows such women to remain in their careers with reduced workloads and responsibilities while they attend to the needs of motherhood.

The mommy track makes sense for corporations, says Schwartz, which can ill-afford to lose experienced professionals, managers, and executives. It has, however, raised a lot of hackles among career women, some of whom see it as a kind of second-class citizenship—another excuse to keep females less well-paid and less eligible for the top positions. Others—men and women both—decry the lack of attention to a male counterpart, the *daddy track,* which would allow men to share more household responsibilities and explore other midlife options.

The upside of this is that the same social trends that mandated the mommy track will bring increases in child care at work, job sharing, flex shifts, and telecommuting—all helping people to share their time and energy between work and families. We'll also see the increase of *eldercare* programs for baby boomers with aging parents. Like most of these developments, the last will be most significant for women, since they are usually the caretakers of elderly parents. None of this is corporate benevolence: it's a reality needed to pacify an aging workforce.

### KEEPING TOO BUSY: THE MIDCAREER WORKAHOLIC

If some people tend to withdraw from commitment to their jobs when doubt and dissatisfaction strike, others do just the opposite—work more. The intense competitiveness of today's business climate and fear of the downward mobility spiral have led to an atmosphere where working at maximum capacity is becoming considered normal.

Baby boomers have been primed for this pattern from an early age. With our educational advantages, we were expected to excel. We had to find ways to stand out from the crowd in big classes, fight the crush to get accepted at the best colleges and get the good job afterward, then try to squeeze through the quickly narrowing window of opportunity in management.

However, the chronic workaholic usually has inadequate energy left for family and other areas of life, and in midlife may find little to sustain him when the promotions dwindle or material rewards fall short. Paradoxically, workaholism can be the perfect coverup for midlife's feelings of alienation and loss. The typical reappraisal of values, the normal and healthy doubts about the meaning of work, fears about aging and the future—all can be deferred if you simply don't have time to think about them. Both Change Resisters and Stimulation Junkies may be inclined to put off dealing with issues of satisfaction and fulfillment, and bury them under an avalanche of work.

In truth, there's a fine line between the dedicated, emotionally healthy worker and the workaholic. It's generally accepted that the workaholic is emotionally disconnected and overinvested in his work, seeing it as his primary or sole reason for being. Such people can be an employer's dream. As long as the workaholic employee is producing, businesses tend to reward such behavior with promotions and financial gain, setting people up for burnout if they fail to look out for their own well-being.

One trait of the workaholic is an obsession with the quantity of work performed, as if that alone could give it meaning. A client named Susan fits the profile. On several occasions she would say things like, "I worked on a proposal all weekend. I started on Friday evening, worked till one in the morning, got up at six and worked the whole day. Sunday it was the same. I finally finished at ten o'clock."

What struck me about such comments was that Susan mentioned nothing about the quality of her work, speaking only of the time that went into it. She seemed not really to care how the proposal was received—as if what mattered wasn't whether she landed the job but how much effort she had expended. When I pointed this out, she responded angrily. "You sound just like my father. No matter what I did, he always found something wrong."

On reflection, Susan realized that the amount of time she put into her work was her defense against any criticism of it. Since there was no guarantee that people would like her work (and she was primed to expect failure because of parental criticism), she felt she could at least insulate herself by insuring that everyone knew she'd worked herself into the ground.

The choice to withdraw from work in any way is threatening to baby boomers, conditioned to competition as we are. Yet confronting workaholism is a midlife imperative. There's the issue of stamina, for one thing: pacing and planning have to replace achievement through sheer effort. It's also important to recognize overwork as a device to shut out the inner voice of discontent. The key is learning to evaluate your work on the basis of quality rather than quantity. This leads you to look inward, to ask how you feel about the work, rather than getting sidetracked by details of how much, how big, or how fast.

## THE IMPOSTOR SYNDROME

This is a related phenomenon to workaholism, and even more specific to baby boomers around midlife. By the mid-1980s it had become so widely recognized that the American Psychological Association held a symposium on it at their national convention. Briefly, *impostors* are generally in their mid-twenties to early forties who, despite success in their careers, feel like they are faking it.

In essence, the impostor syndrome is an unresolved struggle to reconcile high achievement with low self-esteem. Baby boomers may feel ambivalent about career success because their self-image hasn't developed at the same rapid pace. They often rose rapidly in a career environment that didn't allow for gradual development of skills and confidence. They were brought quickly through the management ranks without a chance to form relationships with mentors, and thrust into positions of power or expertise before they were psychologically ready.

George, at forty-two, seemed, on the surface, to know what he wanted and how to achieve it. A partner in an accounting firm, his work brought him financial and material rewards, travel, and stimulation. But George felt like an impostor.

> You know, even when I was doing my best work at the firm and making them a lot of money, deep down inside I didn't believe that I was worth what I was earning. It seemed like anybody could have done what I was doing. And I was never sure if I was the only one feeling that way, or if everyone else really did too.

The impostor may also feel that he hasn't achieved the standards of adulthood in other areas of his life—putting off family commitments, not being in a position to own a home, perhaps. So how can he be trusted with the responsibility for corporate budgets, for the management of other people, for keeping the wheels of commerce spinning? As one man put it, "How can I be the head of a company if I'm not grown up yet?"

George's comments address another facet of the impostor syndrome, the conflict of past values with present lifestyle.

> The other day I was going through some old pictures from college, and I had to laugh. I looked like such a hippie. Back then I never would have believed I'd turn out the way I did. I miss the commitment I felt back then, the strong feelings about civil rights and equality and intellectual curiosity.

Baby boomers who espoused counterculture values during the sixties and early seventies may have entered mainstream culture in many ways—a responsible career, home and family—yet not really feel a part of it. Their earlier self-image was built on the moral platform of social conscience, opposition to the Vietnam War, belief in sharing the wealth, but as they ascended in worldly terms, they often lost the accompanying sense of rightness and purpose. It's not unusual for people in their twenties and thirties to be concerned with worldly success; what is unusual is that a whole generation came to adulthood with a high level of social awareness. We feel its loss like a hole in our identity.

The impostor syndrome often goes hand and hand with workaholism, a shield against being found out. In severe cases, the person's sense of self may be so fragile that the slightest hint of exposure can provoke devastating bouts of depression and anxiety. Cynthia, a forty-six-year-old financial planner with a lot of authority, told me she felt "caught between the need to maintain the image and the urge to confess that it's all done with mirrors." Prone to overestimate any risk to her facade, she pulled away from relationships, as if admitting her fears to anyone could make them come true.

Some deliberately opt out of this oppressive situation after they realize it is threatening their well-being. Quitting while they're ahead—like a gambler in Vegas—can be an immense relief, as if they have been fortunate to have gotten away with pulling the wool over people's eyes for so long. Others, who can't make the conscious decision to quit, may unconsciously arrange it through self-destructive behavior, such as crippling substance abuse or financial transgressions that leave a flagrant paper trail.

This perceived conflict between success and fundamental values can intensify at midlife, as the need for meaning reasserts itself. This can lead in many directions: a radical career switch, a decision to get off the treadmill entirely, a reestablishment of old values. George, for example, decided to volunteer at a preschool run by his sister-in-law. He also arranged his schedule so he could go back to school for some courses he regretted missing as an undergraduate. To relinquish some status at work while placing himself in new environments where he had little status was a courageous and constructive move for him.

## BURNING OUT

Feeling overwhelmed, undervalued, and frustrated about work happens to everyone sooner or later. When these feelings are chronic and persistent, it's usually a sign of job burnout. Baby boomers in midlife are particularly vulnerable because of their high expectations and the need to set themselves apart.

Burnout usually proceeds through gradual stages as the learning curve of a career flattens out and the challenge wears off. The first stage is increasing stagnation, as routine aspects of one's work begin to dominate and its demands start to outweigh the rewards. The feeling of overload becomes more common.

In the second stage, reserves are severely tapped and emotions frayed. One often displaces frustration about work onto coworkers, bosses, or the institution itself. Personal health may become an issue, with an increase in stress-related illness or injuries.

Unless the situation is addressed, stage-three burnout is nearly inevitable. Someone suffering from full-scale burnout is beyond anger and feels crushed under an avalanche of impossible demands, loss of control, alienation, and isolation. At this point frustration is replaced by apathy, a hopeless and helpless feeling like that of a child who has given up calling for his parents in the night. Victims assume there's no solution to their dilemma, and their distress is often manifested in self-sabotage at work—an unconscious cry for help.

Sarah, who was forty-five and had been a nurse for twenty years, came to see me out of a growing despair about her work. She had a twenty-year-old daughter about to leave home, a husband increasingly indifferent to her concerns, and feelings she was reluctant to admit.

> With my daughter leaving I don't need to earn as much as I used to. Nursing has always been difficult, but it used to be challenging and rewarding as well. Now it's just a drain. I hate going to work, and I've started showing up late and being sick a lot, which isn't like me at all. I've got so much responsibility and so little power to make any real difference. I suppose this is the point where a lot of nurses start to move into administration, but I'm not sure I even want to continue in the health care field.

Certain careers, like social work, sales, teaching, and health care, are particularly prone to burnout. The workloads are heavy, the hours long, the system is a bureaucratic nightmare, and in health care, human beings get sick and die despite the dedicated efforts of practitioners.

In Sarah's case, the work itself was part of the problem, but she had also set herself up for burnout by asking too much from her job. As her daughter and husband became more distant, too much of her self-esteem had to derive from work. Sarah recognized this and made some changes, transferring to another service in her hospital and signing up for a series of weekend hikes. Taking action on the work front gave her the momentum to make some painful but necessary changes in her home life as well.

If you recognize the symptoms of burnout in yourself, the first step should be to analyze where it's coming from. Is burnout inherent in the work? Is the problem your attitude toward the work? Or is it simply that you and your job don't mesh well? Sometimes all three are involved. Armed with a better understanding of the situation, you're equipped to make the primary decision: to stay and try to revitalize the work, or to leave. Remember that the getting-out option always exists, whether or not it's the right one right now. Realizing that you're not hopelessly trapped can help you tolerate a stressful situation.

## Working Options for Midlifers

### SHOULD I STAY OR SHOULD I GO?

This is rarely an easy decision, and any move should be considered with great patience. Beware of the impulse to change everything at once; the master skill of tolerating ambiguity is essential here. Careers are built over a lifetime, and decisions to change them need to be considered and lived with for as long as it takes to see all the angles. Factors such as economic needs and responsibilities to others should be carefully weighed.

Try to follow this general plan in deciding whether to leave a work situation. First, identify as specifically as you can what is bothering you about your job. Is the work itself boring, or overwhelming? Have you plateaued, or been pushed into a role that denies personal satisfaction? Are you resenting your superiors or feeling ignored by them?

Next, try to separate how much of your dissatisfaction is external and comes from the work situation, and how much is internal or related to other issues in your life. Do some of the same negative feelings come up in both your work life and family life? Making these distinctions can be very difficult when work is closely bound up with identity. It's easy to blame a specific job for not fulfilling our needs, but we need to look at the larger picture of changing values, the loss of our youthful self-image, and the hard work of de-illusionment.

My friend Andrew said something in passing that made me realize he was using his work as a scapegoat for some fundamental midlife regrets. A general contractor with a background in fine art and design, he was having to do time consuming and unrewarding administrative tasks to manage his growing business.

> I used to feel like I was involved in a variety of things, that I could talk in an intelligent and stimulating way in any setting, about architecture or photography or painting or music. Lately I seem to have become much narrower. I can talk with plenty of authority and humor about my work, sell myself to clients easily and entertain them at the same time. But in other situations I feel dull, as if I have nothing to say. My business has so taken over my life that I don't feel confident outside that arena.

Andrew's comments reflect a narrowing of interests, which happens to many people over time. In early adulthood, your energy gets spread around in many directions. As you get older, your focus does tend to narrow, especially if you have a family and a demanding career. At midlife comes the urge to take a broader approach to life again—but that all-consuming job seems to stand in the way. Rather than resenting your work, try to identify other areas you'd like to explore; if you care enough, you'll make room for them.

After analyzing the sources of your discontent, the next step is to improve your current situation. This calls for a realistic view of your powers and limitations. Midlife is a time—often the first time—when we have to accept that some things about ourselves and our lives may be beyond changing. Just identifying the source of a problem and accepting that you have no control over it can relieve a lot of frustration. And sometimes merely seeing the problem clearly can help resolve it.

Any leavetaking impulse born out of anger should be carefully scrutinized. When something happens in a work situation that threatens one's emotional attachment to a job, it's like being hurt in a relationship: the impulse is often to run away.

A client of mine named Larry was forty-eight and a vice president of sales for an apparel company when it was acquired by another manufacturer. I was consulting on a transition program there when he sought my counsel.

> I know I'm making a mess of things, but I can't seem to help myself. I've been here fifteen years and it's felt like family to me. The acquisition didn't really come as a surprise and, truthfully, the new owners have brought in some good stuff. They're progressive and forward-thinking, and I'm happy to still be here, since they let a lot of people go. But what puzzles me is how angry I am. I'm only forty-eight—I shouldn't be too old to learn new ways of doing business.

Larry's negativity and anger about the takeover got in the way of seemingly trivial things. The computers the new owners brought in became a symbolic stumbling block; Larry had a computer at home, but he resisted being asked to learn a new skill at work.

One thing's for sure: if I don't get my act together, I'll be history. My new boss is a real innovator, and he's been looking over my shoulder a lot lately. I'm not making it any easier for myself.

Actually, I was getting bored with how things were going before, thinking about maybe making some kind of change myself. We have an early retirement program; I considered that option to set up some kind of business. But I decided I didn't want the risk, so I'm trying to see if I can get with the program here.

Larry's conflicted feelings reflect a common struggle between the urge to learn something new and the fear of leaving the proven path. The stage was already set for him to be reconsidering the role of work in his life, and the acquisition easily became the target for his midlife ambivalence. He did have some insight into his situation, not making the new management entirely the villain. I hoped he could use this to his advantage; if he did leave, it should be by his own choice, rather than feeling pushed out. To Larry's credit, he was giving the contemplated move the time and consideration it deserved.

While you're carefully weighing the pros and cons in your own case, keep in mind that you can only do so much—the rightness of any decision is never guaranteed. At some point you may need to make a leap and count on its momentum to take you where you want to be.

### HANGING IN

If you decide that leaving your job isn't the answer, the task then is to revitalize your present work. Usually this calls for recapturing some of your earlier enthusiasm for it, the challenge and the learning. Perhaps reeducation is the answer, or a lateral transfer that requires new skills. Or maybe there's a different way to do the same old thing. A new approach that involves some risk can bring new excitement to your work.

Begin by looking at what you could do to change the existing situation. What causes of stress could you eliminate? Talking frankly with supervisors and coworkers can be very fruitful. It takes some courage to admit to being unhappy at work, but it usually comes as no surprise to those working around you.

Be realistic about what you do and don't have control over. If you and a boss or coworker just don't get along, there are ways to make living with the situation easier, but hoping the irritation will magically go away won't help. If a job requires tight coordination within a large group of people, you may not be able to streamline it down to one or two contacts, but there probably are skills and technologies available to make the task more efficient and less burdensome.

When considering what would help you feel more satisfied with your job, remember the basic human needs that work should satisfy. One of these is a sense of connection to others; perhaps focusing on teamwork and the success of the team can revitalize your work. Ego needs such as pride in your performance shouldn't be overlooked: doing a terrific job within the limits of your ability is a worthy goal.

Perhaps most important to acknowledge is the existential need for meaning. If your work expresses something heartfelt in you, the nature of the work hardly matters. You are the ultimate judge here, and how your work feels to you is all that counts.

## SABBATICALS

There has been a fair amount of press coverage on the increasingly accepted phenomenon of companies granting extended paid or unpaid leaves to business executives and professionals. Sabbatical programs are part of corporate policy at IBM, Apple, Time-Warner, and several large legal firms.

The purpose for taking the time off varies, but, as a June 1990 *New York Times* article points out, it is rarely simple leisure. Some use the time to explore a long-cherished interest, like a law partner who took a six-month sabbatical to learn Bach's violin sonatas. Some use it as a testing ground for a major life change they are contemplating, like an attorney who undertook rabbinical studies with the intent of abandoning his law practice. (He eventually went back to his firm, but with a changed sense of identity.) Others want the opportunity to renew ties with their families through travel, or, like the executive who went off to teach corporate finance at a business school, to "put something back into the system that had given so much to me."

Apparently, this practice rewards not just the people who take sabbaticals, but also their employers, who anticipate a more energized level of performance when the employee returns. Six months or more of paid leave is still a privilege restricted to relatively few high achievers—but many more people can work out ways of arranging to take extended leaves through working part time, relying on a spouse's income, or other creative solutions.

The underlying purpose of any such extended break from one's working routine is an investigation of identity—a way to find out who you are apart from the structure of what you do. As Apple CEO John Sculley, who spent nine months on the coast of Maine studying photography, designing a barn, and puttering around with a boat, expressed it, "Too many people treat CEOs as some kind of exalted, omnipotent leader. The real danger is that you start believing that stuff. In Maine, people at the wharf treated me like any other summer resident who couldn't dock his motorboat correctly."

## CHANGING JOBS OR CAREERS

Let's assume that you've done your best to improve and revitalize your work situation, that you've searched your soul and accepted your flaws—but you're still unhappy at work. Then it may be time to leave. If you've decided that a change is in order, what comes next? Well, it depends on the reasons for the change and how profound the change needs to be.

There are basically three levels of movement to consider. The first is when you are basically happy with the kind of work you do but unhappy about where you're doing it. This suggests finding a similar job in better circumstances, as it does for the two women below.

One, a children's book editor, had been passed over for a promotion to department head, which it was widely believed she deserved. In her case, ego needs dictated accepting an offer from another company, which offered her a slightly higher salary but, more importantly, a psychological clean slate free of resentment. The other woman is a geologist with a large engineering firm, who felt that its administration was unusually insensitive to its employees' needs. Similar positions existed at other firms, so her goal of finding a more nurturing environment held little downside risk.

This kind of career fine-tuning is more common early in one's working life and, therefore, calls for careful consideration in midlife. One might be breaking emotional bonds of a long-held job, or perhaps giving up seniority-based benefits. But the corporate world of today encourages mobility, and the midlifer needs to evaluate whether his loyalty to a job and company is valued.

The second level of change involves moving from one kind of work to a different, but related, kind in the same industry or profession. My friend Marty, a computer consultant, came to this point after running through five jobs in two years. It generally took about three months for the new situation to lose its charm, and as the first symptom he would begin referring to his boss as "that (expletive) idiot."

After job number five began to go bad, we had a long talk, out of which grew the understanding that he was simply no longer willing to take direction from an authority figure. He was frustrated by not being in charge, and any reminder of this was enough to provoke his anger. This insight eventually gave him the necessary push to risk starting his own consulting firm.

The third type of change is more thoroughgoing and difficult: seeking out an entirely new career. We can scarcely do justice to all the factors involved in such a complex transition, and suggest taking advantage of the resources that exist specifically for this purpose: career-changing manuals, counselors, and organizations, some of which specialize in midcareer transitions.

Such counseling and tests are good at measuring aptitude and matching abilities with appropriate industries. They cannot, however, tell you where your hidden passion lies, or measure the degree of your commitment to change. You can only evaluate this yourself, and doing so is vitally important, because the stress of changing careers at midlife can tax even the most motivated person. To overcome the hurdles you'll need desire, support, resourcefulness, and luck. It's critical, too, to take stock of both your life situation as a whole and of the cumulative impact of change on many fronts. Will your health, finances, family life, and friendships all bear the strain of a major career change?

We'll focus on how to locate your passion in the next chapter, but one source of clues is to look back through your life for interests that have remained strong and sustaining, something that has evolved over time.

If you decide a career change is the right move for you, expect it to take time and a great deal of effort. What's the payoff? Think of the many sides to your personality, and how many of them find expression through your work. Is there a musician or an artist in you who can't see the light because you're crunching numbers all day? Is there an athlete who doesn't get to feel the joy of physical movement because you're confined to an office? Is there a caring person who is adept at working with others, but is stuck in a job that is isolating?

These are just a few examples; the idea is that visualizing the destination can help motivate the journey.

## THE ENTREPRENEURIAL OPTION

In 1989 there were more than 40,000 businesses started on the Pacific Coast alone. We have no figures at hand to tell how many of these entrepreneurs are people in midlife, but they must account for a substantial percentage. The current business climate encourages entrepreneurism, with staff cuts dictating more work for outside contractors. Beyond that, being in business for oneself is synergistic with midlife needs. The urge to try something new, to stretch one's capacities, to achieve more control over one's destiny, to seek fulfillment and the freedom from corporate schedules—the vision of these rewards leads many midlifers to strike out on their own.

Starting a business isn't quite as simple as finding something to market and having business cards printed. It may be the most difficult challenge many will ever face—financially, logistically, and emotionally. At worst, entrepreneurial endeavors can be lonely, scary, and ultimately unsuccessful. The entrepreneur often works in a vacuum with only his instincts to trust. It can be a long time between meals, and deferred gratification is hardly filling. The emotional rollercoaster is exhausting; exhilarating highs followed closely by stomach-wrenching lows. One's belief in oneself is tested over and over. The rewards can be great, however: the thrill of personal accomplishment, freedom from the whims of daddy megacorp, and a sense of control that no other working option offers.

Would-be entrepreneurs are often preoccupied with the concrete challenges—who, what, how, and where. They may neglect to do their emotional groundwork, to find out what it takes not just to start but to sustain a business. Good entrepreneurs ideally have a strong sense of self-esteem and need to achieve. They love to solve problems and can live with frustration and ambiguity. They should also have strong people skills, communicate well (and forcefully if necessary), and be good at evaluating and taking risks. This doesn't mean gambling on the longshot, but finding risks that offer a reasonable chance of success. It takes a keen eye to maximize payoff while minimizing exposure. Finally, the good entrepreneur knows when to listen to his gut and how to integrate instinct with what the *experts* say.

These are just some of the coping skills the successful entrepreneur will need. You will also need a support system that's as sturdy as steel; family and friends will feel the strain and may be called on to make sacrifices. On the other hand, the agenda you set for yourself can be more flexible than one imposed by an employer, and the entrepreneur can creatively balance business and family needs with other avocations and goals, such as travel and recreation. For some people, it's an ideal way of working out the midcareer challenge.

## *Welcome Back: Women Reentering the Workforce*

Baby boom women are natural candidates for reentry, because they became adults in an atmosphere that emphasized meaningful work and social responsibility. Sitting on the sidelines after the kids are gone or have become more independent usually isn't seen as a viable option. Such women will also benefit from the increasing need for trained workers resulting from the birth dearth.

Reentry won't necessarily be easy, however. Many women find that they face sex or age discrimination, limited job options, and reduced compensation; financially, they may scarcely be better off or even worse off than when they left the workforce. They also must deal with the resentment of men who fear competition, or perceive them as lightweights or dilettantes, and corporate environments that can be unaccommodating of their needs. Another psychological challenge is that a woman's reentry position may be lower than the level she achieved before leaving, amounting to a kind of dues she must pay. In midlife, this can feel like a terrible burden.

Reentering women usually have to deal not only with the job situation but with family resentments and her own sense of guilt about not being available to their families. Joan had been a magazine editor and had left her job at around age thirty to stay home with her son. When he was a junior in high school, she decided to resume her career. Both her husband and son were very resistant at first. "Mike became so threatened by my need to work outside the family that he started having an affair. We really had a rough time, but eventually he came around. I think my enthusiasm must have been contagious sooner or later—being back in a magazine office reminded me of when I'd been a young editor starting out, before I was married, and allowed me to feel a kind of continuity with the person I had been then."

To prepare for reentry, women might consider retraining: going back to school either to retool skills that have grown rusty or to learn new ones. Computer literacy is an especially useful skill for women who have been out of the workforce; instruction is readily available at community colleges and elsewhere.

Take advantage of whatever formal or informal networks are available to you. Talk to other women; find out what are your marketable skills and which you need to cultivate; follow one contact to others. The best situations are often unadvertised because they are made known by word of mouth and filled before they become public knowledge.

## Crossing the Bridge

I still drive across the Golden Gate Bridge every day to my office, and there are still days when I ask myself what I'm doing it for. On one level, of course, I know: I have a wife and young child to take care of, and some rewarding but costly hobbies to feed. But although these are important, they're not the basic pull that keeps me motivated to work. If that were so, I'd probably still be comfortably ensconced in my secure, profitable, hospital-based practice. These days things aren't always so comfortable, but they are always interesting. I'm learning a lot, and discovering capabilities I didn't know I had.

How you respond to your midcareer challenge will be as uniquely personal as mine has been. The bottom line, though, is that midlife's demands for personal growth must be met somewhere in your life. If circumstances dictate staying in a job that doesn't provide much nourishment for your changing needs, you'll have to maintain it as well as possible and look elsewhere for satisfaction. Baby boomers, though, are more inclined to demand that their jobs meet the test of passion, and to make changes if they don't.

# 9

# The Fire That Lights The Way

## Finding
## Your Passion

*If I could only remember that the days were not
bricks to be laid row on row, to be built into a solid
house, where one might dwell in safety and peace,
but only food for the fires of the heart.*
EDMUND WILSON

If you think of people known to be extraordinarily energetic
and productive in later life—Picasso, Vladimir Horowitz,
philanthropist Armand Hammer, Mother Theresa, scholar
and educator Joseph Campbell, Margaret Mead, actress Jessica Tandy—what do they have in common? I think it is the
quality of passion that they bring to their lives and endeavors.
And we need not look to the glitteringly accomplished for
proof of its power; each of us knows people whose lives are
given shape and meaning by something they are strongly
moved by and committed to.

At no time does passion play a more critical role than in the
later stages of midlife. As we emerge from the crucible of identity testing, the difficult period of shedding youthful illusions
and roles, where do we find the spark that lights our path into
the future, the glowing core around which our identity re-
forms? This is where the *pull* must kick in: the feeling of

being drawn strongly toward something is the surest way to move beyond our fear of the unknown.

For baby boomers, any postmidlife vision not grounded in passion has small chance of taking root. This generation has been motivated by passion from the start, a sense that it was not just accepted but necessary to care deeply about things like human rights, the war in Vietnam, the environment, sexual fulfillment, job satisfaction, and the relevance of institutions. It's no surprise that we are entering midlife feeling passionate about finding new avenues for self-expression, about not fading away into invisible old age. The dark side of this is that we also experience the depression and anxiety of midlife intensely, whereas our parents may have been more resigned to their losses. In any case, the baby boom seems predestined by its history to experience midlife with passion.

## More Than a Feeling

What exactly do we mean by passion? The Merriam-Webster dictionary defines it as "strong feeling," but that phrase seems inadequate to capture its essence. It's easier to describe what it does—to energize, motivate, serve as a guiding force around which to organize our lives. We recognize it by its absence; when passion is lacking, life seems dull and without spice.

It's probably easiest to identify passion by the role it plays in people's lives. My friend Jeff's passion is bicycle racing; I see it when we ride together, how it keeps him going long after I'm willing to quit. He has sacrificed promotions and advancement at work to keep time free for training, but he doesn't see these as sacrifices.

For another friend, Jennifer, it's music. Playing the piano invigorates her when she feels tired and empty. It frustrates her too—but in the way a love affair is sometimes frustrating. Her commitment is obvious: she gets up an hour early on weekdays to practice and sometimes works through the night composing, but rarely complains about being tired. She recently bought a piano with money she might have used for vacations, but like Jeff, there was never any doubt about her choice.

It has been said that anxiety is widespread today because of the plethora of choices we face, but passion acts like a filter, distilling what we most want and removing the anxiety-provoking excess of choices. Passion makes people feel powerful and directed, committed, in control, challenged, alive, and effective. The feedback of these positive feelings is what keeps us devoted to the activity or effort that provides them, and is strong enough to outweigh any sacrifices involved.

The strength of a passion varies, of course; it can be an all-consuming force in our lives, as for many creative artists, or a more limited source of satisfaction. Some passions last a lifetime, but it's common for them to change, or at least evolve, over time. My friend Stewart, for example, was dedicated to sports car racing in his twenties and thirties, but about five years ago his interest started to shift from racing to collecting and trading in vintage cars. His love for classic automobiles has only changed in the way it is manifested.

Midlife is a predictable time for passions to change, and this can be threatening, especially if an interest fades before something else has emerged to replace it. We may reflexively continue a certain kind of behavior after it has stopped being gratifying, just because it provides structure. But it's natural and necessary to reexamine and relocate our passions in midlife, since they follow from the changes in our values. The real test is whether they continue to challenge us, to let us grow. Challenge is the cutting edge that hones our sense of identity. If a long-held passion continues to challenge us, it will endure—if not, it will give ground to others.

Conceiving how we want our lives to unfold after midlife is like launching a mission. It is an endeavor that calls for both philosophy and practicality—daring flights of imagination and hard-nosed goal-setting. And the fuel of this mission is passion. The solutions we seek at this stage aren't just temporary first-aid from the stresses of transition; they are major choices—in careers and relationships and pursuits—that will ensure our continued growth. These decisions are lent urgency by the time-consciousness of midlife: how many more chances will we have to make them?

To make the second half of life as rewarding as it can be, the groundwork must be laid in midlife. This is true on the physical level—taking care of ourselves now makes a healthy old age more likely—and the same holds for psychic rewards. A passionate interest that is worthy of your valuable time in and after midlife takes time to develop and blossom. As Gail Sheehy points out in *Passages,* "there are no golden years if there has been no anticipation in midlife of the need to cultivate parallel interests. A man retired at 65 doesn't suddenly pick up a camera and revive himself with a second career."

## Finding Your Passion—Where to Begin?

When we were younger, we used to discover what we cared about from external sources: parents, teachers, political activitsts, the media, our peers. Some of these passions stuck, some didn't. By the time we reach fortysomething, we are usually better equipped to discover within ourselves what moves us most deeply. Our judgments are based more on experience and less on youthful assumptions. We need to bring all this accumulated self-knowledge to bear on finding where our passion lies at midlife.

If past experience is one major tool for uncovering passion, another is dreams of the future. This is where the role of myth becomes important. In an article in *Psychology Today,* Sam Keen writes:

Myth is the cultural DNA, the software, the unconscious information, the program that governs the way we see "reality" and behave. . . We need to reinvent ourselves continually, weaving new themes into our life narratives, remembering our past, revising our future, reauthorizing the myth by which we live.

To envision the future we must reenter the realm of myth, resurrecting our hero or heroine. Some aspects of our myth are inherited from our families: "My family never encouraged us to take risks. That's why I've always played it safe in making choices." Or: "I guess I'm destined to suffer in silence. That's the way I see it played out. I'll be the good soldier, put in my years, keep my mouth shut, and retire quietly." Myths that come from cultural stereotypes are potent too, such as "Dave is a typical male, always pushing, closed off, a real brute." Or, as a client described herself: "I'm a typical Asian woman. I've never felt comfortable being assertive."

We have to acknowledge how much of these inherited myths we have permanently internalized, but by midlife we are free to use mythmaking more creatively. The primary function of myth at this time is to free us from the narrow confines of our thinking and let us see ourselves as larger-than-life figures in a story. As in classical mythology, objective reality needs to be subservient to our feelings about what is significant. We should pay attention to mysterious signs and portents, try to identify the large themes and key turning points.

Dreams are very important: Just as they hold the key to the hero's quest in many myths, they are the raw material of our emerging mission. The reborn hero of midlife takes his or her cue from dreams and visions that come to the surface around this time. As we saw in Chapter 4, these are expressions of parts of our identity that have been denied or unrealized, and now need to be heard.

The reborn hero of midlife is rarely a total stranger. Many

people don't allow themselves to follow where their passion leads, fearing they will turn into someone they don't recognize, with dangerous or unpredictable impulses. More often, assuming you are reasonably self-aware, the new version of your hero or heroine should seem like a very old friend who has been out of touch for a long time.

This raises the issue of being realistic about your life situation. Some factors are beyond changing, and sometimes "following your bliss," as Joseph Campbell puts it, may have negative impact on others. Ignoring that we are connected to other people and institutions is a poor basis for healthy, sustainable growth.

If you see certain life circumstances as standing in the way of passion, but no way to change them, don't give up. Such a dilemma can force us to look elsewhere for relief, and the most creative midlife solutions are often found in wholly unexpected places. Feeling trapped in a work situation may be the commonest case: you want more than anything to chuck it and run, but responsibilities prohibit this. The answer often lies in finding an energy boost in some other area of life.

### DODGING THE OBSTACLES

"Find your passion/Make it happen," the popular song goes. Sounds simple, but changing even one piece of an established life structure—a new job, say, a move to a new location, or starting a new relationship—can be a tremendous effort. It's a mistake to underestimate the inertia that one needs to overcome in revamping a life structure at midlife. As we try to locate the dreams that will lead us onward, some familiar obstacles may get in our way.

*Denial* is the most basic of all roadblocks to change. It allows us to magically believe that no problem exists, even in the face of overwhelming evidence. Like a heavy blanket, it can smother our perceptions and feelings about our life situation. For example, the boredom and despair that can lead to a job change can be erased by denial as the moment of decision draws near. Denying what's wrong with a relationship can negate any attempts to imagine something better.

*Resistance* is a more sophisticated defense, in that one can acknowledge the problem and entertain solutions, but never act on them. The excuse may be as flimsy as cardboard, but is reinforced by the fear of the unknown.

A favorite tactic of someone involved in resistance is the *Yes, but* . . . game, which gives a nod to the suggested solution and immediately explains why it won't work. I once pointed out to an overworked executive that while his family life was his chief satisfaction, he worked seventy hours a week and spent much of his leisure time volunteering on a neighborhood committee. He responded, "Yes, but what if I took more time off and didn't know what to do with them?" When I reminded him that last year he and his daughter had gone camping and had a great time (and shared other interests as well), he came back with, "Yes, but what if I don't enjoy doing those things with her anymore?"

*Avoidance* occurs when we use a distraction to quell the urge for change. A woman I once worked with was released from her public relations job at a hospital at age forty-one, and came to see me after a year of procrastination about finding a new position. She was well qualified, bright, energetic, and reasonable about what she wanted. Each time she scheduled an interview, however, she would find some way to avoid it. Once she had a particularly good shot at a job that fulfilled many of her wishes—and canceled an interview at the last minute. The excuse was that she had an appointment for an estimate to get her carpet cleaned! This struck me as a cry for help, and when I confronted her about her avoidance of returning to work, she finally began talking about her anguish at being dropped from her former position. She hadn't truly assimilated that rejection, but the feelings came out only when she got close to having what she really wanted.

*Criticism* can be deadly to the pursuit of passion. People in midlife are often ridiculed, and the feelings and changes they must grapple with minimized. What you are going through may be dismissed as a *stage*, trivialized in the same way that childhood traumas often are. Underlying much of the criticism directed at midlifers is that what you want might seem threatening to other people. They react by labeling your experiments, your seeking, as foolish or destructive. Try to see such criticism for what it is—a projection of someone else's fear of change—and not let it deter you from your quest.

These obstacles to passion can appear at any time of life, but almost invariably arise at midlife. The closer you are to making a major change in your life, the louder will be the voices, internal or external, warning you of disaster and urging you to stay on the safe path. They may be come out as attempts to recapture feelings or situations appropriate to the past but now outgrown. They may be the voices of family, friends, or spouses who erect barriers to prevent you from acting on your impulses. It is your responsibility to sort out the useful warnings from those likely to keep you stuck.

### SOME TECHNIQUES FOR LOCATING PASSION

The luckiest people are those who seem to know where their passion lies. Perhaps what moves them hasn't changed significantly with the advent of midlife, or they have a conscious dream waiting in the wings and the resources to pursue it. For many of us, it's not so easy. Here are a few specific ways to do some prospecting for the precious commodity of passion.

*Pay attention to your dreams.* The driving force of midlife resolution comes from the unconscious. The conscious mind is good at framing problems, identifying feelings, and implementing solutions. But it needs inspiration from the unconscious; dreams can bring to light buried urges and point in unexpected directions. The problem for most people is recalling them in enough detail to be useful, so this is an excellent time to keep a dream notebook by the bed. It takes some practice and concentration to get the content down before it disappears, but even small clues can be important.

The dreams that reveal passion need not be those that come with sleep. Daydreams and fantasies are even more explicit guides, especially if they're of long standing. In moments of boredom or stress, do you envision yourself on a stage? Living in the mountains? Taking a kid to the museum? Coming home for lunch? Studying martial arts? Fantasies are often kept in an unrealized state by practical contingencies, but it may be time to get more creative with solutions. Even if you can't live out your daydreams as fully as you imagine them, some kind of approximation or surrogate may well be within reach.

*Keeping a journal* is another way to tap into the unconscious. This kind of journal is a little different than a diary; it's a way to set down your thoughts and feelings rather than a record of the day's events. You might choose to focus on one question each day, such as, Where have I found the greatest satisfactions in my life?, or What traits would I like to nurture in the second part of my life? Or it might be something more immediate, like, What would I do if I had a month off from work?

You can also use the journal to review your day's activities and, more specifically, your reactions to them: what felt good and what didn't—and why. Whatever you write about, let the writing be a free-association process. Try to be as uncritical as possible. Let your thoughts flow and follow them, not make them fit into any particular line of reasoning.

*Use ritual creatively.* By ritual I mean any repetitive activity, whether it be an exercise program, a daily walk, a religious service, or a hobby. All can serve the same purpose: to create a space where we can turn off the mind's mundane chatter and let our thoughts float, allows unconscious impulses to surface. Even commuting to work can function this way, and lower the stress of driving in traffic as a bonus. If you have a small tape recorder, you can use it as a mobile journal.

*Meditation and visualization exercises* can be very effective methods of getting in touch with deeply buried impulses. The following exercise is a fairly standard meditation technique that people use for different purposes.

Find a quiet place where you won't be disturbed and get into a comfortable position; loosen any clothing that binds. Let your eyes close slowly and focus on your breathing. Notice the sound of your breath and, with each exhalation, let the tension flow out of your muscles.

When you feel comfortably relaxed, imagine yourself in a soothing environment, perhaps on a beach or in the mountains. Bring all your senses into play, imagining the sights, sounds, smells, and tactile sensations of the place: the scent of pines or ocean, the sun on your skin. Make the scene as vivid as possible.

Now focus on a calming word or phrase and repeat it quietly each time you exhale, perhaps a word such as *relax* or a phrase like *floating lightly.* As you continue to relax, begin to follow the images your mind produces. You might imagine you're looking at a movie screen with no control over what you see; the images simply roll on. It might be scenes from your life, perhaps images that relate to future events. Make a mental note of any picture that you find especially interesting.

Many people find, when first attempting such exercises, that they become distracted by current problems and worries. Their frustration and distress that they're not "doing it right" shortcircuits the relaxation process still further. If you find your mind wandering back to your unpaid bills or that big meeting tomorrow, don't let it throw you. Gently leave that thought and try to focus on what you want to be thinking about.

After fifteen or twenty minutes, you can leave your meditation and let yourself come back to the here and now gradually. Count backwards from ten to one, and as you approach one, open your eyes slowly. Sit quietly for another minute or so, recalling some of the images you've seen. Don't try to analyze them yet, but record them in a notebook for review later on.

Don't expect to find your answers in the course of one exercise. The kind of feedback you're seeking comes from making ritual, meditation, or visualization a regular (preferably daily) part of your life, a form of training in which you conduct an ongoing dialogue with your unconscious. The medium, in a sense, is the message. Over time you'll begin to see a pattern to the images that come up, a repetition of certain themes. These are messages that warrant close attention. The follow-up work of recording and reviewing the material is important, as is remaining open and nonjudgmental.

*Observe other people,* especially those who seem to have found new rewards through some deliberate action taken in midlife. Your friend took a health-care job in Asia for a year, taking her young child along. Your colleague at work negotiated six months unpaid leave. Your neighbor quit her demanding advertising job to open her own antique store. Try to put subjective preconceptions aside and take the approach of an anthropologist looking at your own culture. You might imagine that you're from another planet, as a way to avoid comparing yourself with others. You're looking for a wide variety of input rather than trying to emulate someone else's mission.

*Talking about what you want* serves its usual purposes of articulating unspoken feelings, soliciting feedback and endorsement, with the usual caveat of being careful not to give outside feedback too much weight. Such conversations can be in the context of informational interviews about a prospective job or location change. They can involve getting reactions from people who know you very well and less well—what's called longitudinal versus cross-sectional feedback. Or you can do your talking in the more structured context of support groups or therapy.

*Try your hand at some creative art.* This can be a wonderful way to jump start your unconscious, and the arts are a unique avenue for emotional expression. Midlife is a great time to take up a musical instrument, or perhaps start to paint or draw or sculpt. Talent and technical skill are secondary to the act of expressing yourself in some nonlogical, right-brain mode. There's a certain boldness that comes with age and experience, and with doing something outside one's primary field.

*Structured classes in personal growth* are available in most communities. They require widely varying commitments of time and money, so do some research and choose carefully. A client told me about an interesting class that combines personal mythmaking with creative craft. The group meets weekly over a year and each member slowly constructs a human figure, a doll, that represents him- or herself. Various materials and techniques are used: for example, the feet are sculpted from clay and fired; the large organs woven in basketry or sewn. And the personal choices expressed in how each part is made are fertile ground for group discussion.

Ultimately, the process of finding your passion has less to do with technique and method than with attitude. No single endeavor can guide us unerringly to our individual path, but putting your heart into the search will eventually point the way. Simply taking the time to explore questions like, Where am I going, and who is going with me? has a directive quality. Follow where the path twists and beckons, rather than the shortcut you *think* will get you there quickest. I like to think of the old story about the man who is looking for his wallet under a streetlamp. A friend approaches and asks, "Where did you lose it?" He replies, "I lost it down the street, but the light is so much better here."

## Taking Action

*Just Do It.* These three words succinctly express the most helpful advice we can give about launching your mission. They are borrowed from the popular series of TV ads for a running shoe company depicting nonprofessional athletes competing fiercely. The message is: live life to the fullest, don't waste a day, use all your capabilities, and don't let fear hold you back.

Of course, there's more to getting your mission off the ground than the exhortation to *just do it,* but the truth is that action itself is empowering. Even if you don't feel totally committed to your new mission, the energy of setting it in motion can help convince you of its viability. If you're headed in the right direction, you'll feel it. Behavior that works is self-reinforcing.

Jenny is an example of someone who took the leap. At thirty-eight, she was recently married and had reached a plateau in her work. She was grappling with the decision to have children or to try for the fast track in her career in marketing. Her husband wanted children but she had never envisioned a way to do both.

> At a sales conference last spring, a speaker gave a presentation on marketing techniques. She had started her consulting business after spending fifteen years at a company. When I met her after the speech, she was so convincing and encouraging. It gave me the idea that I could move to a consulting position and structure my time to allow for a family.
>
> I had a lot of doubts about going out on my own. While I was agonizing, the company made the decision for me by announcing they were going to be moving their headquarters out of the city.
>
> So I just did it. I started small, working with a group of clients I had dealt with before. I was kind of amazed that people didn't question my qualifications. They just assumed I knew what I knew and gave me the benefit of the doubt. The first job scared me to death—but then I saw that I really had something to offer and the business started to take off.

Which comes first: the belief that a change is possible or the behavior that makes the change believable? Both are essential, but you can start with either. They are complementary forces, each stimulating and reinforcing the other. Without behavioral support, belief is impossible to sustain for long; by the same token, taking action without believing that things will work out reduces the chances of success. In Jenny's case, she did what turned out to be the right thing for her, and the confidence and commitment followed. She postponed the baby issue for a few years, but by the time she had her child, the business was running smoothly enough.

Commitment can be a scarce and precious commodity in

midlife. Our experience of hard knocks in life so far, and our growing awareness of limited time, can make any risk loom large. Sometimes breaking a commitment down into smaller components can render it less formidable. That is, if you can't commit yourself to a major, overarching life change, resolve to take some intermediate step that can lead you there.

Andrew, the contractor we met in the last chapter, found this a good way to proceed. He had gone to school in fine arts, moved into construction to support himself and his family, and eventually built a thriving general contracting business incorporating some design work. He came to realize that an architectural degree would give him more clout and allow him to design plans without a middleman, but he wasn't in a position to go back to school full-time. So he started out with classes at night, finding those with credit that could be applied toward a graduate degree, and with his practical background he was able to put together the necessary requirements at his own pace.

Many women reentering the workforce do well to take it a step at a time, too. A client of mine wanted to return to school for an advanced degree in social work after being a wife and mother for twelve years, but was daunted by the two to three-year commitment. She expressed many doubts about whether she still had the skills to study, her ability to follow through, whether it was the right move, whether she would even like it. When I asked her to think about what level of commitment she could be comfortable with, she realized she could free up the time to take a few classes, and work up to more if she chose.

There's no point in beating yourself up if you can't make the commitment to a major change all at once. That's a good way to get stuck and discouraged. Take on what you can, and start the ball rolling. The experience of following through on even a small commitment can snowball.

What it comes down to, though, is the imperative to do it. I sometimes ask my clients what they would do if they had only a short time to live, say, two years. The answers vary—some talk about travel, others about projects they'd like to finish, or about leaving some kind of legacy—but no one has any trouble considering the question seriously. Even if we're talking about forty years rather than two, the awareness of limited time resonates with people in midlife. We can harness the energy released by this awareness, use it to illuminate what matters most to us, and then take the first steps in that direction.

## RESOURCE MANAGEMENT

Since it's important that your first step be a successful one, don't neglect to consider the resources you'll need: financial support, social support, logistical support, and so on. Try to predict where you may need extra help. In some areas you'll probably have abundant support; in others you'll need to be more creative. Support in one area can compensate to some extent for lack of resources in others.

Jeff was a recently divorced father, aged forty-five. At first, the shock of his wife's leaving and the logistical demands of caring for his young daughter were nearly overwhelming. He lived from day to day, almost hour to hour, feeling that he was always in crisis management.

> I'd be at work and get a call from school saying Karen was sick and I had to pick her up. I really questioned whether I could maintain custody of her, if it was the right thing to do. But I knew deep down that she was the most important thing to me. That hadn't always been true, but as I went through the divorce, it became more clear.

The bottom line for Jeff was to make it work somehow. His family provided good support; his sister came to stay with them for a month and help them get organized. Jeff worked out a deal with a neighbor to share daycare, paying a larger portion since the neighbor was on a tight budget. In return, the neighbor handled more of the logistics, made sure things went smoothly.

> At this point it seems to be working OK—who knows what it will look like in six months? I do know that Karen and I have formed a terrific relationship. My values have changed, and how I relate to Karen is just the tip of the iceberg. People at work tell me they see a difference too—which is funny, because work is actually less important to me now. At any rate, what's happened with me and Karen seems to have taken some of the edge off me at work.

Jeff's mission found him, in a sense, rather than the other way around. Sometimes the path where our passion lies can be right in front of us without our being aware of it until we stumble on it. But the lesson of Jeff's experience applies in any case. Knowing that you have resources to call upon can make the commitment to change easier. And using those resources to good effect in one area can have unexpected benefits in another; in Jeff's case, at his job.

## SETTING GOALS

Specific goals are the nuts and bolts of launching your mission. Once you have a clear idea of what you want, you need to set goals that will enable you to achieve it. The best insights, the most inspiring vision, will remain forever distant if no milestones mark your progress.

Goals are desired objectives that can be attained through a certain course of action. They may be internal changes that affect how we see ourselves and the world, or external changes in our life structure: what we do, where, and with whom we do it.

It's important to distinguish between different kinds of goals. Abstract goals, such as, I want to be a better person, are fine for inspiration but useless in developing a specific plan. They must be translated into something concrete; for example, What might a good person do? The more specific and measurable a goal is, the more effectively it can guide our behavior. A handy test is to ask yourself: if someone were following you, would he be able to observe your accomplishment of a goal?

It's tempting to keep goals nonspecific, but that's a cop-out. In my work with baby boomers in midlife, this is one of the biggest stumbling blocks to progress. I'm not sure why, but it may have to do with the safety of abstractions. Some remain in this Never-Never Land of unachievable goals; the more fortunate move on.

One way to approach goal-setting is in stages. At the first level, goals can be vague and diffuse; later they are honed down. If you set a goal that can't be made more concrete, ask yourself why. If it's because you don't want to put yourself to the test of measurement, or because there is no relevant measure, the goal need not necessarily be scrapped but should be examined closely. Such a goal is highly unlikely to motivate behavior unless you take it to a level where action is possible.

Any goal should have a time estimate pegged to its accomplishment. Consider the various goals described to me by Les, a forty-one-year-old systems analyst.

> By this time next year, I want to be out of my current work situation, no longer working for Company X. This may involve a move the East Coast, maybe not, but whatever it takes, I want to make it happen.
>
> I know I have to get moving on it, talk to some head-hunters and revive the networks I had earlier. I've got some resistance to doing that. I hate to admit I'm looking for a new position; it always gets back to the company you work for. But it's a chance I have to take.

I've got a call in to a buddy at a rival company. He went through the same thing about three months ago, so he should know the state of the business. I'll try to get some recommendations from him about who else to call—maybe someone who helped him.

Les describes three kinds of goals, defined by their time requirement.

*The long-range goal* is to be in a new work situation in a year. Often, long-range goals can be even more distant: some people work on five- and even ten-year plans. I feel, though, that plans made so far in advance are increasingly unrealistic is a world that reinvents itself every few years. Besides, unless you are highly disciplined, goals projected for more than a year invite fuzzy thinking and procrastination. Setting the deadline so far off weakens the imperative to get moving. One year is a pretty good rule of thumb for a long-range goal, and has symbolic meaning for most people. In some circumstances, however, a year may be too long; six months or even three might be more appropriate.

*Intermediate goals* are stepping stones to the long-range goal. In Les's story, cultivating his network and contacting headhunters were intermediate goals; accomplishing them would help bring about his long-range goal of changing his job. Achieving an intermediate goal provides a sort of way station along the path, a place where we can rest a bit, savor the achievement, and reconnoiter before moving on. Any long-range goal big enough to change your life structure will also tax your motivation, and success in reaching intermediate goals helps to sustain motivation over the long haul.

*Short-range goals* are the very first steps—the things we plan to do this week, today, or this morning, depending on urgency and opportunity. For Les, making that phone call to his buddy was a short-range goal aimed at alerting and widening his network. Such goals can be thought of as *instrumental behavior,* the means toward an end. Sometimes they seem small and distant from the final goal, but even if it's hard to see the connection, they are crucial links in the chain. Keeping your final goal in mind can help you see how the links connect.

This kind of planning—identifying goals and then working backward to determine specific behaviors—is sometimes criticized as lacking creativity and spontaneity. But being methodical in your planning need not rule out the creative leaps that characterize successful launches. Just the opposite is true: a good, solid plan frees the mind for creative improvisation. The action you take in pursuing short-range and intermediate goals is a process of trial and error, providing information, stimulation, and most important, feedback on what works and what doesn't. Movement towards a goal rarely proceeds in a straight line; creativity lies in the twists and turns.

Sometimes the creativity lies in being alert and responsive to opportunities. Molly had been wanting to leave the giant law firm she worked for to set up her own practice. In the course of her personal discovery process, she met another attorney who lived in the same suburban area and was also ready for a change. In talking with Virginia, Molly came to realize the potential advantages of working outside the city, and the two eventually set up shop together.

### REINFORCEMENT

In working with Les, I encouraged him to think about giving himself rewards for attaining his short- and mid-range goals. While the big payoff may lie down the road, baby boomers have never gone in much for deferred gratification, and I believe that periodic rewards are necessary to sustain motivation while you're working toward a larger goal.

Reinforcement can take many forms and need not be elaborate. Les rewarded himself with occasional weekends out of town and a scheduled break during the workday. Another client would set a daily goal of making a certain number of networking calls, and treat herself to a walk by the ocean after getting them done. The number changed from day to day depending on her energy level and how many leads she had—there's no need to be rigid—but she always had something to look forward to at the end of her quota. The carrot on the stick is effective for most people.

## CONTINGENCIES AND MIDCOURSE CORRECTIONS

In my work with people in midlife, I've rarely seen someone end up exactly where they thought they were headed at the beginning of the transition. Or if they did, it was by a much more circuitous route than they could have imagined. I compare what usually happens after we launch our mission to a rocket launched toward the moon: it doesn't head for its goal in an unwavering line but must take readings and make corrections throughout its trajectory.

We too must allow for midcourse adjustments, accepting that we cannot plan for all contingencies. Your family situation may change unexpectedly; a work opportunity may arise; a new avocation might become a dominating passion; or a path you've committed to exploring could turn out to be a dead end. Your long-range goal may require slight revision or drastic revamping as a result.

A client, Laura, was compelled by circumstances to make a major adjustment. She had been working as a stockbroker until age thirty-nine, and had always loved it. Even when it seemed like drudgery or when burnout threatened, it never entirely lost its thrill for her. In stressful times, she would remind herself that she didn't have to sell stocks forever, and she had formulated a plan that would allow her to get out before she was fifty, with a comfortable cushion to see her through the transition.

> Then I had my car accident and major back surgery. I was out of work for a year, and the hospitalization and rehab used up a lot of my resources. I would get depressed thinking how hard I'd have to work to make up the lost ground, and I started to dread going back.
>
> I went to this exercise studio regularly as part of my rehab, and it became like a second home to me. When I had the chance to buy it I was frightened at first. Something inside me was saying, "Yes, yes!" but it was so different than anything I'd done before. But it felt so good to be excited about something, and a little research showed it was a good investment. I pulled every string I could find to scrape up the capital, and it's been everything I could have asked for. I really look forward to going to work—and I've recruited some of my former fellow traders as customers!

The catalyst for Laura's career change was more dramatic than most, but the basic motivation was the same (she could just as easily have gone back to the brokerage house). To extremely goal-driven people, the need to change course may seem like failure, but that's far from true. Keep in mind that we change simply by virtue of participating in midlife transition. What we want as we emerge from the transition process will almost certainly be different from what we wanted upon entering it. It's crucial to accept and accommodate those changes to avoid discouragement and demotivation.

### A QUESTION OF BALANCE

We have mentioned balance as one of the guiding principles of midlife, and it's certainly critical here in the later stages. We began this chapter on the lofty plane of myths and heroes, and ended up closer to the ground, discussing goal-setting, motivation, and reinforcement. There's no incompatibility; like right and left-brain capabilities, they must work in tandem: the mythic and the practical, the abstract and the concrete. The people in midlife who come to see me tend to be over-balanced to one side or the other: all vision and no plan, or detail-obsessed and lacking a larger sense of mission. That's probably why they feel stuck and in need of therapy. However, the two modes can alternate, vision and planning taking the dominant role in turn. But keep in mind that you need both to get where you want to go.

# The Far Shore

## Life After Midlife

*The future becomes the present. The present becomes the past.*
*And the past becomes eternal regret, if you don't plan for it.*
TENNESSEE WILLIAMS

The question I hear most often in my work with midlifers has to be, Is this ever going to end? Will I ever have any stability in my life again? The answer is yes, of course. Sooner or later, like Jonah emerging from the dark belly of the whale, you come through the stormy sea of midlife and find yourself on its other shore. Since life doesn't work like a one-hour TV drama, there is no clearly defined boundary you will cross. The realization probably won't come like a bolt from the blue, as in, Hey, I'm not going through midlife anymore! More probably, you'll become aware of a gradual subsidence of turmoil and change, and that you've more or less settled into a new—or slightly revised—life structure.

What does it look like on the other side of midlife? Well, it's almost certainly going to be quieter than the process of transition, but beyond that lies a lot of variation. The quality of midlife resolution is determined largely by the work you have, or haven't, done in the transition. If you do no more than just hang on, the force of transition will move you through it, push you along as surely as a wave washes you toward shore. Knowing this is often enough to salve the anxiety that comes from losing one's bearings.

But simply riding out the storm and hoping you land somewhere close to where you started is far from the most effective kind of transition management. You may put on a new life structure, but it probably won't be a very good fit, since you haven't resolved the problems that made the old one uncomfortable. Or, if some have been resolved by circumstances, you're left with the feeling of having no control.

A client of mine, Joe, who was a Vietnam veteran, talked about the danger of trying to get through a crisis unscathed and unchanged:

> In Vietnam we all thought we could just do our time, survive, whatever it took, and then just come back and resume our lives. But what happened over there was more than lost time. The experience changed you; there was no way you could come back and pick up the pieces as if nothing were different.

Midlife isn't exactly comparable to combat, of course, but Joe pointed out this similarity to me.

> For the last couple of years, I've been waiting for my life to regain some sense of reality, some normality. As though it could go back to being what it was. But two years down the road, I've got to admit that the end of my transition doesn't look much like I thought it would.

If you pay attention to the process, on the other hand, if you invest yourself in it and do the necessary work at each stage, practice the master skills and get serious about seeking your mission, then your postmidlife resolution represents a real step up the growth ladder and brings tremendous rewards.

## *What If It Doesn't Happen?*

We don't want to dwell on the negative at this point, but it's vital to realize that failure to deal with the issues raised in mid-life can have far-reaching consequences. At best, it means expending a lot of energy on damage control that could be better used elsewhere; at worst it can poison the next stage of life and leave one stuck in a negative mindset that becomes ever harder to break out of.

David, who started seeing me at age fifty-two, was one of my most difficult clients. Ten years ago he'd been a successful attorney with a family; now he was divorced, broke, and functioning only marginally in his profession. Our meetings had a stuck quality, which was no surprise: David was stuck in every sense of the word, and it took a long time to get any real communication going. At first he would listen to me only when I was willing to accept his perspective on the world.

> I've been had by everybody—my wife, my partners, my kids. Nobody has appreciated me or the work I've done. All people care about is what you can do for them. I don't know why I even try anymore—nothing good ever comes my way. I feel like the world is passing me by, and there's nothing I can do to get back on the merry-go-round.

David was a bright guy whose professional history indicated that he had a lot of talent. But he fiercely resisted my attempts to get him to look at his own role in what had happened to him. I avoided a crisis by not confronting him, and things started to open up when David hit bottom. It all happened in one week: he was censured by the state bar for mismanaging a case; he lost a custody battle for his children; and he was cited for contempt for refusing to cooperate in the hearing. With his career and his support system both in shambles, David was finally forced to consider his situation more objectively.

I don't know how things got so bad. Well, actually, I guess I
have to admit that I've been pushing to see how bad it could
get. It was like I wanted to push it to the point where someone had to stop me. And I wanted vindication that life
wasn't fair. I probably could have cooperated along the way
and prevented some of this. But I've been so furious, and
making things worse seemed like the only way to fight back.

His insights focused on his marriage, and the way its troubles were projected onto his work.

My wife kept insisting that things weren't working between
us. I actually felt the same but never admitted it to her; I was
pretty threatened by her taking the lead. I guess it goes way
back to my need to be in control. It seemed like making concessions was giving up control.

When she said she wanted a separation, it was like something snapped. I stopped taking care of business at work. I
was tired of the whole law industry, anyway; I used to fan-
tasize about taking off and never coming back. I think I
took out my anger toward my wife out on some of my
clients.

David is a classic example of how long-standing personality
traits influence our perspective on current situations. His fear
of change combined with his need for control caused him to
engage in a huge amount of resistance and denial that were ultimately self-defeating. As he started to lose most of what mattered to him, he was unable to respond except to make things
worse, cutting off his nose to spite his face.

Eventually, David put some of the pieces back together, but
the trauma he had experienced damaged him profoundly. If
you have a hard time dealing with change at forty and don't
work through this, it's not likely to get any easier at fifty or
sixty. An unsuccessful resolution to midlife transition is really
the lack of resolution; its legacies are the same problems that

often come up during the transition itself. Let's review them and see what happens if they are left unattended to. This should encourage you to pay attention to warning signs early.

## UNWELCOME LEGACIES:
## QUALITIES OF AN UNSUCCESSFUL RESOLUTION

*Alienation.* People who fail to resolve midlife issues feel left behind. They move farther and farther away from their cohorts who have come to terms with transition. They feel old instead of vital, used up instead of useful. It becomes a vicious circle: feeling alienated keeps them from getting the support they need, which makes them feel even more alienated.

*Anxiety and depression.* The prevailing discomforts of passage increase instead of abating, as they should. One's awareness of time running out becomes more acute, as do the urge for resolution and intolerance of negative emotions. In other words, one's emotional state gets worse and one's tolerance for it is compromised. For some, increased anxiety and/or depression are masked by outward apathy. What they put out, unfortunately, is matched by what they get back from others.

*Resistance, denial, and despair.* The person who hasn't resolved midlife acts out by refusing or being unable to move on with life. The defense of avoidance becomes ever more seductive. It's like watching a man walking down railroad tracks, knowing eventually a train will come along. The stuck person engages in lots of self-defeating behavior; his senses are dulled by the weight of helplessness and hopelessness. The best warnings are met with passive (and sometimes active) resistance.

*Distortion of time perspective.* Nostalgia Buffs tend to get lost in longing for more comfortable times, others in vague dreams of a better future. Such time warps are different from the constructive use of memories and visions, in that they are not grounded in reality or linked to specific goals. Because the wishful time zone doesn't apply to the present situation, it inspires frustration more than comfort. There's nothing wrong with the gentle nostalgia some people feel for times past, as long as they've made peace with the present.

*Detachment and defensiveness.* This is the negative flip side of midlife's interiority, the necessary work of looking inward. A person like David, who comes to see himself as a victim of life's slings and arrows, uses detachment as a defense, building walls between himself and others to avoid closeness. Underlying his withdrawal are cynicism and skepticism about the world and other people's motives. Like all defenses, this means of protecting oneself is ultimately more dangerous than the original threat.

*Impotence and insecurity.* Failure to resolve midlife issues can lead to a belief that one is fundamentally flawed and helpless to change it. People in this fix suffer from lowered aspirations and practice avoidance to keep their sense of impotence at bay. Their behavior is largely ruled by defenses designed to protect their fragile egos.

It's easy to recognize someone who hasn't adequately resolved the important issues of his or her midlife transition. They are people who seem to be fighting the passage of time, not with intelligence and resourcefulness but with brute force; people past fifty who are still trying new identities on a weekly basis, or are still trying to relive their youth in inappropriate ways; people who continue to waste their energies in self-defeating behaviors. Or worst of all, people who seem to have simply accepted defeat and given up.

Remember the basic tenets of stage theory: each transition has its particular tasks to accomplish, and failure to resolve the issues of any stage will come back to haunt the next life structure. Since midlife is the single most important transition of adult life, the price of an unsuccessful resolution will be commensurately high—as will the payoff of a successful one, as we're about to see.

## What Does a Successful Resolution Feel Like?

With more detail in the following sections, we might describe it as a feeling of *energized calm*. There is a renewed sense of purpose and meaning to life, an acceptance of oneself and circumstances that earlier we wasted energy in fighting. Many people talk about their lives seeming less effortful, almost a sense of floating.

Perhaps the most fundamental quality of a well-resolved life after midlife can be summed up in a paradox: we feel at the same time more independent of others and more connected to them. Midlife brings us to point in the lifelong process of individuation where we recognize how profoundly alone we are in the world, how little the judgments and opinions of others matter in comparison to our inner sense of who we are and how we're doing. Once we've absorbed the impact of this realization, however—and it can be scary enough to send people into full retreat from transition—it can remove some of the barriers that kept us apart from others.

A successful resolution need not be one that turns your entire life upside-down. Major change can be limited to one area of life, or subtle adjustments in different areas may make the whole system hum. A client named Jean has such a success story.

Midlife crept up on Jean. She was too busy to notice it, running a successful retail enterprise on one of San Francisco's most fashionable streets. Merchandising was her forte, but her rent was soaring and her profit margin shrinking. So she did what she had always done in a crisis: bore down harder, worked longer hours, cut back on expenses.

I was going through all the motions, and it seemed like such a chore. One day, while going over some promotion ideas with a consultant I'd hired, it hit me in the face: I didn't want to do this anymore. I finally understood why it had become such an effort to stay afloat—my heart just wasn't in it any longer. I'd ignored the signs and assumed I felt flat because I was tired from the long hours. The truth was, I was depressed. Maybe whatever had fueled my desire to succeed with the store was just used up; maybe I had proved myself to my family, my friends, the world. Whatever—the drive was gone.

Jean's despondency soon lifted in a burst of energy as she held a going-out-of-business sale, sold her lease, and tied up her loose ends in less than three months.

Once the store was gone, real fear set in: What do I do next? Doing nothing seemed unthinkable, so I had to get busy. I must have gone through six different life plans in the next six months. Each seemed like the right move, but when the novelty faded I'd be off in a totally new direction. I just followed whatever impulse came by. One day I even found myself entertaining the idea of opening another store, thinking maybe it was just the location, or the merchandise, that was wrong before. That's when the alarm went off, and I had to face what I was doing.

Like many midlifers, Jean felt the seduction of the familiar in times of pressure, even though she knew it was an empty well. It may take some people one or two trips back to the well to convince them it won't quench their thirst, but if they're paying attention, the message sinks in eventually. Jean's phase of grasping at impulses reflects that other common midlife urge: to escape. But she was smart enough not to confuse escapist illusions with substantive evolution.

After the plan-of-the-month phase, I was exhausted. But I must have gotten something out of my system, because I started to be more comfortable with not knowing where I was headed. I could slow down and just accept whatever came next. What a relief!

Between the siren song of old solutions and the lure of fantasy escapes, Jean found some solid new ground to break. When we last spoke, she was working as a manufacturer's representative and loving it. The flexibility and mobility were welcome after being tied down to her store, and she could use her merchandising savvy effectively. She didn't know if she'd be doing it forever, but she felt committed and challenged again—with enough energy to spare for volunteer work with a small-business counseling service.

Jean had some advantages going for her in making a successful transition: she's not a Change Resister but someone who finds it relatively easy to take risks, and her present-time orientation is strong. The toughest master skill for her was that of tolerating ambiguity and lack of resolution, but this came more readily too, after some practice.

Something else to keep in mind as we review the qualities of a successful resolution is that *successful* and *unsuccessful* are relative terms. Midlife isn't a pass-fail course, though some people will land radically toward one or the other end of the spectrum, their life after midlife dramatically improved or steeply in decline. Most people who enter midlife in basically sound psychic health will be transformed positively to some degree; how much depends on both circumstances and how much you give to the process. The only true measure of success is how you feel about your life afterwards.

## ACCEPTANCE

Life after midlife is best seasoned with a heavy sprinkling of acceptance—acceptance of the self and its limitations, of the world around us, of the process of transition, of the seasons of life and life's finitude.

Self-acceptance is the central principle from which the others spring. It's achieved through the process of de-illusionment—giving up the outworn, inherited, or wishful ideas about ourself that we carry around like so much heavy baggage. When this happens, people talk about the freedom and sense of relief they feel. Self-acceptance is largely responsible for giving life after midlife a calmer, less driven quality.

Self-acceptance generally extends to greater acceptance of the world and other people. During midlife, the struggle to gain control of a life in turmoil is often expressed by the urge to control other lives; this becomes much less of an issue after midlife. One of my clients, John, described his experience.

> I'm fifty-seven now, but I can remember when I first started going through my forties. It was hell. I kept trying to keep everything and everybody in place. Well, it didn't work. I'd known that change was inevitable, but never really accepted it.
>
> Then my wife died at only forty-two, when I was forty-five. My first reaction was trying to control things even more. I was frightened and angry, and looking for someone to blame. I was, truthfully, angry at her for leaving me and angry at myself for being so lost without her. I used my anger to manipulate people and distance myself from them at the same time.

When I asked John what had changed for him, he replied, "It just came to me that nobody cares about you if you get too far away. There are only so many years you have here on this planet, and the bottom line is you have a terrific responsibility to enjoy them. I realized that I was wasting time trying to control things; that it's an unpredictable world and even the best efforts don't guarantee things will go right."

Learning to accept the limits of our time on earth is important midlife work. This doesn't mean that its end is celebrated or anticipated. It is simply acknowledged, like the walls of a room. And as those walls define the meaning and use of the space within the room, so the end of life helps us to value the space that exists within its boundaries, and use it well.

## BALANCE

Staying in balance during transition is a struggle—balance between body and mind, home and work, internal and interpersonal life, the rational and the emotional. We are like someone crossing a stream on a narrow log; as long as we maintain forward momentum, one foot in front of the other, we can progress with only minor tilting. When we get stuck, however, slight deviations can throw us way out of balance.

Midlife transition is dynamic, our balance is constantly shifting. We feel more connected to the past one day, and focused on the future the next. We get entranced by what's going on internally, then distracted by what's happening in the world around us. We feel in charge, completely on top of things, and then, with mercurial speed, lose all sense of control and feel at the whim of any passing influence.

After midlife, our balance becomes more solid. There's still a dynamic tension between opposing forces, but the conflict is more subdued, and we don't veer so far from the center. We are better able to integrate past and future, our roles at work and in the family, our responsibilities to ourselves and others.

Another way to look at balance is in terms of psychological growth. Human experience balances on three legs: the first is *emotion,* the feelings that are both stimulus and response to our world. The second is *cognition,* the thought processes that help us organize our experience. The last leg is *behavior,* the actions that influence and are influenced by our surroundings.

As we move through the life stages, our development in these three spheres occurs at uneven rates. At times our behavior is more mature than our feelings; at other times we may come to certain insights far in advance of our ability to act on them. Often, feelings are the first to change, followed later by intellectual and behavioral manifestations. In any case, only rarely are all three in synch.

Life after midlife—after any transition, for that matter—is characterized by more balance in this psychological triumvirate. It may be a temporary stasis, but it nevertheless produces a sense of coherence and calm. As a friend of mind put it, "It's nice to wake up on two consecutive mornings with the same set of principles."

The balance among thoughts, feelings, and actions is the cornerstone of optimal mental health, and is evident at the times when we feel most comfortable with ourselves. Remember, though, that it's a fluid and dynamic balance; if you try to hold onto it, you'll lose it. By its nature growth depends on movement.

## THE EVOLVED IDENTITY

The Who am I? question comes up in so many ways during midlife. We may leave or lose a job situation we identify with strongly; a familiar family role may change radically; the death of the youthful hero may leave us temporarily bereft. But the end result of the midlife identity shuffle—if we have questioned honestly, listened to our inner voice attentively, and experimented boldly—is that our core identity comes through tempered and stronger, our fundamental beliefs more solid. Paradoxically, this reaffirmed sense of self allows one to be more flexible, to continue experimenting, to work out compromises among conflicting needs. By contrast, the person whose postmidlife identity is insecure may rigidly cling to old principles, a self-defeating tactic.

During the years preceding midlife, our identity tends to be closely focused on our individual accomplishments, the climb up the ladder. Life after midlife usually brings an expansion of identity beyond the self, an increased identification with family, community, and cultural institutions. This shift may be especially notable in men, who have generally been more narrowly focused on career goals than women, and is related to easier acceptance of the world and our place in it. Baby boomers who have strongly resisted belonging to their cohort may find no further need for such resistance. This reconciliation with the outside world provides comfort and anchoring as we grow older.

A reorganized system of values is central to the identity that evolves out of midlife. Many baby boomers find themselves downgrading the high value they have placed on materialism. They may have achieved material success and found it wanting; for others, the turn of events has kept expected success out of reach. But in general, this generation is beginning to revise the long-held American principle of More is Better—to fit both the economic realities of the day and the awareness that satisfaction in later life won't derive from mere accumulation. To recall terms introduced in Chapter 8, affiliation and existential needs take precedence over status needs in the second half of life.

There are other rewards of the midlife identity quest: insights that add to our self-knowledge, a sense of emotional resilience. We learn about how we think and what goes into our decisions; about the importance of timing, and how difficult decisions may become easier as time clarifies the issues.

We learn better how to short-circuit our weaknesses before they lead us too far down the wrong paths. Fran, a former client, was disappointed by the end of a relationship, but proud that she had avoided her usual pattern of holding on too long. "I guess I'm learning, because it used to take me longer to get the message, to pick up on the signs. It doesn't hurt any less, but at least I figured out what was going on before I got in any deeper."

The sense of owning one's life—not as an onerous responsibility but as a joyous gift—may be the grand prize of life after midlife. Feeling at ease with oneself and subject to no one else's judgment leads people to discoveries and accomplishments never dreamed of before.

## PASSION AND THE POSTMIDLIFE MISSION

Midlife transition is full of passionate feeling, the kind that flares up hotly: anger and rebellion against the limits of life, enthusiasm for trying out new identity roles, wild, vague hopes for the future. The passion that comes with resolution is slower burning and longer lasting, for the values, people, and activities that have been tested and survived.

Sometimes the chief objects of our passion are recently discovered; what we care deeply about after midlife can be very different from what we cared about before. We feel the need to conserve and focus our energy, and any piece of our life structure that doesn't meet the litmus test of passion may be jettisoned. This testing process may also prove the strength of an old passion. Elaine, a forty-six-year-old teacher, had such an experience.

> My relationship with my husband went through tremendous changes in the past few years. First I found out that he was having an affair. I came apart about that, but then realized I was being kind of a hypocrite; I hadn't been intimate with anyone but not for lack of trying.
>
> When Bob and I separated for six months, I did a little dating but didn't get interested in anyone. Finally, Bob and I started trying to work it out. We had a lot of anger toward each other but we got through it. The effect of the whole process on the rest of my life has been enormous. When you start to look at what you really care about, you can get quite a shock. I had come so close to losing my marriage, largely because I'd stopped asking myself what I wanted from it, and working with Bob to make that happen.

As we discussed in the last chapter, passion is the fuel of our postmidlife mission. We start with a vision of how we want the second half of our life to look—at least the early stages of it—and move on to specific time-linked goals that will help us achieve what we want. The passion we invest in our mission keeps us moving ahead, counteracting the inertia that is commonly supposed to overtake people as they age.

## ENERGY AND OPTIMISM

People who have successfully negotiated midlife feel a renewed sense of energy and confidence. Transitions are fatiguing, and afterwards much of the emotional energy that went into resolving questions and doubts is released for other uses. Pierre, a fifty-one-year-old retailer who left his job as vice president of marketing for a computer manufacturer, remembers what it was like.

> What I remember most about going through midlife was how tiring it all was. It seemed like I was running through quicksand. Simple decisions, like whether to go to a party or not, or which movie to see, would tax me.
>
> When I left the company and opened the store, I was amazed at how much energy I suddenly had. It was like night and day—all those insignificant decisions went back into perspective. It's not that I stopped worrying, but the worries were more reality-based. The decisions I was making about the store had some significance.

Much of the energy that the midlifer turned inward is now directed back out toward the world. Family and friends often note this change with relief: many a spouse has remarked that his or her partner became unreachable and unavailable during midlife, and the return is like a breath of air.

The mentoring urge we've talked about is also connected to this outward redirection of energy. A word of caution, though, about midlife graduates who turn into missionaries, zealously preaching the gospel of changing values and life re-organization to everyone around them. I question how re-solved they really are, since an important midlife lesson is that everyone's experience is unique. There is no right path. The optimism of life after midlife is akin to the feeling of having weathered a terrific storm. Lois, forty-nine, started seeing me while she was getting divorced.

> I was so dependent on Jack. He made my decisions, or-ganized our life. I can't blame him totally because I let him do it. That was the relationship model we both learned from our parents.
>
> When I tried to take a stronger role, all hell broke loose. We tried counseling, but Jack was so negative. Finally we started divorce proceedings, and I can't tell your how furious he was. I was scared to death, but put up a brave front. Every time he'd tell me I couldn't make it without him, I would puff up and get even bolder. Inside, I had serious doubts, but I knew I had to try.
>
> It's been six months since the divorce was final, and to be honest, not a day goes by that I don't think about what I went through. I'm just getting on my feet again, but no way would I go back to the old situation. I just have a feeling things will work out, and you can't put a price on that. I be-lieve in myself—at least most of the time.

The optimism of life after midlife is different from the bra-vado of youth, based on limitless possibilities, or the confi-dence of the power-oriented thirties. It is a belief tempered by experience and the knowledge that more bumps in the road lie ahead. Like the professional athlete who acknowledges his opponent with respect, the midlife graduate knows that opti-mism is a relative commodity. We can revel in the ease that fol-lows transition, while knowing that it won't stay easy forever.

## LIVING IN THE PRESENT

As we've mentioned, our time orientation tends to swing widely during the transition process. We salve anxiety with memories of the past and boost ourselves out of depression by dreams of the future. Midlife resolution, though, strengthens our orientation to the world of today. Operating in a real-time mode is another good thumbnail test of a successful resolution: the better we've adapted to change and the more solid our new life structure, the more firmly rooted we can be in the present.

This can be manifested in many ways. People who are present-oriented avoid denial, which signals a lack of resolution. They take good care of their bodies rather than putting off health maintenance (unlike the client who once said to me: "I don't worry much about my health. By the time I get sick there will be a cure for everything"). They look after themselves financially, aware that to procrastinate on this issue is a setup for dependency or disaster. They continue learning because they enjoy the accumulation of knowledge and skills, and because they know it is adaptive in today's world. They enjoy leisure on a regular basis, not waiting until retirement to find appropriate and gratifying relaxation. They are connected with the people who surround them in the present, reaching out to others in an exchange of spirit, ideas, and assets. And they stay productive, knowing that it is the primary basis for self-esteem.

## SPIRITUAL GROWTH

Until quite recently in history, spiritual faith served as a primary support for people moving into the second half of life. Baby boomers, more dramatically than any previous generation, have perceived organized faith as largely irrelevant to their lives—yet the pull toward and more spiritual dimension around midlife is a primordial, persistent human need. The reason is obvious: it is the need to transcend the newly discovered limits of our own bodies and the limited span of our lifetimes.

Jung's essay "The Stages of Life" makes some powerful arguments about the spiritual needs of later life, including the usefulness of some kind of belief in life after death. This can be an uncomfortable subject in our age of scientific rationalism, but it bears thinking about. For one thing, as Jung points out, "proof of this kind is a philosophical impossibility. We simply cannot know anything whatever about such things." He persuasively offers a more practical reason:

> I have observed that a life directed to an aim is in general better, richer, and healthier than an aimless one . . . As a doctor, I am convinced that it is hygienic . . . to discover in death a goal towards which one can strive, and that shrinking away from it is something unhealthy and abnormal which robs the second half of life of its purpose . . . From the standpoint of psychotherapy it would therefore be desirable to think of death as only a transition, as part of a life process whose extent and duration are beyond our knowledge.

The forms of spirituality available to us today are more diverse than ever, responding to the needs of a widely educated, global society. Some people in the second half of life find comfort and community by returning to the religion they grew up in. Others are attracted to Eastern spiritual practice, forms of pantheism, or ecological ideas about the unity of life. Some identify with ancient mythology or adapt its ideas into a personal mythology. For many people, the spiritual dimension that comes with postmidlife may go no farther than recognizing that we are part of a world bigger than any individual. Rather than feel compelled always to set ourselves apart, we can find solace in the universality of human experience.

## PUTTING IT ALL TOGETHER

All the above ingredients of life after midlife function together in a kind of psychic ecosystem. Balance leads to present time orientation, which leads to energy, which leads to optimism, and so on. Together they describe a picture of fully rounded psychic health that is probably unattainable at any earlier time of life. This is the great promise of midlife transition—the promise that can be achieved by actively managing your transition and directing its power, as we've stressed throughout.

Let's take a moment now to look ahead. So far we've been addressing primarily the fortysomething folks, those looking forward to the resolution of midlife or perhaps even just entering transition. How does our promising picture of life after midlife carry over into the fiftysomething years, or even later?

## The Promise Ahead

From the insights of some age scouts, groundbreakers in the generation ahead of ours, baby boomers can get hopeful clues about what lies in store. In a recent interview, television commentator Hugh Downs, echoed many of the qualities we've been discussing.

> The main thing about getting older, if you work things right and aren't unlucky with your health, [is that] you'll acquire techniques and accumulate wisdom that will make your life better than it was when you were younger. That's what I'm after now . . . I know that the time will come when I'll see some decline of powers, and I hope I can cope with that. I've got plenty to go to. If I get so I can't fly an airplane or ride a horse anymore, I've got a lot of reading to do and a lot of music to listen to, and it won't bother me to pull back.

Feminist author Betty Friedan has shifted her own focus a little in recent years, writing and speaking on the rewards of aging.

> I find that life is getting more adventurous, more interesting, as I become freer to really be myself in ways I never dared before. After long years of asking and looking for answers, observing and participating, you do acquire a certain wisdom and strength. Life can open up in surprising ways, especially if you let yourself keep meeting new challenges.
>
> What's the difference if you make a mistake? You know it won't kill you. You know that you can laugh it off—and so will other people.

In both sets of comments we hear acceptance—not the depressed tone of resignation but a peaceful coming to terms with age that relies on diverse resources. We hear energetic optimism and pride in the learning gained over a lifetime. We hear a rhythm of engagement with the world that keeps the music moving forward.

We've seen that the need for meaning has been important to the baby boom generation throughout their lives, and is at the center of creating a postmidlife mission. Each mission is individual, yet can we generalize about the purpose of later life and its connection with what happens in midlife transition? Various writers have suggested such ideas, including Jung:

> A human being would certainly not grow to be seventy or eighty years old if this longevity had no meaning for the species. The significance of the morning [the first half of life] undoubtedly lies in the development of the individual, our entrenchment in the outer world, the propagation of our kind, and the care of our children. This is the obvious purpose of nature . . . Culture lies outside the purpose of nature. Could by any chance culture be the meaning and purpose of the second half of life?

Ken Dychtwald, in an article first published in *New Age Journal,* gets more specific. Referring to a philosophy evolved from the European tradition of adult education, he characterizes the *troisieme age* or third age of human life as a "less pressured, more reflective period [that] allows the further development of the intellect, memory, and imagination, of emotional maturity, and of one's spiritual identity."

> The third age is also a period of giving back to society the lessons, resources, and experiences accumulated over a lifetime. From this perspective, the elderly are not seen as social outcasts but as a living bridge between yesterday, today, and tomorrow—a critical evolutionary role that no other age group can perform.

In other cultures and other times, the oldest humans traditionally have been the spiritual guardians of society, its link between this world and the next. As baby boomers move through midlife and on into the third age, it will be interesting to see if our urge to bring spirituality into our own lives will also bring it to the larger society currently so in need of it. Given our influential history, it wouldn't be surprising.

Midlife transition doesn't just prepare us for the life structure immediately following; it lays the groundwork for all of our remaining life. The discomforts and drives that take us by surprise and threaten to disrupt our current lives are like clues in a whodunit. If we ignore them, the journey into later life can be like stumbling out of the sunlight into a horror movie. But if we pay close attention to them, the intricate mystery of living in harmony with time will reveal itself gradually and gracefully.

## The Dance of Change

"There is no steady, unretracing progress in this life. We do not advance through fixed gradations, and at the last one

pause. . . . But once gone through we trace the round
again . . . Where lies the final harbor, whence we unmoor
no more?"

Herman Melville

If Jung's speculation about death being just another transition
is right, then there is no final harbor. And whether it's right or
not—regardless of whether death is the final rest—what we
know of life is change. As structure grows out of transition, so
inevitably another transition will follow from it. They are
locked in a symbiotic dance, each one's demise signaling the
other's revival.

As we leave midlife, it's good to keep in mind that other
transitions lie down the road, and we should never become too
sedentary in any resolution. Daniel Levinson's scheme of life
stages proposes an *age fifty transition*, followed by the latter
part of middle adulthood, and finally a *late adult transition* at
around age sixty to sixty-five.

Gail Sheehy's book *Pathfinders* continued her exploration
into late-adult transitions, using terms like the *Freestyle
Fifties*, the *Selective Sixties*, and the *Thoughtful Seventies*. As
the baby boom rolls on, no doubt there will others. As we enter midlife, it's not necessary to know the exact parameters of
these future transitions, only that they will occur.

The constancy of change in our lives doesn't mean that we
can't enjoy its periods of stability; on the contrary, it allows us
to appreciate them all the more. We have to remember that
change is inextricably linked with our capacity to feel passion,
to feel alive; it's like the salty ocean in our life's blood. As
Spenser said in the eighteenth century: "For all that moveth
doth in Change delight." So take delight in the midlife voyage,
and in the new landscape it brings you to, and look forward to
the next fruitful journey.

# Recommended Resources

When the first feelings of midlife hit me, I attempted to read my way through the confusion. The books listed below were helpful. I pass them on to you in the spirit with which I learned to use them. That is—they are guides, nothing more, nothing less. Like all guides, they can point out a course, describe some of the markers along the way, help prepare you for your transition. They cannot make the crossing for you.

Bardwick, Judith M., *The Plateauing Trap* (New York: Bantam, 1986)

Bridges, William, *Transitions: Making Sense of Life's Changes* (Reading, MA: Addison-Wesley, 1980)

Campbell, Joseph, ed., *The Portable Jung* (New York: Penguin Books, 1976) Originally published by Viking Press, 1971.

Dychtwald, Ken, and Joe Flower, *Age Wave* (Los Angeles: Tarcher, 1989)

Erikson, Erik H., *Childhood and Society* (New York: Norton, 1950)

Gould, Roger, *Transformations: Growth and Change in Adult Life* (New York: Simon and Schuster, 1978)

Jaffee, Dennis T. and Cynthia Scott, *Take This Job and Love It* (New York: Simon and Schuster, 1988)

Jones, Landon Y., *Great Expectations: America and the Baby Boom* (New York: Ballantine, 1980)

Jung, C. G., *Modern Man in Search of a Soul* (New York: Harcourt Brace Jovanovich, 1933)

Levinson, Daniel J., *The Seasons of a Man's Life* (New York: Ballantine, 1978)

Merser, Cheryl, *Grown-Ups* (New York: Signet, 1987)

Nichols, Michael, *Turning Forty in the '80s* (New York: Norton, 1986)

Shames, Laurence, *The Hunger for More* (New York: Times Books, 1989)

Sheehy, Gail, *Passages: Predictable Crises of Adult Life* (New York: Dutton, 1976)

Viorst, Judith, *Necessary Losses* (New York: Ballantine, 1986)